JEWISH LIFE
AND
AMERICAN CULTURE

SUNY series in American Jewish Society in the 1990s
Barry A. Kosmin and Sidney Goldstein, editors

Jewish Life
and
American Culture

Sylvia Barack Fishman

State University of New York Press

Cover photo:
Julie Hilton Danan and family—reading Torah
by ©1999 Lori Grinker, Contact Press Images

Published by
State University of New York Press, Albany

©2000 State University of New York

For information, address State University of New York Press
State University Plaza, Albany, New York 12246

Production by Dana Foote
Marketing by Dana E. Yanulavich

Library of Congress Cataloging-in-Publication Data

Fishman, Sylvia Barack, 1942–
Jewish life and American culture / Sylvia Barack Fishman.
p.   cm. — (SUNY series in American Jewish society in the 1990s)
Includes bibliographical references and index.
ISBN 0–7914–4545–3 (hardcover : alk. paper) — ISBN 0–7914–4546–1 (pbk. : alk. paper)
1. Jews—United States—Identity.   2. Judaism—United States—History—20th century.
3. Jews—Cultural assimilation—United States.   4. Jewish way of life.   5. United
States—Ethnic relations.   I. Title.   II. Series.

E184.36.E84 F57 2000

305.8924073—dc21   00–021943

10 9 8 7 6 5 4 3 2 1

This book is for all my children
Lisi and Josh
Elie and Suzanne
and Joseph

and my children's children
Joshua, Leor Barak, and Ari Shai . . .

CONTENTS

TABLES AND FIGURES

Figures

FOREWORD

Jewish Life and American Culture is the sixth monograph to be published in the series "American Jewish Society in the 1990s," based on the Council of Jewish Federation's (CJF) landmark 1990 National Jewish Population Survey. The survey yielded a vast array of statistical data on the demographic, social, and religious characteristics of the Jewish American population. It is being used to provide, in a number of monographs, an in-depth assessment of the major changes and trends in Jewish American life as it approaches the end of the century. To a degree, this monograph series parallels past undertakings by teams of social scientists who analyzed the demographic and social data emanating from United States decennial censuses. A monograph series focussing on the Jewish population is, however, unique. Although a national survey similar in nature had been conducted in 1970, that project yielded comparatively few reports and those were in limited areas of concern.

Recognizing the importance of a comprehensive assessment of the total Jewish American population as the basis for an effective planning agenda, the concept of a national Jewish population survey in 1990 was first considered in 1986 by CJF's National Technical Advisory Committee on Jewish Population Studies (NTAC). The idea was further promoted the following year at the World Conference on Jewish Demography held in Jerusalem, at which plans were developed for a worldwide series of national Jewish population studies undertaken in or around the decennial year. An American survey was seen as a key component of this series. In 1988, CJF officially agreed to conduct a national Jewish population survey in 1990, parallel to the federal decennial census. ICR Survey Research Group of Media, Pennsylvania, was commissioned to conduct the three-stage survey.

In contrast to the 1970 national study, NTAC decided to insure public access to the 1990 National Jewish Population Survey (NJPS) data as early as possible and to actively encourage wide use and analysis. The success of that effort is evident in the large number of analyses that have been completed or are in process. To date, more than 150 items extensively based on NJPS, such as journal and magazine articles, dissertations, and papers for professional meetings, have been written. These encompass such varied topics as aging, apostasy, the baby boom generation, children, comparisons with international Jewry, comparisons with the larger American population, denominations, fertility, gender equality, geography, intermarriage, Israel connections, Jewish education, Jewish identity, life cycle, mobility, occupation, philanthropy, Sephardim, social stratification, and women's roles. A number of these topics are expected to appear as monographs in the series.

From the outset, NTAC envisioned that a number of scholars would independently produce monographs utilizing NJPS data for in-depth assessment of topics having special relevance for the understanding of Jewish life in America. While planning for the various stages of NJPS, NTAC therefore concurrently acted to identify potential monograph writers. Public notices were placed in a variety of academic journals and invitations were conveyed through a network of professionals, both within and outside of Judaic disciplines. Although funds were raised for the data collection, survey execution, and data processing, no financial support was available for subsidizing data analyses, except for a summary report, *Highlights of the CJF 1990 National Jewish Population Survey.* Thus, potential monograph writers knew from the beginning that they would be participating on a voluntary basis, dependent on whatever resources they could themselves muster. The dedication of the authors to the completion of their respective monographs is gratefully acknowledged. While drawing on basically the same set of data, authors were free to establish their own analytic categories and to apply their own perspectives in interpreting the data. They were also encouraged to draw not only on NJPS, but also on comparative data from other sources, such as local community surveys.

In selecting authors, efforts were made to insure coverage of key issues and a diversity of topics and to avoid serious overlap in coverage of the same topic. A screening and approval process, in collaboration with the editors at SUNY Press, was administered by the series editors, Dr. Barry Kosmin, Director of the Institute for Jewish Policy Research in London, England; and Dr. Sidney Goldstein, Chair of NTAC and G. H. Crooker University Professor Emeritus and Professor Emeritus of Sociology at Brown University.

Jeff Scheckner, Administrator of the North American Jewish Data Bank at the Graduate Center of the City University of New York (NAJDB) and Research Consultant for United Jewish Communities (formerly the Council of Jewish Federations), with the help of the series editors, coordinated the activities of the monograph writers by arranging meetings at which authors discussed technical aspects of the data and their preliminary findings, fielding daily inquiries about the data set, and circulating periodic informational updates. Much of this activity was necessitated by the fact that NJPS is both a large data set with a complex weighting system (see the Appendix) and that definitional issues complicate any analysis of contemporary Jewish populations. The work of the monograph authors was further enhanced through the coordination of a "buddy" system by which other scholars associated with NJPS provided academic peer review to authors at various stages of manuscript preparation.

The intense interest generated by the initial release of NJPS findings has already significantly affected deliberations within the Jewish American community among communal service workers, religious and educational professionals, and lay leaders. At the same time, the results of early reports have elicited considerable attention among those in the larger American community whose interests focus on the changing religio-ethnic composition of the population and the role of religion in America. This series is intended to provide a comprehensive, in-depth evaluation of American Jewry today, some one hundred years since the massive waves of Jewish immigrants from Eastern Europe began to change the size and character of Jewry in the United States. During the intervening decades, continual change has been the hallmark of the community. The profile of the Jewish population in the 1990s that NJPS delineates both provides a historical perspective and points to the challenges of the future.

Barry A. Kosmin	Sidney Goldstein
Director	Population Studies and
Institute for Jewish	Training Center
Policy Research	Brown University
London, UK	Providence, RI

April 2000

ACKNOWLEDGMENTS

One of the most pleasant aspects of finishing a book is thanking the people who have helped along the way. This book draws on many different sources of research data; the length of my list of thank yous is a delightful circumstance for me, because each person named here has made a significant contribution to my work.

Sidney Goldstein and Alice Goldstein of the Population Studies and Training Center at Brown University read my entire manuscript with wonderful attention; their wise suggestions were invaluable. The core of *Jewish Life in American Culture* is based on data from the 1990 National Jewish Population Survey, and I am delighted to thank Barry Kosmin and Jeff Scheckner, of the Graduate Center, City University of New York, and Sidney Goldstein, who directed the 1990 NJPS. Throughout the writing of this book, I have benefited from the friendship and guidance of Shulamit Reinharz. Serving as codirector with Shulamit for the International Research Institute on Jewish Women, established in 1997 at Brandeis University by Hadassah, has been an exhilarating opportunity. Thanks also go to my colleagues at the IRIJW, Susan Kahn and Helene Greenberg.

I owe deep gratitude to several friends and colleagues who carefully read an earlier essay, *Negotiating Both Sides of the Hyphen: Coalescence, Compartmentalization, and American-Jewish Values*: Jonathan D. Sarna, Charles Liebman, Benny Kraut, Pamela Nadell, and Louis Dickstein each generously made extensive comments that greatly enriched *Jewish Life and American Culture*. As always, I am grateful to my colleagues in the Near Eastern and Judaic Studies Department at Brandeis University, especially Antony Polonsky, who, as chair of the department during the writing of this essay, provided a lively and supportive environment for research and teaching. Nancy Zibman's care and diligence made possible this book's index.

This book draws on research done in several different settings, and I am pleased to thank the persons who facilitated that research: my cross-country "Voices for Change" focus group research was sponsored by Hadassah's National Commission on Jewish Women, ably chaired by Shulamit Reinharz and facilitated by Brandeis colleagues Amy Sales and Suzanne Shavelson, with the competent support of Shirley Kalb, at the Hadassah Department of Strategic Planning. The Wexner Foundation sponsored my research on Jewish professionals, and it was a pleasure to work with Larry Moses, Rabbi Maurice Corson, and Ferne Katelman. A report that I wrote as an IRIJW research consultant for the Morning Star Commission, a project of Hadassah Southern California, was the outcome of a working relationship with Commission Chair Joan Hyler, Commissioner Claudia Caplan, and HSC Morning Star project director Dr. Mara Fein.

At Brandeis University, Sylvia Fuks Fried was always willing to lend a helpful hand. Jonathan Ament, Paula Ducarret, and Tova Neugut worked energetically and efficiently preparing tables and citations. My students were frequently a source of inspiration, and I am delighted to note their intellectual contributions in this book's text and notes.

My family is now, as they have always been, the joy and light of my life. My husband Phil read the manuscript and helped me wrestle with the difficult issues discussed here. Where we disagreed, his loyal opposition helped me to clarify my thoughts and words. This book is dedicated to my children, in love and admiration, and to their own darling children, who carry the future in their little hands.

INTRODUCTION
ANALYZING THE EVIDENCE

This book examines the social psychology of Jews relocating the boundaries of American Jewish ethnic identity. My research reveals and juxtaposes two critical ongoing adaptive processes. Observers have noted that American Jews compartmentalize, often becoming inattentive to one world when functioning within the perceived boundaries of the other. I argue that contemporary American Jews increasingly employ a very different coping technique, which I call "coalescence." Coalescence is a pervasive process through which American Jews merge American and Jewish ideas, incorporating American liberal values such as free choice, universalism, individualism, and pluralism into their understanding of Jewish identity.

Compartmentalization and coalescence, two contradictory methods of negotiating the interplay between secular and Jewish aspects of life, share the capacity to reduce the discomfort of cognitive dissonance. They are linked also by the fact that many American Jews do not utilize one or the other response exclusively, but make use of both in differing situations. I propose coalescence as a model and an interpretive tool to elucidate the sometimes dramatically shifting meanings of certain behaviors vis-à-vis Jewish identity: a number of behaviors which were correlated with weak Jewish identification several decades ago today carry neutral or even positive associations.

Indeed, behaviors such as educational and occupational achievement, which were linked at midcentury with assimilationist tendencies, are now most characteristic of Jews who are, relatively speaking, among the more ethnically distinctive segments of the American Jewish population. This is because coalescence allows highly educated, highly achieving Jews to feel that their achievements bond them to, rather than separate them from, their Jewish ethnicity.

Coalescence has not sprung out of a vacuum. I compare contemporary American Jewish coalescence with syncretism in other Jewish societies and historical periods. Coalescence is built on ever-increasing levels of accommodation to Western mores in modern Jewish societies, especially in the United States. However coalescence comprises multifaceted Jewish ethnic identity reconstruction on an unprecedented scale, due to both internal and external transformations. Many Jews have minimal awareness of historical conflicts between traditional Jewish attitudes and Western egalitarian ideals. Moreover, American culture incrementally reflects the influence of Jews, further lessening a sense of discrete realms. Today few rewards accrue to rejecting Jewish identity. I suggest that as Judaism is Americanized, and America is Judaized, the permeable boundaries signifying Jewish ethnic identity are reframed.

Finally, I demonstrate that context changes the impact of coalescence. Among populations whose Jewish enculturation has been minimal, little remains of distinctively Jewish behaviors and values. Some American Jews react to such sweeping Americanization by attempting to reseal the boundaries that divide Jew from non-Jew, and even the observant Jew from less observant coreligionists. However, my data show that in Jewish social subgroups that actively promote formal Jewish education, Jewish peer activities, Jewish activities within the home, and Israel connections, American and Jewish behaviors and values characteristically thrive side by side.

An Interdisciplinary Methodology

In *Jewish Life and American Culture* I employ an interdisciplinary methodology called triangulation, which casts a wide net to bring together data culled from three different types of sources in the social sciences and humanities, including (1) statistical studies (survey research), (2) qualitative data culled from interviews and focus groups, and (3) cultural artifacts found in popular and material culture, literature, and film.[1]

I have generated statistical data by gender and age group from the 1990 National Jewish Population Survey (NJPS) to provide information about major trends in the lives of contemporary American Jewish men and women, in addition to citing several important recent studies based on the 1990 NJPS data.[2] Survey data are also included from interviews with 280 Jewish professionals which I conducted in 1994 for the Wexner Foundation, illuminating the differing worlds inhabited by rabbis, Jewish communal workers, and Jewish educators, and the client populations they serve.[3] This book cites qualitative data from several different sources: (1) data from fourteen focus-group conversations that I conducted across the United States in 1994 for the National Commission on Jewish Women spotlight the attitudes of specific subgroups of Jews;[4] (2) interview data from a series of 120 semistructured interviews that I conducted with Jewish women in diverse geographical areas from 1990 through 1992 speak to individual perceptions;[5] and (3) focus-group data generated by the Morning Star Commission are useful in determining the impact of media images on Jewish and non-Jewish women and men.[6]

These quantitative and qualitative data are supplemented with participant-observer ethnographic notes and with both scholarly and general analyses of contemporary trends; each are clearly indicated. I explore the clues provided by American-Jewish cultural artifacts and material culture, as revealed by magazines and advertisements, to provide insights into what "real people" are buying, reading, and thinking about. In addition, fiction and film are often referred to in this book to provide two different kinds of data: first, as a signal or indicator of trends that may not yet be statistically measurable, and second, as a means to illuminate the personal realities underlying quantifiable trends.

Literary and cinematic sources are a prism through which to view social and political change. This approach is innovative, but is gaining increased scholarly attention. Political scientist Catherine Zuckert, for example, notes that in 1993 "more than one hundred political scientists signed a petition calling for the creation of a section within the American Political Science Association devoted to the study of politics and literature. There are now more than 250 dues-paying members of the section." Zuckert comments that literature is especially useful for those "concerned with establishing norms and standards," investigating "values," and seeking a reflection of "the way we see the world, and thus what we do in it."[7]

The distinguished historian Yosef Hayim Yerushalmi warned, "The divorce of history from literature has been as calamitous for Jewish as for general historical writing," because neglecting literature impoverishes "the image" of history by concentrating on "explanation" and omitting "evocation."[8] It should be noted that no less a pioneering figure in the sociology of American Jews than Marshall Sklare paved the way for this technique. In his prophetic 1964 article on intermarriage, Sklare lamented the fact that sociologists were often misled by their exclusive reliance on statistics into thinking that intermarriage would remain an insignificant trend, whereas novelists were already more accurately describing intermarriage trends which were at that time only a weakly measurable reality:

> . . . the present state of endogamy seems to have been grasped more firmly by the novelists than by the sociologists. Even a hasty rundown of the work of such writers as Bernard Malamud, Saul Bellow, Philip Roth, Leslie Fiedler, Bruce Jay Friedman, Neil Oxenhandler, etc. reveals how much recent American fiction has dealt with marriage or the strong possibility of it between a Jew and a gentile.[9]

Another axiom of this book's methodology is to focus on diverging subgroups of American Jews. Although it is important to look for large trends, when too many disparate groups are yoked together statistically, the differences between them are lost—and the resulting picture is misleading. Recent analyses of American Jews, for example, have sometimes ignored the critical role of age in determining American-Jewish experience. The fact is that the "Gentleman's Agreement" America of the first half of the twentieth century has given way to the "Seinfeld" era of the century's closing decades. Younger American Jews as a group have a different relationship with their own Jewishness than their elders, and those differences are reflected both statistically and in qualitative and cultural materials.

Not least, the methodology of this book incorporates analysis of gender role construction as a factor in the construction of contemporary American-Jewish ethnicity. Recognizing that religious and cultural definitions of Jewish attitudes and behaviors have for centuries been androcentric, this book looks at both male and female experiences in their commonalities and differences, as they evolve and define contemporary American-Jewish societies and culture. While this study often compares statistics on men and women, it places particular emphasis on the relationship of women to their Jewish and American identities, in response to the primarily male-centered nature of many earlier studies. Thus, *Jewish Life and American Culture* is both a general study of the contextualized Jewish lives of contemporary American men and women, and also a study that focuses on Jewish women's experiences in particular.

Identity Construction, Coalescence, and Compartmentalization

Jewish Americans provide particularly interesting examples of the ways in which ethnic and religious minority groups negotiate conflicting behavioral prescriptions and belief systems from both sides of a hyphenated identity, coping with simultaneous pulls toward assimilating and maintaining a distinctive heritage. Jews have often been perceived by themselves and others as a singularly divided and fractious people. Despite the frequently articulated sentiment that all Jews comprise one people, American Jews at the end of the twentieth century have established at least five commonly recognized official branches of Judaism: Orthodox, Traditional, Conservative, Reconstructionist, and Reform,[10] and also include in their midst a substantial number who see themselves as secular, cultural, or unaffiliated Jews, altogether outside the rubric of organized religion.

Moreover, not only are American Jews divided externally into differing religious groupings, many of them feel that they are divided personally and internally as well, as they struggle with competing ideas, impulses, and yearnings. As Philip Roth puts it, "inside every Jew there is a mob of Jews":

> Divided is nothing. Even the goyim are divided. But inside every Jew there is a mob of Jews. The good Jew, the bad Jew. The new Jew, the old Jew. The lover of Jews, the hater of Jews. The friend of the goy, the enemy of the goy. The arrogant Jew, the wounded Jew. The pious Jew, the rascal Jew. The coarse Jew, the gentle Jew. The defiant Jew, the appeasing Jew. The Jewish Jew, the de-Jewed Jew. . . . Is it any wonder that the Jew is always disputing? He is a dispute, incarnate![11]

Contradictions have characterized the lives of the people who became twentieth-century American Jews even before they arrived at these shores. First Western and later Eastern European emancipation had plunged many Jews in their countries of origin into the process of mediating between differing lifestyles and value systems, especially between secularized humanistic Christian and traditional Jewish modes of behavior and attitudes.[12] That struggle was dramatically intensified and broadened when European Jews emigrated to the United States in large numbers, and confronted an increasingly tolerant and open society which offered them genuine opportunities—provided they adapted to American cultural norms. Significantly, these norms were not only behavioral—American clothing, eating habits, manners, secular education—but ideological as well. As Philip Gleason notes, "to become an American a person did not have to be of any particular national, linguistic, religious, or ethnic background. All he had to do was to commit himself to the political ideology centered on the abstract ideals of liberty, equality, and republicanism."[13]

From intellectual leaders to popular writers, the mainstream American ethos seemed to advocate the blending of diverse ethnicities into what Emerson called "a new race, bent on creating a new religion, a new state, a new literature, which will be as vigorous as the new Europe which came out of the smelting pot of the Dark Ages."[14] Members of minority ethnic groups struggling out of their respective ghettos were encouraged to resemble as much as possible Americanized white Protestants of European background.[15] Horace Kallen, whose 1915 essay on culture and democracy in the United States became a foundational statement on cultural pluralism, remembers the enormous assimilative pressure he experienced as a young student:

> When I was a student, I was very largely an assimilationist, living under the handicap of being called a Jew. To be a Jew in certain American institutions of that time was not easy, and most of the young Jews in the colleges of my day were not visible as Jews; they tried to conceal the fact that they were Jews."[16]

Some American-Jewish leaders argued passionately for a synthesis of American and Jewish values. Louis Brandeis suggested that the Jewish spirit "is essentially modern and essentially American," and that "loyalty to America demands . . . that each American Jew become a Zionist."[17] More common were the assumptions of Reform religious leaders, transferring and further developing the patterns of post-emancipation German Jewish adaptation in America's promising environment, who suggested that radical surgery could render traditional Jewish modes of life consistent with American mores, producing a "concordance of Judaism and Americanism," in the words of Reform leader Emil Gustav Hirsch. Kaufman Kohler, German-born and -educated American Reform rabbi and president of Hebrew Union College, extolled "American Judaism," which to him spelled "a triumph of the world's two greatest principles and ideals." However, he warned, the incorporation of "the wandering Jew," the "former Pariah of the nations" into full American life could only take place if American Jews eschewed "Orientalism" and rid themselves of the "Medieval garb," "alien form," and "seclusiveness" of "Ghetto Judaism."[18]

For most American Jews, the confrontation of Americanism and Judaism created feelings of conflicting expectations, and American Jewish life continued to embody contradictory trends. Jewish immigrants and their children yearned to be "real Americans," yet most refused to completely relinquish their ties to Jewish ethnicity, culture, and religion. Committed to family and community, American Jews were also individualistic, well-known for their entrepreneurial imagination and energy. Preponderantly liberal, often seen as socialistic in their leanings, they also became known as avid and at times conspicuous consumers.[19] Indeed, it often seemed as though cultural tension was in itself an important ethnic marker for American Jewish life. In the 1950s and early 1960s, when the melting pot ideology still permeated mainstream America, religious and cultural boundaries seemed all too solid to many American Jews. Several generations of American Jews could identify with Philip Roth's sharp awareness of differences, and his mixed attitude of "contempt" and "veneration" toward a "nosegay of shiksas" or a "pride of shkotzim," as he reflected, "These people are the Americans."[20]

Constructing Contemporary Jewish Identity

Today, multiculturalism rather than the melting pot is the politically correct ideology. Americans believe that they celebrate ethnic and religious differences. Jews, like other white ethnic groups in the United States, currently enjoy an environment which in some ways offers unprecedented freedoms for the expression of distinctiveness. Ethnic identification, once subject to the dampening efforts of disapproving assimilationists, attracts positive scholarly and popular attention. Immigrant groups, once urged to suppress distinctive characteristics in favor of the melting pot, are now frequently encouraged to preserve their ethnic heritage. Robert Bellah and his colleagues have celebrated "ethnic and racial communities, each with its own story and its own heroes and heroines," because such communities provide structure and context in an otherwise anonymous and impersonal society; they urge individuals who are not fortunate enough to have been born into such ethnic and racial communities to access a different kind of community of memory through regular church attendance.[21] And yet members of the Jewish community, as dramatically evidenced through quantitative research such as the 1990 National Jewish Population Survey, through qualitative studies, and through cultural artifacts, have not become more distinctive in this tolerant environment, but have, instead, by and large become more and more like the mainstream Americans described by Roth.

Herbert J. Gans noted decades ago that for Jews, as for other white ethnic Americans, ethnicity is largely voluntary and symbolic, rather than externally enforced.[22] The voluntary, symbolic nature of ethnicity has become more pronounced as the years pass and educational, occupational, and social boundaries within American society have become increasingly permeable. Scholars building upon the work of Peter Berger, Thomas Luckman, Malcom Spector, and John Kitsuse utilize constructionist theories of ethnicity, which view ethnic identity as fluid, continually being negotiated and renegotiated. They analyze the ways in which ethnic identity is constructed "out of the material of language, religion, culture, appearance, ancestry, or regionality." The constructionist view of ethnicity[23] does not negate the shaping forces of history, group conflict, persecution, or religious belief, but it asserts that members of an ethnic group are not merely passive recipients of an unchanging ethnic identity. Rather, ethnic group members as individuals and as members of the group, responding to "demographic, political, social and economic processes," are engaged in the ongoing task of diminishing or reconstructing social boundaries, of changing the meaning of these boundaries, and of reassessing and revitalizing the definition of their own ethnicity.[24]

As Mary Waters puts it, far from being a "primordial characteristic, ethnic identification is, in fact, a dynamic and complex social phenomenon," incorporating both "choice and constraint."[25] For many white Americans, despite historic persecutions, ethnic restrictions are actually minimal today. White Americans may be educated by their ethnic social group, they may believe themselves to be biologically linked to their ethnic group, and yet they do retain the option of disassociating themselves entirely from that group, or of maintaining only very weak ties. Unlike persons whose ethnicity marks them with unmistakable physical characteristics, ethnic white Americans, says Waters, "do not give much attention to the ease with which they are able to slip in and out of their ethnic roles. It is natural to them that in the greater part of their lives, their ethnicity does not matter. They also take for granted that when it does matter, it is largely a matter of personal choice and a source of pleasure."[26]

Ethnic groups not only differentiate themselves from other social groups by constructing boundaries, they also provide meaning and identity for those who perceive themselves and are perceived by others as ethnic group members. Group membership may imply certain restrictions or constraints, but membership rewards include a sense of place and meaning. Still, for Jews the memory and sometimes the present reality of antisemitic discrimination persists, and the task of sustaining viable, distinctive value systems and behaviors when aspiring to full emancipation in an open society evokes complicated and often seemingly inconsistent attitudes and behaviors. When individuals or societies attempt to negotiate identity on both sides of the ethnic-American hyphen, they employ a variety of strategies that help them cope with what they perceive as diverging demands.

Compartmentalization: One Model for American-Jewish Negotiations

One coping strategy that has often been utilized to explain the functioning of American Jews is compartmentalization—a process whereby an individual employing two contradictory value systems either utilizes them in serial and separate fashion or becomes inattentive to their contradictions. Indeed, compartmentalization has been attributed to American Jews with such regularity that many social scientists regarded it as a defining societal characteristic. According to observers such as Berger,[27] Heilman, and Cohen,[28] compartmentalization has enabled individuals and groups of individuals to feel that they are both Jewish and American. At nonsectarian or frankly Christianized work or social settings that seemed to demand acculturated "American" behavior, Jewish individuals often acted according to what they perceived as American societal guidelines. In contrast, in their homes, in places of worship, and in friendship groups composed primarily of others from their religious and/or ethnic subgroup, individuals often acted according to the distinctive guidelines of their subgroup's culture. This strategy facilitated feelings of comfort in two different worlds through avoidance of the discomfort of trying to bring those two worlds together.

Qualitative research supports the idea that numerous contemporary Jewish women and men still feel divided within themselves and find compartmentalization a useful technique for conflict resolution. For example, among the National Commission on Jewish Women focus-group participants, individuals who worked or lived in primarily non-Jewish environments almost always kept their Jewish ethnicity a secret until they were sure they would not be subject to any negative repercussions as a result. As one Oregon woman put it, "It is only when I feel comfortable and when I know who I am dealing with that I will reveal my Jewish background."

For some, contemporary uses of compartmentalization are a continuation of the historical American-Jewish experience. Thus, one Atlanta Jewish woman in her forties echoed the voices of earlier Jewish immigrants as she remembered Jewish languages and Jewish concerns being confined to her home as she was growing up:

> There were three children in my whole class that were Jewish. It was important that you fit in, so like my father . . . his parents spoke Yiddish and

Hebrew and all of that, but they [my parents] didn't want . . . if they spoke Yiddish or Hebrew they didn't want anyone else to know. . . . I learned very quickly from the other children [in school]. At Christmas time they all sang, we were exposed to it in school. I can remember somebody telling me you'd better sing that Christmas carol. To the point about Jewish people being the chosen ones, we've got a Catholic neighbor, and she said that her priest told her that the Jewish people were on the last row when it comes to being selected [by God].

For some American Jews the conflicting values demanding compartmentalization differ from those that galvanized Jewish life in the past. Nevertheless, despite this apparent change of issues, the psychology of compartmentalization still is precipitated by fear of embarrassment: contemporary American Jews are usually not afraid of being embarrassed by immigrant relatives, but they are often anxious over being linked to other images of Jews that might embarrass them, such as pushy Jewish women, or overly militant Israelis, as seen in films, television, or the evening news.

These anxieties sometimes have a gendered component, as both men and women are likely to project negative characteristics on Jewish females, deriving images from literature, films, and popular culture. Riv-Ellen Prell suggests that "the stereotypical suffocating mother or whiny and withholding wife express ideas about how Jewish men understand their own place in American society": "Jewish women, in these stereotypes, symbolize elements of 'Jewishness' or 'Americanness' to be rejected. Jewish women represent these features precisely because of their link to Jewish men, whom they do and do not resemble.[29] Paula Hyman analyzes this phenomenon, which she calls "the sexual politics of Jewish identity":

> Faced with the need to establish their own identities in societies in which they were both fully acculturated and yet perceived as the other because they were Jews, Jewish men were eager to distinguish themselves from the women of their community, whom they saw as the guardians of Jewishness. The negative representations of women that they produced reflected their own ambivalence about assimilation and its limits.[30]

Corroborating Hyman's assertion, Jewish male participants in focus groups implemented by the Morning Star Commission, for example, often spoke about Jewish women in language consistent with negative stereotypes. Some pictured Jewish women as aggressive, articulate, and demanding; others pictured Jewish women as the chubby makers of "killer chicken soup." One male Jewish focus-group participant asserted that even when Jewish women were attractive, "they aren't really gorgeous." Several stated that they would like Jewish women to be "not that complicated," quiet attentive listeners, and more sexual beings who would "give a one-night stand without asking for a commitment."[31]

Many women mentioned similar images, and expressed their vehement desire not to be perceived as "Jewish American Princesses" and not to be seen with women who might be perceived that way. A significant number of Jewish women in the

"Voices for Change" focus groups had internalized pejorative stereotypes of Jewish women, and projected these negative stereotypes onto other Jewish women. At the same time, such women compartmentalize by trying to make themselves oblivious to the extent to which such stereotypes could be attached to them. For example, a single career woman spoke about being embarrassed by other Jews who seemed pushy or materialistic, yet ignored her own tendencies in that direction:

> The religious aspect leaves me cold, as does the monetary aspect [of American Jewish life]. I think I stopped going even to High Holidays [sic] when I was in the seventh grade because it became apparent to me that the mink coat was more important than the service. . . . [and yet] I drive a BMW, I have four mink coats, a safe deposit box full of jewelry, and most of the time I don't have a dime in my pocket. It occurred to me that the reason I don't have any money in my pocket, I don't want anyone to think I am a JAP.

The State of Israel also has been subject to image problems, which have been internalized by many American Jews. Some "Voices for Change" focus-group participants assigned to Israeli Jews the "job" of being good Jews, a moral light to the nations, while they arrogated for themselves and other American Jews the right to maintain typically American entrepreneurial goals. For example, one Reform woman with children and a career spoke with candor about her own ambitions, her individualistic career goals, and her impatience with people who tried to tell her what to do—and then pilloried Israelis for being too concerned about themselves: "Israel exists for the purpose of representing American Jews. When Israelis oppress others or when they are too materialistic or not idealistic enough, I am very displeased with them. They should be more idealistic, more concerned with others. I do not feel they are representing me to the world the way I would like to be represented."

Coalescence: An Alternative Strategy for Coping with Conflict

The compartmentalizing model for conflict resolution continues to be utilized as a coping mechanism in some ways and by certain types of Jews. However, for many American Jews, the use of compartmentalization has declined. This book introduces a new model, called coalescence, to focus on a strategy that large groups of American Jews employ to deal with the interplay of secular and Jewish elements in their lives.

The term coalescence is used here to describe an often unrecognized phenomenon, foreshadowed in earlier periods of Jewish history, which now permeates American Jewish societies. Coalescence builds upon and supersedes adaptation, a process of acculturation in which the elements of two disparate value systems exist side by side within an individual or society, and whereby "original and foreign traits are combined . . . with either a reworking of the patterns of two cultures into a meaningful whole to the individuals concerned, or the retention of a series of more or less conflicting attitudes and points of view which are reconciled in everyday life as specific occasions arise."[32] Adaptation implies a continuing awareness of difference; the person who adapts Jewish tradition to contemporary American life remains aware of the differences between the two value systems, and privileges one or the other as the situation seems to demand.

During the process of coalescence, in contrast, the "texts" of two cultures, American and Jewish, are accessed simultaneously, much as one might access two different texts on a single computer screen. These values systems coalesce or merge, and the resulting merged messages or texts are perceived not as being American and Jewish values side by side, but as being a unified text, which is identified as authoritative Judaism. In coalescing American values and Jewish values, many American Jews—including some who are very knowledgeable and actively involved in Jewish life—no longer separate or are even conscious of the separation between the origins of these two texts.

The scope and nature of coalescence differs from its diverse antecedents. Although it has evolved from previous incidence of merging messages in modern Jewish life, as a phenomenon it is both familiar and different. Coalescence today takes place in a context where there is a lack of attention to the sacred versus the secular origin of ideas, and thus it is different from synthesis, which sought to deliberately bring together immersion in Judaic knowledge and law combined with familiarity with the best and finest of secular Western humanistic thinking and behavior.[33] Coalescence is also reminiscent of, and yet less harsh and overt than the radical surgery and removal of "Orientalism" which Reform Jewish leaders ever-so-consciously advocated, in order to make Jewish lifestyles more consonant with American mores, in their enthusiastic, Westernized rearticulation of Judaic values and behaviors.

Coalescence grows out of, and yet is different from, the gradual Westernizing embourgeoisement of Jewish households, first in Germany[34] and then in the United States, as consumerist material culture was drawn into the service of Jewish identity and Jews consciously adapted their Jewish religious environments to American ideas of propriety. It is foreshadowed in the evolution of Conservative synagogue worship, with its deliberate bringing together of Jewish tradition, exemplified by Hebrew liturgy, with American aesthetics of decorum.[35] In domestic spheres, coalescing behavior eventually became the American norm, as women found Jewish celebrations of the seder service more acceptably American when they were conducted in a kind of consumerist "house beautiful" setting, complete with flowers and expensive linens and china. Luxuries

> symbolized the faith in social progress that moved many Jews seeking to fit into American society. The ritualized demand for new products gave newcomers reason to believe that they were 'greening themselves out,' upgrading their level of material life in the manner of urban Americans. Passover thus enabled immigrants to retain an important element of communal identity while it sanctioned a basic American attitude.[36]

Prescriptions for American Jewish synagogues and American Jewish seder services encouraged the accommodation of both sides of the equation—Jewish and American, as "kiddush cups brought from the Old World mingled with the 'good dishes' and the Community Silver (actually silverplate) purchased in the New."[37]

Coalescence extends into elite Jewish environments, and is not limited to marginally committed Jewish populations. Because coalescence permeates virtually all strata of American Jewish life, from Orthodox through Reform, from well-educated leaders through the Jewish masses, it differs from the confusion about Jewish traditions that Marshall Sklare and Charles Liebman each observed years ago among minimally educated American Jews. The tendency of the common American Jew to blur distinctions between Jewish and American values was described first by Sklare in the late 1960s in his incisive analysis of "The Image of the Good Jew in Lakeville," in *Jewish Identity on the Suburban Frontier*,[38] and then in the early 1970s by Charles Liebman in compelling analyses of folk and elite religious belief systems. Sklare noted that suburban American Jews with minimal Jewish education tend to cherish those "Jewish" values that they find first in liberal American culture and then, only secondarily locate in Jewish historical culture and texts. In contrast, Sklare correctly noted, those Jewish values and behaviors that did not fit easily into an American lifestyle or map of beliefs were simply ignored, or labeled as "minor" by laypersons.

Sklare felt that this blurring of American and Jewish values was facilitated by the poverty of Jewish educational opportunities. He saw poor Jewish education as the "bete noir" of Jewish life in the suburbs, leading to a lack of distinctiveness and ultimately an erosion of group boundaries.

> At first glance the ideal of Jewishness predominating in Lakeville seems to be that of the practice of good citizenship and an upright life. To be a good Jew it means to be an ethical individual; it also means to be kind, helpful, and interested in the welfare of neighbors, fellow Americans, and of humanity at large. . . . while the ethic identified by our respondents is certainly intrinsic to Judaism, it appears that the motive power for their making such an identification comes from the general culture. . . . [Thus,] while the Lakeville Jew may be following certain Jewish sources when he formulates his ideals, the lack of distinctiveness inherent in his model of the good Jew is capable of eroding away group boundaries.[39]

Liebman ascribed the bringing together of disparate elements as part and parcel of the folk religion of American Jews, and he contrasted this widespread blurring of boundaries among the uneducated Jewish masses with the more clearly demarcated belief systems of the Jewish elites. Indeed, two decades ago Liebman was hopeful that the tide had turned, and that the leaders of liberal Jewish movements—unlike the Jewishly ignorant or apathetic masses—had discovered the power and importance of Jewish cultural distinctiveness:

> The prevalent notion in American life is that a "religious" person is someone who behaves morally. . . . Moralism, the stress on universal standards of ethical behavior as opposed to particularistic standards of proper ritual practice and faith, dominates the religious culture of America. . . . perhaps a majority of

American Jews are indifferent to the demands of the Jewish tradition, and far more attuned to the cultural standards of urban, middle-class America. (To some degree, they even create those standards.) But these Jews do not set Jewish standards, nor do they pretend to. They neither control Jewish institutions and communal organizations, nor dictate the norms of American Jewish behavior.[40]

In contradiction to Sklare's and Liebman's assessments however, contemporary data indicate that many among today's elite strata of liberal Jews share certain perceptual commonalities with groups of American Jews who are minimally educated in Jewish history, culture, and tradition. The distinction that Liebman draws between the Protestantized stance of uninvolved Jews, positing that morality and religiosity are synonymous, and the more definitively Jewish stance of Jewish leadership, which values ritual observance for its own sake, is primarily valid among those who identify themselves as Traditional, Conservative, or Orthodox.[41]

Perhaps the widest remaining gap between elite and folk expectations exists in the Conservative movement, in which rabbinic elites approach near-Orthodox standards of behavior, while their congregants are largely satisfied to designate such religious behaviors to their clergy. Arthur A. Cohen in his novel, *The Carpenter Years,* brilliantly depicts this dichotomy between a small-town Conservative rabbi and his congregants: "It was as if he had been appointed to come out from New York to be himself a Sabbath for the Jews. . . . He was tired of being something apart: a utensil of God."[42] In contrast, Reform and Reconstructionist leaders and their congregants may both look to social action and universalist principles of *tikkun olam* (perfecting the world and repairing its ills) as the sustained mission of Jews and Judaism in modern times, utilizing their free choice to select from traditional Jewish rituals only those behaviors they feel may contribute to a meaningful Jewish experience.

As we have stated, this book utilizes statistical data, interview and focus-group materials, and quotes from fiction and film to tell the story of how American-Jewish lives arrived at their present hyphenated condition. Chapter 1 discusses the process of coalescing American and Jewish values within various American-Jewish societal subgroups. Subsequent chapters present detailed information, illustrating the status of American Jews in areas such as secular education and occupational achievement, Jewish formal and informal education, patterns of family formation, ritual observances, and organizational activities. Interwoven through these detailed explorations of specific areas of American Jewish life, the recurring motif of coalesced contemporary American-Jewish values and behaviors provides a unifying theme.

American-Jewish family values, for example, comprise an important case of coalescence. We will see that in the realms of personal choice, marriage and family planning, the American community has relocated its ethnic boundaries. Rather than being defined as a community that is highly prescriptive in its gender role construction, American-Jewish men and women today tend to be characterized by relatively permeable gender role constructions.[43]

American-Jewish attitudes toward secular education represent another striking example of coalescence. We will trace the trajectory of secular education, which first facilitated alienation from traditional Jewish lifestyles, and later was incorporated by American Jews into at a coalesced myth of themselves as "the people of the book." Within this coalesced vision, the historical conflicts between sacred and secular learning dissolved, and the two bodies of knowledge were perceived as enjoying a fruitful coexistence.

We will see that even in their relationship with their own organizations, American Jews have a coalesced, consumerist psychology, rather than a traditional notion of communal duties. Contemporary American Jews, including many lay leaders, often approach organizations looking to have particular familial, social, or spiritual needs met. Perhaps more than Jewish professional leaders would wish, the voluntaristic nature of American society has been thoroughly incorporated into the Jewish communal world.

Not only have American Jews created a coalesced American Judaism, they have also created a distinctly Jewish notion of what defines the true America. In the Jewish view of American values, the National Rifle Association, pro-life militants, white supremacists, and perhaps even right-wing Republicans are perceived as "un-American," despite the fact that these groups see themselves as the quintessential definition of flag-waving American feeling and behavior. The American hybrid preferred by Jews provides a comfortable fit for Jews and Judaism. Thus, negotiating values on both sides of the hyphen, American Jews have created a coalesced conception of America, in their own image.[44]

ONE

COALESCING AMERICAN AND JEWISH VALUES

American Jews are typified by a mostly liberal package of attitudes, which they often articulate as traditional "Jewish" values; indeed, American Jews have been associated with activities on behalf of social justice and with liberal political attitudes for much of the twentieth century. Jewish liberalism may to some extent be self-protective and linked to Jewish feelings of vulnerability, and it is surely connected to the involvement of Jews in socialist and union movements, but it is also nonetheless related to a coalesced American-Jewish tendency toward altruistic spiritual ideals. As historian Stephen Whitfield comments, "the historical record and the data of political science disclose that Jews are more susceptible than other voters to a vision of human brotherhood, to ideologies and programs that can be packaged in ethical terms, and to politicians who can present themselves as apostles of social justice. More so than other Americans, Jewish voters are inspired by ideals that can be contrived to echo the prophetic assault upon complacency and comfort."[1]

Jews from every wing of the Jewish denominational spectrum tend to be more politically liberal than Christians who occupy the same place on their own religious continuums. While a numerically small neoconservative trend has emerged among a group of Jewish intellectuals, their cause has not attracted a nationwide, grassroots following among Jews. Additionally, some traditionalist Jews have exhibited politically conservative leanings in recent years, especially in recent New York elections; however, they seem to be responding to specific local factors.

Decades ago Marshall Sklare noted that liberal American Jews "locate the source of their ethic in Judaism," although the "motive power for their making such an identification comes from the general culture."[2] Contemporary American Jews continue to articulate the belief that their liberal American values are ultimately traceable to the "essence" of prophetic Judaism. As one participant in a 1995 American Jewish Committee educational program commented:

> My personal identity generally has been as an American, rather than as a Jew. I have always considered religion as a strictly personal matter. The values of fair play, justice and hard work have been foremost in my mind. About ten years ago I got "religion" and realized that Jewish teachings were the basis for my so-called American values. Furthermore, I became impressed with the humanity of Reform Judaism.

The liberal attitudes of the majority of American Jews emerge in a variety of venues, not least in national presidential election results, which consistently place Jews overwhelmingly in the Democratic camp. Thus, an analysis of national elections from 1972 through 1996 showed that Jewish voting patterns were idiosyncratically liberal and distinctly different from other white Americans, as seen in Table 1.1.

Beyond alliegance to the Democratic party, Jewish coalesced notions of free will, individual choice, and commitment to social justice at times emerge in liberalisms that seem to go far beyond their original components. Thus, according to a *Los Angeles Times* survey immediately after elections in 1996, California Jews overwhelmingly supported Proposition 215, the California ballot measure that would legalize marijuana for medical use. Three-quarters of Jewish voters supported Proposition 215, compared to 54 percent of Catholics and 44 percent of Protestants. Even more revealing were statements by the leadership supporting the proposition. Bill Zimmerman, the Los Angeles-based campaign manager of the proposition, explained the Jewish vote by saying "Jews are always in the forefront of struggles for social justice." Marsha Rosenbaum, a former drug researcher who has written two books on the subject and now heads the West Coast branch of the Lindesmith Center, a policy institute promoting alternatives to America's "zero tolerance" drug policies, asserts that two-thirds of the leaders in the drug reform movement are Jews. Rosenbaum feels that Jews characteristically try to provide "a voice for people who aren't spoken for."[3]

Relocated Boundaries and Contemporary Social Trends

Many coalesced beliefs are already well established in American Jewish society. However, contemporary liberal movements, such as ecologically correct Judaism and Jewish feminism, provide ideal windows through which to view the actual processes first of conscious adaptation and eventually of unconscious coalescence. An adaptation-in-progress and potential arena for coalescence is found within the work of a small but passionately committed group of Jewish thinkers who are forging a form of environmentally sensitive Judaism. Formulations of eco-kashruth bespeak concerns about oppressed farm workers, unwholesome herbicides, the ravaging of the land, and cruelty to animals.

Of particular interest is the organization *Shomrei Adamah* (Keepers of the Earth), which has close ties to the Reconstructionist Rabbinical College. Calling themselves "the first eco-Jewish organization," its leaders publish curricula and run summer trips to make mainstream Jewish Americans more aware of biblical and rabbinic texts that can be construed as "deep ecology in Judaism—really!"[4] While the ideological foundations of eco-Judaism are often linked to the universalist, social activist pronouncements of the Hebrew prophets, the authors of eco-Judaism are also influenced by their American cultural milieu. They are continuing the process of creating a Judaism that harmonizes with liberal American values. They may consciously seek to avoid elements dissonant to American values, such as those exhibited by some "traditionalist religious groups" who harbor what Arthur Green characterizes as "attitudes harmful to the social order" and "protracted antagonism toward others." Such dissonant Jews cause "embarrassment over the nationalism and Israelocentrism of their own tradition and of their compatriots, the Jewish traditionalists."[5]

Similar blending is found in some segments of the "Jewish renewal" movement, which is especially prominent in some coastal California communities. As Jack Wertheimer notes, the Jewish renewal movement "is part of a larger movement that since the 1960s has sought to merge Eastern religion, the self-actualization movement, and the counterculture outlook with Jewish religious traditions, particularly with Jewish mysticism."[6] Jewish renewal groups try to incorporate joy and spontaneity into their ceremonies and services. Where tradition conflicts with particular creative aspects of religious expression, expressivity is considered paramount and traditional behavior is viewed as less compelling than the desired spiritual atmosphere. Significantly, such communities often assert that their activities are "authentic" because they foster the spiritual values of movements such as Hasidism. Spiritual authenticity, rather than revolutionary change, seems to be the desideratum when such movements discuss their own rationales.

While the Jewish renewal movement is often perceived as emanating from the Reconstructionist movement, it has had a significant impact on Conservative and Reform Jewish communities. Temples affiliated with each wing of American Judaism sometimes incorporate spiritual melodies derived from the Hasidic world into their worship services. Devotees of the more austere "classic" Reform mode of worship are not always happy with these innovations, claiming, perhaps with unconscious irony, that such melodies are not part of their "tradition."[7] Similarly, previously sedate Conservative congregations sometimes develop new institutional personalities, blending equal parts of exuberant prayer styles and communitarian good works projects—and attracting larger numbers of previously unaffiliated young adults in the process.[8] Zionism also is affected by ecological issues, as evidenced by advertisements for a Jewish National Fund and World Zionist Organization sponsored conference, the Fourth Annual Eco-Zionism Conference at the University of Texas, March 1999.

Within some Orthodox communities as well, the concepts of eco-Judaism have made significant inroads, especially among young people who have been influenced by American ecological movements. Such communities are likely to emphasize the biblical and rabbinic sources for ecological concerns in order to legitimate their attitudes and activities. Some reject the eating of kosher meats, such as veal, which putatively are produced through methods that involve cruelty to animals. Many opt for vegetarianism, calling on those texts in Jewish tradition that hail vegetarianism as a higher form of *kashrut*.

Thus, eco-Judaism and renewal interpretive communities are involved in the work of boundary relocation and "inventing tradition," which Eric Hobsbawm suggests is a critical activity in transitional societies. Tradition "invention" does not imply that its authors are fabricating attitudes and behaviors that have no foundation in the group's past, rather that the ways in which the innovative values and actions are conceptualized and emphasized differ significantly from past modes. Ironically, in order to be successful, the enterprise of inventing tradition often demands that ancient precedents, rather than innovativeness, be emphasized in the "spin" or public packaging of ideas and behaviors. Ordinarily, such new/old traditions more effectively achieve legitimacy, widespread approval, and permanence when they can be routinized, so they acquire the status of "invariance."[9] For thinkers within liberal American religious movements, however, such routinization may in itself be problematic, since it conflicts with the American-Jewish ideal of free choice and rejection of coercive dogma.

Incorporating Egalitarianism into American Judaisms

Far more overtly sweeping changes have been effected by Jewish feminists. In terms of family life and personal decisions, American-Jewish attitudes toward women have already undergone a culturewide, coalescing transformation. Jews have become the most predictably liberal group vis-à-vis women. American Jews, for example, are overwhelmingly committed to equal educational and occupational opportunity for women, and to reproductive choice.

In the religious realm as well, American-Jewish life has been transformed by American feminist goals. The Jewish community has been struggling for the past three decades to make American Judaism more feminist in its structure and liturgy. Reformers aim to juxtapose Jewish and feminist values in order to improve Judaism, which is perceived as wanting in this regard. As women move into positions of power and public prominence in worship services or synagogue politics, or as reformers work to change Jewish liturgy so that it incorporates references to biblical women, or reflects women's unique experiences, or uses gender-neutral language, they are quite conscious of the fact that they are drawing from two distinct belief systems. Wherever they can, they try to find precedents to lend traditional legitimation to their activities, but even in the absence of such traditional precedents most of them see the egalitarian moral imperative as being so compelling that they must and should proceed with change.

For the majority of American Jews today, egalitarianism is an accepted moral value—even a sacred or religious value. *Halakhah* and egalitarianism actually comprise parallel and often competing continuums of moral behavior for American Jews, as indicated in the model of Normative Religious Groups below in Figure 1.1.

As Figure 1.1 illustrates, for those Jews on the radical right, who reject the ideals of pluralism and consider only certain kinds of Orthodox Jews to be authentic, only *halakhah* is sacred, and egalitarianism has no moral hold. Many among this group espouse such antiegalitarian ideals as rebuilding the Temple in Jerusalem and reinstating the Priestly class, and reenforcing gender role distinctions far beyond the mandates of rabbinic law. Right wing Jewish groups often make a show of ostentatiously rejecting gender equality, as though to perform a symbolic exorcism of modernity by eliminating the principle of gender equality from their midst.

In contrast, for those Jews on the radical left, who wish to remake Judaism as a completely egalitarian belief system and to reincorporate female deities and woman-centered liturgies rejected by early monotheistic Jewish thinkers, only egalitarianism is sacred and *halakhah* has no moral hold: a vision of Judaism as a woman-friendly, species-friendly, earth-friendly, nonhierarchical belief system completely takes the place of traditional, patriarchal Jewish values and behaviors.

It should be noted that egalitarianism can refer to issues that are not related to gender. Socioeconomic status and professional or lay status may also affect egalitari-

	Normative Religious Groups				
L					R
Radical Left	**Normative Reconstructionist**	**Reform**	**Conservative**	**Normative Orthodox**	**Radical Right**
Remake Judaism as completely egalitarian belief system. Reject hierarchies of gender, status, socioeconomic factors. Remake Judaism as woman-friendly, species-friendly, earth-friendly religion. Re-incorporate woman-centered elements rejected by patriarchal, monotheistic, hierarchical Judaism.	Egalitarianism sacred principle. Reject most hierarchies: status, gender, religious functionaries. Regard Halakhah as system created by men with considerable historic & inspirational interest, but not binding. Reject outright paganism & witchcraft.	Egalitarianism of gender accepted, but status differences exist for institutional needs. Marked differentiation between religious functionaries and congregants. Socio-economic status can make difference. Halakhah object of study, can provide choices, but not binding.	Egalitarianism of gender accepted by most, but not all. Women may be required to live up to higher standards to "qualify." Hierarchies of religious functionaries, congregants. Most do not distinguish between priestly class and the *Yisrael* remainder of congregants. Socio-economic hierarchies matter institutionally. Halakhah cherished guideline for religious life, however seen as organically developing, responsive to changing social conditions.	Accept many halakhic hierarchies: priestly class distinctions part of regular worship service. Separation of men and women in worship & some other environments. Religious functionaries respected but often share values & lifestyles with congregants. Socio-economic hierarchies matter, but learning may provide alternative status. Halakhah system developed by rabbinic Judaism binding. Liberalization of gender roles achieved only by finding legal precedents.	Rebuild Temple, reinstate priestly class. Re-enforce gender role distinctions. Reject idea of expanding women's roles even with rabbinic guidelines. Women urged into silence, modesty; symbolic exorcism of modernity. Halakhah only guideline; little incursion of outside standards. Reject pluralism; draw lines between different grades of Orthodox Jews.

Figure 1.1 A CONTINUUM OF TWO SACRED PRINCIPLES IN AMERICAN JEWISH RELIGIOUS LIFE: RABBINIC LAW—HALAKHAH—AND EGALITARIANISM

anism: for example, a fully gender egalitarian Reform congregation may function via dramatic differences in participation between the professional Jews—rabbi and cantor—and the congregants, whereas a gender nonegalitarian Orthodox congregation may be very egalitarian in terms of religious functioning, with male congregants leading services, reading from the Torah, and giving sermons. Similarly, a gender-egalitarian Conservative or Reform congregation may accord very high status to wealthy philanthropists, and may not treat less affluent congregants in a truly egalitarian mode.

As this chapter will show, the great majority of American Jews fall into normative religious groupings which comprise the mainstream continuum: normative Reform, Reconstructionist, Conservative, Traditional, and modern Orthodox Jews. For these normative religious groups, the sacred notions of both *halakhah* and egalitarianism are often in conflict and require ongoing negotiation.

Egalitarian Visions of Orthodox Life

Evidence that American values are being coalesced not only into liberal environments but into Orthodox communities as well is particularly significant, since Orthodoxy has been presumed by many eminent Jewish sociologists to be the great stronghold of compartmentalizing behavior. Heilman and Cohen, for example, conclude their study of modern Orthodox Jews by stating, "Most American Orthodox Jews have had to live with contradiction. They have done this, as we have said, by compartmentalizing their lives."[10] However, in contrast to this assumption, observing the behavior of American modern Orthodox Jews quickly ratifies the suggestion that American Orthodoxy is far from untouched by coalescence.

While compartmentalization certainly continues among Orthodox Jews, many modern Orthodox Jews have coalesced far more American values and behaviors into their version of Judaism than either they or non-Orthodox Jews frequently realize. It is possible that modern Orthodox Jews are ideologically disposed toward coalescence because of a neo-Orthodox foundational commitment to a version of synthesis that differed greatly from that espoused by American reformers, as Sir Immanuel Jakobovits, former Chief Rabbi of the British Commonwealth explains:

> *Torah im Derekh Erets* [dual excellence: Judaic learning combined with secular refinement and knowledge] was indigenous to the West in Germany and the Anglo-Saxon communities. . . . I regard modern Orthodoxy as a philosophy of synthesis rather than of compromise, authentically in the tradition of the Rambam, followed by a long line of philosopher—or *Wissenschaft*—savants down to Hirsch, Hoffman, Epstein and J. B. Soloveitchik in the modern period.[11]

Unlike coalescence, the concept of synthesis that was espoused by many classical Judaic thinkers was based on the assumption of a deep knowledge and understanding of two great world traditions—Judaism and Western humanism—and an ability to bring these ways of understanding the human condition and humane responsibility into fruitful interaction within a vibrant, unflinchingly Jewish interpretive framework. Within coalescence, in contrast, the interpretive framework through which Judaism is evaluated is primarily derived from contemporary secularized Protestant American culture.

In some modern Orthodox institutions today, compelling commitments to egalitarian organizational principles, group consensus, self-determination, individualism, and feminism have made observable inroads, as practitioners struggle with two competing modes of conformity and with their own desires for autonomy as individuals and as a group. This confrontation is very American. As Alexis de Tocqueville noticed 150 years ago, Americans are powerfully motivated by both individualism and conformity, and tend to turn ideas and beliefs in upon themselves, wanting at the same time to be in harmony with the group, and yet to be inner directed. De Tocqueville noted that democracy and social equality lead to individualism, because they allow people to "imagine that their whole destiny is in their own hands."[12]

Across the normative denominational spectrum, on the right as well as on the left (but often struggling with differing issues), Jews try to incorporate and accommodate American and Jewish ideals. Writing in the black-hat Orthodox educational *Torah Umesorah* publication, *Jewish Parent Connection,* headmaster Rabbi Berel Wein asserts that "there is much in Americanization that can be good for Jewish society in the United States and Israel":

> The fatal error of the first generation of immigrant Jews to this country was in not being choosy and selective about "Americanization." The acceptance of "Americanization" whole, of being absorbed in the "melting pot" of American society has cost us dearly. . . . That painful lesson of history should now be apparent to us all. Therefore, our generation of American Jews must be choosy in accepting "Americanization." . . . We cannot hide from "Americanization," and all its ramifications. But our ability to be selective, the necessity of encouraging holiness, of teaching our children how to say no . . . will preserve Torah values and life within our midst. Americanization per se is not the problem."[13]

Rabbi Wein's balanced view of juggling American and Jewish values places him firmly on the normative American-Jewish continuum of values, and demonstrates the validity of Walter Wurzberger's analysis of the "two opposite approaches" represented by contemporary Orthodoxy:

> On the one extreme we have the position of the Hatam Sofer that *hadash asur min ha-Torah.* Any form of innovation, any concession to modernity, any deviation from the traditional life-style is the very antithesis of Torah. On the other extreme, we have the position of Rav Kook who maintained that *hehadash yitkadesh.* Embrace the new by all means, but do so selectively. Make sure that the *hadash* [new] can be integrated within our religious perspective, not only without doing violence to that perspective but actually contributing to its enhancement.[14]

Like other American Jews, modern Orthodox Jews are pulled between individualism and conformity, but they have two systems that demand their conformity: contemporary culture and rabbinic law.

Symptomatic of coalescence within Orthodox life is the proliferation of women's prayer groups (*tefillah* groups) in and around Orthodox congregations in many American communities. *Tefillah* groups are the embodiment of a consciousness that has coalesced Jewish and American values in complicated ways. From traditional Judaism comes the value of daily prayer (Maimonides, Nachmanides, and other religious authorities prescribe private daily prayer for women);[15] however, traditional Judaism does not envision women as members of a congregation or as needing participatory group settings for prayer. The consciousness of women as a spiritual group, rather than spiritual individuals, is drawn from contemporary American feminist cultural values, and the desire of women to work together to change their own destiny is derived from the most cherished American beliefs in self-sufficiency and the responsiveness of fate to individual courage and resourcefulness.

The coalesced nature of women's *tefillah* groups, and the attitudes and behaviors they exhibit, is underscored by the fact that the Orthodox religious framework is also nonegalitarian in ways that are not directly connected to gender.[16] The protocols of traditional rabbinic decision making are hierarchical, and in their unameliorated form fly in the face not only of feminism but also of such democratic, egalitarian principles as the rule of the majority or consensus building. When Orthodox women began to organize women's prayer meetings, from the early 1970s forward through the 1990s, although they have been perceived by many outsiders as being "feminist" in their behaviors and motivations, most of them have depended on a male rabbinic adjucator (*Posek*) to give them "permission" (*heter*) to pursue their group agendas by creating religious rulings in their favor.

This tension between feminist and Orthodox norms continues, although, in true coalescing style, it is often unrecognized. Amongst themselves, in decisions not halakhic in nature, women's *tefillah* groups operate according to feminist principles of consensus building and egalitarian empowerment. Where halakhic decisions are concerned, however, they accept the normative hierarchies of Orthodox life.[17]

Responding to the issue of women conducting their own Torah service, as well as to the perceived feminist influence in the evolution of prayer groups, for nearly three decades Orthodox rabbis as individuals and in groups have issued statements prohibiting or permitting participation of women in *tefillah* groups.[18] Contemporary rabbinic prohibitions often have a sociological rather than an halakhic basis: prayer group participants have been accused of lacking appropriately pure motivation, of looking for power rather than for spiritual expression, of rejecting their foremothers or traditional Jewish notions of femininity, and of having been influenced by the "licentiousness of feminism." In their sociologically based castigation of women's group prayer, right-wing rabbis display their own forms of coalescence. Ironically, in contrast, rabbinic defenders of women's *tefillah* groups usually eschew ideological arguments and set forth the halakhic precedents for each element of the prayer groups' activities.

Egalitarianism and Coalescence within Conservative Judaism

While coalescence in the Orthodox world is striking particularly because it is so unexpected, it is within Conservative Judaism that the tension between the sacred principles of egalitarianism and *halakhah* is often most poignant. The American Conservative movement at various junctures in its development has consistently reiterated the principle that rabbinic law has an "authority" unmatched by "social, ethical, and cultural" trends.[19] At the same time, Conservative Judaism has also frequently articulated the principle that Judaism develops "organically," that it has always responded to profound social changes, and must continue to respond. The prominent Conservative rabbi and scholar Robert Gordis traced this Conservative ideological balancing act back to the "positive-historical Judaism" of the nineteenth-century German liberal-yet-traditional rabbi Zacharias Frankel, whose conservationist ideas Gordis expressed as follows:

> Judaism within the ages was not static and unchanged, but, on the contrary, the product of historical development. This complex of values, practices and ideals, however, was not to be lightly surrendered, for the sake of convenience, conformity or material advantage, masquerading as love of progress. A positive attitude of reverence and understanding toward traditional Judaism was essential. Changes would and should occur, but they should be part of a gradual, organic growth.[20]

It is thus the legacy of Conservative rabbinic leaders to find themselves excruciatingly pulled between juxtaposed modern Western and historical Jewish values. The struggle within the Jewish Theological Seminary (JTS) in moving during the 1970s toward Conservative ordination of women, finally accomplished in 1985, brought to the forefront the conflict between American and traditional Jewish standards of evaluating appropriate behavior. When women who wanted to become Conservative rabbis wrote to the JTS faculty urging the ordination of women, they declared themselves "seriously committed to Jewish scholarship and to the study of Jewish texts" and "committed to the halachic system." They emphasized practical communal reasons for ordination of women: "there are many communities where we would be fully accepted and could accomplish much toward furthering a greater commitment to Jewish life."[21]

In the great controversy which rocked leaders and scholars at JTS, some rabbis insisted on retaining *halakhah* as the unwavering standard against which all demands must be evaluated. Some of these rabbis eventually left the seminary in protest. The attitude that prevailed allowed women to be ordained, provided they pledged themselves to a standard of halakhic near-perfection, thus showing themselves to be exceptional women. Within this formulation, the halakhic status of women as a class of Jews remained unaffected. In contrast, Gordis took the intellectual giant step of using egalitarianism as a moral standard against which *halakhah* itself must be measured:

> For many, if not for most people today, the principle of the exclusion of women as witnesses is morally questionable. In a society where women were

sheltered and had little experience or contact with the world at large, there might perhaps have been some basis for regarding their testimony as inexpert and therefore inadmissible. To defend such a principle today is, for most people, morally repugnant and sexist.[22]

Gordis insisted that rabbinic law must be brought "into conformity" with the ethical demands of egalitarianism, and resistence to this effort was "inconscionable."[23]

Only time will tell whether Judaism and feminism will truly become coalesced in religious spheres as they have in the familial realm, whether an awareness of their existence as distinctive belief systems will be erased and feminism will be perceived as being "part of" Jewish religious thought and behavior. The signs seem to indicate that Conservative Jews, both elites and folk practitioners, may be well on the way toward coalescing Judaism and feminism. For example, a Conservative academic speaking at a conference on gender and Judaism remarked that he believes that worship services that separate men and women are not only "immoral" but are also "nonhalakhick," antithetical to Jewish law. His assertion—resting on a reinterpretation of *halakhah* and contradicting as it does extensive Jewish law which prescribes just such separations—is a clear coalescing of secular and Jewish norms of moral behavior. According to such coalesced "Jewish" belief systems, egalitarianism is not only a sacred moral principle but a sacred moral Jewish principle. Among the papers presented was one that urged feminists not to retreat from an intellectual and spiritual confrontation with the halakhic system:

> . . . the halakhic system, even during its centuries as an exclusively male domain, functioned along two parallel trajectories, as a system designed to serve a functioning community, and as system designed to point to and actualize an ideal of unity. For many centuries rabbinic Judaism worked well within that tension for its men. The challenge before us now is to see if a transformed rabbinic system can work both for women and men. . . . However much women may have been excluded from positions of power in law historically, this historical exclusion has ironically led to self-exclusion in our contemporary moment. . . . Halakhah, like American law, still requires feminist revision.[24]

Free Choice and Reform Coalescence

The incorporation of the values of individualism into American Jewish life has often proceeded in an unselfconscious mode. Living in a culture that privileges individual choice over family or community, American Jews quickly absorbed the individualistic ethos, but frequently did not perceive it as being in ideological conflict with their Jewish ties. American Jews often articulate their attachment to a Judaized America and an Americanized Judaism in personal terms: America gave them the right to break free of familial ties, to pursue their own education and occupational dreams, to postpone marriage, to choose romantic partners according to their own preferences and orientation. American individualism has been thoroughly coalesced into the value systems of many American Jews. Free choice, that birthright of individualism, is not perceived as being in conflict with Judaism. On the contrary, it is often perceived as being an intrinsic axiom of Judaism itself.

Among Reform Jews, free choice was a frequently invoked Jewish value by participants in the 1994 National Commission on Jewish Women focus-group discussions, as many women who spoke of "Judaism" ascribed to Judaism attitudes and activities that were primarily American rather than Judaic in origin. They stressed the values of individualism and freedom of choice, and felt that they had learned these values from Judaism. Egalitarianism and feminist issues were often on the front burner of their Jewish consciousness. Women talked about how much more receptive Jewish environments are to women now than they were years ago. One commented, "My mother never felt comfortable going to synagogue; there was no place for her." In contrast, she said, "I feel now I can do things that were not allowed before. They now have equivalent services for girls."

Reform women felt proud and happy about the leadership role that Reform Judaism has played in promoting egalitarianism within Judaism. The coalescence of traditional Jewish values—the importance of worship and text study—with American feminist values giving women equal access to these activities, was clear in their words:

> In the present moment I am involved in synagogue membership and working as an adult and belonging to a group of Jewish women who get together informally to study. Initially, two years ago, our goal was to do a women's Seder. After that we spent six months planning for a weekend Shabbat which has to be, without a doubt, the highlight of my experience as a Jewish woman. From that point on, we have embarked upon a course of study which includes meeting once a month reading the Torah and realizing we don't have to be Torah scholars to read Torah. . . . one person brings in material from a psychological point of view. I am a media specialist at the Reform day school here and so I bring in that kind of material because that is what interests me. Someone else may bring in something from a historical point of view. It is the act of women studying and worshipping together."

In keeping with the Reform movement's concentration on social action as a religious activity, many women commented on civic activities as an important aspect of their Jewish lives. For some, the universalist ethic was paramount: a substantial proportion of Reform participants felt that many Jews worked too hard for Jewish causes and not enough for non-Jewish causes, for what one woman called the "whole world and global group." Typically, this type of Reform participant seemed totally unaware that statistically Jews today are much more likely to work for nonsectarian causes than for Jewish causes. Some Reform women said that they felt that the Jewish communal world is narrow and self-absorbed, and they pictured themselves as rebels because they were more interested in working for broader civic groups. In reality, the rejection of Jewish voluntarism in favor of nonsectarian voluntarism is currently not a rebellion from Jewish norms but a mainstream American Jewish behavior.

Many Reform women mentioned personal, spiritual issues or communal activities as the most salient vehicles for their relationship to Jewishness. They spoke about the warm, supportive feeling they have when they associate with other Jews. One woman said that Judaism provided her with "a womb-like state." Some Reform participants spoke about God and morality; others were actively involved in expanding their Jewish intellectual and spiritual lives. They differed, however, in their assessment of how much classical Jewish education might have to say to them. The Atlanta focus-group participants genuinely believed that the concept of "free choice" is an intrinsic part of classical, historic Judaism—far more intrinsic, in their minds, than ritual observance or rabbinic scholarship. Indeed, a "Judaic" belief system that incorporates the sacred American values of individualism and free choice is one that is shared by numerous elite Reform Jewish leaders and a broad spectrum of Reform congregants. Reform elites are more likely than congregants and lay persons to have a sense of how the messages of secular Western humanism, American dedication to "life, liberty, and the pursuit of happiness," and Judaic values of social activism and *tikkun olam* have been blended in Reform ideology. Congregants are more likely to believe that all of these are written in the Torah somewhere, and to be innocent of more rigid biblical references to the onerous minutia of the "yoke of the kingdom of heaven."

While Reform participants generally agreed that they felt more comfortable with Jewish women, many were quite concerned that they not sound chauvinistic. More than one declared, "I don't see Judaism as superior to other religions. All religions have the same vitality." Many Reform participants said they did not want to raise their children in a ghettoized or parochial environment. They were concerned that their children should have non-Jewish friends and should be able to get along with everyone. Many were more worried about their children becoming too narrow than they were about their children assimilating.

Reaction, Boundary Resealing—and Hidden Coalescence

This discussion has, thus far, focused on increased permeability of boundaries. However, not all movement in American Jewish life is in the direction of making boundaries more permeable. For traditional Jews, boundary resealing between the secular and Jewish worlds is an important, perennial task requiring forceful, even militant vigilance. Such boundary resealing activity is entered into far more confidently and deliberately now than it was three or four decades ago. Many choose to live in densely populated urban neighborhoods, or in isolated suburbs inhabited exclusively by their own sectarian group, so that they can maintain physical separation from persons who do not share the specifics of their lifestyles. Some have their own bus systems to transport them from those neighborhoods to their places of employment. Some groups discourage television viewing or reading of general newspapers, utilizing newspapers circulated by approved Orthodox publishers instead. Schooling is provided within specialized sectarian day schools. From reclaiming the East European insistence that leafy vegetables be officially examined to insure that no insects lurk in their green recesses (*bodek*) to declaring that all tuna fish lacking certification should be assumed to contain fragments of mammalian dolphins, the purveyors of resealed boundaries have found in the kosher food industry enthusiastic, entrepreneurial allies. Their behavior is quite conscious and deliberate, and results in a very effective reinsulation of Orthodox Jews who subscribe to their findings.

It is significant that such activities represent an exaggerated rediscovery and retrieval of stringencies, rather than an ongoing boundary maintenance. They thus go beyond mere insulation, the "lack of adoption of new cultural values and practices, in favor of maintaining a lifestyle based on the standards and norms of the original culture."[25] Jews involved in resealing the boundaries and reinsulating Orthodox communities become ever more acutely conscious of the differences between themselves and their neighbors, even in areas previously thought benign. Like the proponents of eco-kashrut who rediscover ancient Hebraic earth-friendly precepts and present them as the ultimate in authentic Judaism, some of the activists promoting creative rediscoveries—and eschewing—of nonkosher foods and activities might be considered to be working in the realm of Hobsbawm's "invented tradition," albeit with very different goals from their more liberal brothers. Some have suggested that escalating dependence on the authority of coedifed texts and a preoccupation with ritual minutia is being accompanied by a decline in intellectualism. The right-wing Orthodox world, galvanized by perceived erosion on its left flank, searches frantically for invincible and inviolable authority, while rejecting more relaxed parental patterns and familiar folkways.[26] For Orthodox Jews who are motivated to locate ever more stringent food restrictions, the goal is not to make the concept of kashrut more relevant and meaningful to American life, as it is to the eco-kashrut thinkers, but instead to reinforce social cohesion and to legitimate the status of rabbinic authority figures.[27]

This boundary resealing is a critical activity for a group that requires fairly impermeable boundaries, living in a country whose openness constantly threatens to erode boundaries and to render them permeable. However, practitioners seldom understand their behavior as a sociological phenomenon, but perceive their efforts, instead, to be halakhically mandated. This belief itself is linked to the second important task of ethnic groups, that of providing meaning to group members. At least in official written communications, Orthodox practitioners perceive and discuss their own boundary resealing behavior as a religious imperative.

Orthodox Jews are the group most likely to have arrived at the dissonant point that Charles Liebman prescribes for all American Jews who wish to survive as a meaningful group: "Any strategy of Jewish survival, I believe, has to be built around mechanisms that make deviations from contemporary standards of behavior tolerable to the Jew. This is even true for Reform Jews with their minimal level of ritual observance, given the evidence . . . that Jewish commitment of all kinds is associated with religious performance."[28]

To nontraditional Jews, however, the resealed boundaries of the traditional Jewish world are often perceived as an isolationist stance, an un-American and highly distasteful posture with which they do not wish to be connected. One suburban woman, who expressed her Judaism through political social action and has worked hard for decades on separation of church and state issues, spoke bitterly about the habit of Hasidic Jews in a neighboring town to construct apartments so that large family groupings can live side by side: "They build apartment house fortresses, and then they fill them with their parents and their sisters and their children." What might have seemed to her admirable family feeling in another religious/ethnic culture was offensive evidence of Orthodox clannishness among Jews. The great majority of American Jews have internalized the American message of "pluralism" and "tolerance," which approves pride in one's own ethnic and religious heritage, but views as bigotry or racism associating too exclusively with persons who share that heritage. Some non-Orthodox Voices for Change respondents stated they would prefer that their children marry well-educated Episcopalians rather than persons who are clearly visible as Orthodox Jews, such as Hasidim.

It should be noted that coalescing behavior permeates even the resealed American Orthodox world. American Orthodox Jews, as much as they may labor to be not like all the nations, also feel it is their birthright to enjoy pleasures that the nations offer, provided they can be supplied in an externally kosher and socially insulated package. Discussing "Sushi and Other Jewish Foods" with knowing irony, Alan Mintz comments on "the spectacle of sushi-eating Hasidim" and "the still-regnant 'fusion cookery' that is a byproduct of the acculturated status of American Jews."[29] Gourmet international culinary styles, exotic (and expensive) dry wines from far flung locales, and international group vacation opportunities are now available to and enjoyed by pious Orthodox practitioners. Weddings at which men and women eat and dance separately on opposite sides of the room are punctuated by rock music set to Hebrew or Yiddish lyrics. The wigs and clothing of many ultra-Orthodox American women are extraordinarily stylish and au courant. On a less visible level, therapists who work with Orthodox individuals have testified that contemporary American individualistic values and a variety of social dysfunctions have also been incorporated into Orthodox life, albeit perhaps not on as widespread a level as in society at large.

Coalescence within the most secluded American Jewish societies emerges, perhaps unconsciously, in their own words. According to a *New York Times* report on civil disobedience in the Satmar Hasidic suburban community, Kiryas Joel, one rebellious leader explains his vocal dissidence from the community's official policy by saying, "Here we have to fight just to freedomly express our views and educate our children the way we want and practice our religion the way the old Rabbi Joel wanted. This is a fight for our democracy."[30]

Signaling New Trends

Vivid illustrations of contemporary coping strategies such as compartmentalization and coalescence by American Jews are found in literature, film, and popular culture. The continuing American-Jewish tendency to reduce cognitive dissonance by compartmentalizing, for example, can be seen in the rather dramatic forms of internal division, ambivalent feelings, and compartmentalization in characters created by many Jewish artists.[31] At the same time, American-Jewish fiction has signalled contemporary tendencies of American Jews to move beyond compartmentalization,[32] and has indicated, significantly, that coalescence is a phenomenon that affects traditional as well as liberal Jews.

Writing from within a national ethos that promotes multiculturalism rather than the melting pot and in which many boundaries have been dramatically weakened, American Jewish writers have recently depicted contemporary Jews who seem to access texts from two cultures and merge them into a single document. One young writer who is fascinated by this merging is Allegra Goodman, whose short story, "Variant Text," humorously illustrates the process of coalescence. In Goodman's "Variant Text," Jewish day school principal Kineret Goodman, an Orthodox pedagogue who covers her hair with a kerchief in consonance with rabbinical prescriptions for female modesty, articulates the day school's guidelines in the language of coalescence: "This school is governed by the standards of Kohlberg, Piaget, the Rav Soloveichik . . . " She continues by urging a young father to dress his little girl in skirts, rather than dungarees, in an impassioned diatribe that coalesces religious rabbinic, psychological Freudian, and educational Kohlbergian prescriptions:

> The gan is working to teach Yiddishkeit, and that's a complete world picture which includes tsniustic clothes. Attalia has to wear dresses and skirts now if she is to have a healthy sexual and social identity later. Psychologically this is crucial; if she dresses like a boy, she'll never find her place within the peer group and interact normally. That's what we're working for here. We want every child at Kohlberg stage three by the end of the term.[33]

In Goodman's "Variant Text," the protagonist is a self-styled modern Orthodox Jewish man, a voracious reader and rigorous intellectual. One Saturday morning, the story tells us, Cecil, as usual, walks his children to the synagogue:

> Cecil sports an ABORTION RIGHTS button pinned to the lapel of the suit he bought after his wedding. . . . "This is very bad," he says when they reach the shul. Someone is pushing strollers on Shabbat. It's shocking, really, and isn't any different than driving a vehicle or carrying, when you think about it. In fact, there are two strollers on the steps of the building.[34]

Cecil is doubly offended: first more than one congregant has wheeled a baby carriage to the synagogue despite the absence of an *eruv* (a ritual device that renders an entire community private property according to Jewish law and thus an appropriate space in which to carry or wheel objects on the Sabbath). Second, the husband of one woman who pushed a stroller to the synagogue is called up to make a blessing over the weekly reading of the Torah portion. According to the strictest interpretation of Jewish law, a person who participates in any violation of the Sabbath should not receive such an honor; however, this prohibition is subject to much interpretation and is often neglected even in Orthodox congregations. Wearing his "Abortion Rights" pin, Cecil strides forward and vehemently protests what he considers to be a flagrant violation of Jewish law.

By wearing an "Abortion Rights" button in a place of Orthodox public Jewish worship Cecil has surely offended many more people than the husband of the carriage pushing woman who blesses the Torah. Rabbinic law, while notably different than the dogma of the "Right to Life" proponents, also works with different axioms than those of the "Right to Choice" proponents, assuming that neither men nor women own their bodies in quite the mode that is commonly assumed in contemporary liberal circles. The categories and considerations of Jewish law vis-à-vis reproductive rights do not easily match the current debate.

The reader understands this situation to be humorous because it is so incongruous. The reader may well feel that Cecil is spiritually tone deaf—an interpretation that is quite consonant with the story, because Cecil is obtuse as a father, husband, son-in-law, and colleague. He imagines himself to be a feminist, when he is merely equally insensitive to men and women. However, one thing that Cecil is not doing is compartmentalizing the Jewish and secular values that he holds dear. On the contrary, the learned, observant, and politically liberal Cecil is coalescing two value systems. He does not compartmentalize his political liberalism and his Orthodox rigor, as he advertises his pro-choice attitudes in an Orthodox worship setting. Like the vast majority of American Jews (although perhaps not the majority of contemporary Orthodox Jews), Cecil is firmly in the liberal camp. More than any other ethnic or religious group, American Jews are sweepingly committed to reproductive rights, both as individuals and in their organizational statements.[35]

Thus, Cecil's coalesced belief system is very much in the American Jewish mainstream. On the computer screen of life, Cecil accesses American and Jewish values simultaneously and merges their messages.

A similar coalescence is found in Joan Micklin Silver's 1980s film "Crossing Delancey." In one memorable scene, one of the protagonist's Jewish female friends has decided to have a baby even though she is "not yet" living with the child's father. As the baby is a boy, she invites a large group of family and friends to a traditional *brit milah* (ritual circumcision ceremony) in her apartment, complete with refreshment-laden tables and a young rabbi-mohel who gently teaches those attending about Jewish laws and customs. In inviting her friends and family to this traditional ceremony, the young mother coalesces several values from diverging sources: (1) the Jewish ritual requirement for an appropriate circumcision ceremony; (2) the traditional Jewish personal bias toward reproduction; (3) the Jewish communal value of sharing circumcision ceremonies with the community; (4) and the very secular American value of sexual and reproductive choice even for single women. In contrast, the baby's grandmother is not ready or willing to merge these value systems. Presumably more comfortable with the compartmentalization of secular and Jewish values, she refuses to come to the ceremony. Instead, her sister, the baby's great-aunt, comes to and participates in the ceremony, bemoaning both her sister's narrow-mindedness and her niece's daring.

For some viewers, the ultimate symbols of coalescence are found on the television screen. The popular, long-running dramatic series "Northern Exposure," for example, featured several episodes in which frequent protagonist Joel Fleishman, a New York-born Jewish physician, explores his relationship to Jews and Judaism in isolation in the town of Sicily, Alaska. In one episode, Fleishman goes through a great deal of effort to assemble a *minyan* (prayer quorum) of ten Jews with whom to recite the *kaddish* prayer for the dead. However, Fleishman resolves his arduous search by concluding that Jewishness is not an appropriate criterion to determine the persons who comprise his community. Fleishman decides that his community of faith is based on caring, supportiveness, shared feeling and experience, and is comprised of his good, non-Jewish friends in Sicily—not strangers who happen to be born Jews. Gathering Sicily's quirky and lovable characters, Fleishman, with great fervor, recites the *kaddish* prayer, which they respond to with deep, supportive feeling. The desire to recite *kaddish* with a *minyan* is, of course, a time-honored Jewish tradition. The episode's resolution that something as arbitrary as the religion one is born into should not limit religious interaction is pure Americana—and is presented as an appropriate alternative to Jewish law.

The "Northern Exposure" episode should not be presumed to be mere artistic exaggeration; the extent to which television programs reflect coalescence in American Jewish life and values is frequently corroborated by other types of evidence. For example, in a recent op-ed piece in the *Wall Street Journal*, a reporter from the *Journal*'s Boston bureau reports attending a "Cambridge-style Passover Seder, BYOP, Bring Your Own Place Setting." Participants soon discovered "we were missing something else: Jews. There were only three" among the thirteen attending:

> We used modern Haggadot, which describe the exodus from Egypt, but they were not modern enough. Someone complained that references to "lightness and darkness" carried negative connotations for people of color. Susan, an Episcopalian, was complimented for her skillful reading of Hebrew. "I went to divinity school," she explained. . . . We improvised on other matters. A Passover song, "The Ballad of the Four Children," was sung to the tune of "My Darling Clementine" and "La Cucaracha." A new-age prayer was read decrying alienation, anomie, and "the pharaohs of technology." Individuals read special poems or literary passages. We heard a selection from e.e. cummings and a few words from "Candide." A friend suggested I read "the Midnight Ride of Paul Revere," as it combines the theme of exodus with a New England twist."[36]

Qualitative and quantitative research, literature, film and popular culture, and anecdotal materials all indicate that American Jews today inhabit a universe that is substantively different from the contexts of Jewish lives in earlier periods of Jewish history. This transformed cultural context of Jewish existence has had a profound impact on Jewish lifestyles. The coming chapters focus on the details of contemporary Jewish lifestyles and societies in specific areas: secular education and occupational profiles, Jewish education, households and family formation, Jewish behaviors of households, and organizational activities. By focusing on each of these areas and then considering the overall picture they comprise, we can gain insights into the changed equations of American-Jewish life. Perhaps most important, we can increase our understanding of those aspects of coalescence which threaten and those which can contribute positively to a vital American-Jewish future.

Table 1.1 **Jewish Voting Patterns in Recent American Presidential Elections**
Percentages of Jews Voting for Each Candidate

Religion	1972 Nixon/McGovern		1976 Carter/Ford		1980 Reagan/Carter/Anderson		
WASP	76	22	41	58	63	31	6
CATHOLIC	54	44	54	44	50	42	7
JEW	34	64	64	34	39	45	15

1984 Reagan/Mondale		1988 Bush/Dukakis		1992 Clinton/Bush/Perot			1996 Clinton/Dole/Perot		
72	27	66	33	33	47	21	36	53	10
54	45	52	47	44	35	20	53	37	9
31	67	35	64	80	11	9	78	16	3

Source: Exit poll data, adapted from *The New York Times* Nov. 10, 1996. p. 28.

Two

Tracing Educational and Occupational Patterns

Sacred and Secular Education as Cultural Values

The secular educational and occupational achievements of contemporary American Jews, and the comfort with which these achievements now fit into American-Jewish lives, comprise powerful evidence of the phenomenon we are calling coalescence. American Jewish men and women today are unusual in their multigenerational high levels of educational achievement and occupational status. These achievements are understood by American Jews (with the exception of the Orthodox right wing) to be extensions of typical, time-honored Jewish values and behaviors. Essentialist descriptions of Jews as "the people of the book" are commonplace in both scholarly and popular spheres.

Assessing *Assimilation in American Life,* for example, sociologist Milton Gordon (1964) argued, "the stress and high evaluation placed upon Talmudic learning was easily transferred under new conditions to a desire for secular education."[1] The father of American-Jewish sociology and self-described "survivalist" Marshall Sklare (1971) ratified this argument in his seminal study of *America's Jews:*

> Jewish culture embraced a different attitude toward learning from that which characterized the dominant societies of Eastern Europe. This Jewish attitude was part of the value-system of the immigrants. It pertains to learning in general, though in the traditional framework it is most apparent with respect to the study of religious subjects. Learning is seen as a positive good—the more learning, the more life.[2]

On a grassroots level, the myth of a "natural" Jewish affinity for secular education goes as follows. In traditional communities, Jews were "the people of the book," devoting themselves with religious intensity to sacred texts. When Jews came to the United States, they took their characteristic passion for sacred study and reapplied it to secular study with a virtually religious intensity. Jews believed in education, and education rewarded their faith; through secular education, Jews leapfrogged into the professions. Within one or two generations, thanks to their religious faith in and ritualistic devotion to secular education, Jews were radically transformed from Europe's wretched outcasts into middle- and upper-middle-class mainstream white Americans. As an informing myth, this understanding of Jews transforming themselves from the chosen people of the holy books to the secularized "people of the book" has enabled

American Jews to effectively reduce the cognitive dissonance created by living in and feeling loyalty to two worlds at once.

However, the actual social-historical role of secular education in the shaping of American Jewish societies was far more complex. What Gordon calls the "transfer" from "Talmudic learning" to "secular education" did not proceed with the "ease" with which nostalgic hindsight often supplies it. During much of the nineteenth and twentieth century secular education functioned as a facilitator of rupture with the Jewish past. And yet, when Jews are portrayed as the people of the book, distinctions between secular Western and historical Jewish religious traditions of learning are blurred, and a coalesced notion of seamless complementarity emerges as historical "fact."

This is not to diminish the incomparable role of Jewish education as a critically important strategy for accomplishing social goals during many eras of Jewish history. Education functioned as a countersyncretic force as developing Judaism confronted a changing series of surrounding societies, including but not limited to Babylonian, Persian, Greek, Roman, Spanish, Turkish, Arabic, Western and Eastern European, and finally American cultures. Although Jewish communities were demonstrably influenced by elements of diverse civilizations, Jewish written and oral traditions educated for dissonance and provided a matrix into which alien elements could be absorbed—and transformed.

Perhaps most dramatic, after the destruction of the second temple (70 C.E.), educational activities played an increasingly central role in the reorganization and reconstruction of traditional Jewish culture as we know it. Biblical Judaism, with its elaborate network of cultic, Temple-based sacrificial rituals, developed into the rabbinic Judaism of the Diaspora, which emphasized home-based rituals, prayer, and life-long education, within a decentralized structure of communal synagogues presided over by local rabbinic religious and educational authorities. The family, synagogue, and informal study hall (*beit midrash*), as well as formal classrooms in the community *heder* (children's school) and various *yeshivot* (schools of higher rabbinic education) each became "teaching environments" and served intricately interwoven educational functions.[3] Many scholars consider this extraordinary social emphasis on Jewish education as a prime key to "the riddle of the continued existence of Judaism despite the catastrophe which overwhelmed it."[4]

For nearly two thousand years, the study and explication of sacred texts served as a powerful force for social cohesion. Although Jews seldom were truly a community of scholars, scholarship was the ideal, and education shaped the lives of even common Jews. The rabbinic precept that Torah study is equivalent to and leads to all other forms of religiously mandated piety and social responsibility (*Talmud Torah k'neged kulam*) became the much-quoted axiom of a norm of expectation, if not reality. For the elite group of *lerners* (student/scholars) who followed intensive Talmud study into their adult lives, this quintessentially Jewish intellectual activity came to define existence. As Samuel Heilman argues, they really were the people of the book:

> Mirroring the give-and-take of the sages quoted in the Talmud, the *lerners* refer to parallels in other sacred Jewish literature, review supporting commentaries and related codices of Jewish law, evaluate the significance of what they

have read and debate its conclusions. . . . The students' concerns and words merge with the issues and language of the Talmud they review. This is the ultimate step of the process, the point at which life and *lernen* become one.[5]

Physical and intellectual contact with non-Jewish neighbors was limited in many Jewish societies prior to emancipation. In historical Jewish communities, with notable exceptions in Spain and Italy, few Jews enjoyed systematic Western education before the eighteenth century. Lacking other outlets, the brightest Jewish men were likely to find within Jewish text study an intellectual satisfaction that was charged with religious meaning and that linked them to their coreligionists past and present, as Jacob Katz points out:

> As long as the Jew was segregated from the surrounding world, being Jewish posed no problem to him. Hence all religious traditions were accepted naively and unchallenged. Aside from a few rare exceptions like Spinoza (1632–1677), even the most distinguished minds found in the study and observance of this tradition their intellectual satisfaction, presenting as it did a world of faith and thought that corresponded to their own perception of reality.[6]

Jewish societies were profoundly albeit unevenly transformed during the late eighteenth and nineteenth centuries, with advancing waves of social change leading to the emancipation of the Jews in France, Germany, and England, and considerably later in Eastern Europe. Gradually the gates of Western educational opportunity opened to the Jews, providing access to modernity. As Katz emphasizes, the way *Out of the Ghetto* and the "whole program of the Enlightenment" was "an educational one."[7] Emancipators offered Jews the opportunity to emerge from their pariah status, and, through education, to be part of humanity at large.

Standing at the crossroads of modernity, Jews stood between two very different educational traditions: sacred Jewish texts linked them to their national past, while secular Western texts promised them access to the rest of the world. For many, embracing one set of cultural texts meant rejecting the other. The process of Westernization set in motion by educational access was augmented for many European and Russian Jews by sweeping social movements, including socialism, nationalism, individualism, and secular intellectual and cultural trends. Some Jews fled from the piety and isolation of the *shtetl* to the relative personal and intellectual freedom and cultural excitement of urban centers.

For those who saw little intrinsic value in Jewish culture or traditions, historical Jewish civilization was a retrograde quicksand. Antisemitism created a negative image of things Jewish which many of the most Westernized Diaspora Jews themselves internalized. Many nineteenth-century non-Jews in London, Vienna, and the United States believed Jewishness to be essentially pathological, as Sanford Gilman has chillingly demonstrated. Jewish men were perceived as physically weak, hysterical beings, unmanly in their physiologies and psychologies.[8] Antisemitism engraved upon Jewish minds a grotesque image of what Jews had been, and precipitated in them passionate convictions that Jews must change.

Western education was to be the route whereby Jews would learn to leave behind the ignorance and superstition of their religious traditions and folk ways, along with their distinctive clothing, customs, and behaviors. Although *maskilim,* Zionists, socialists, and assimilationists had very different views of the Jewish future, their attitudes toward the past status of Diaspora Jews was similar. The enlightened, emancipated Jews who shaped twentieth-century Jewish history wished to be Jews, but not Jews in the image the Western world had come to know. Diverse Jewish groups felt that the image of the Diaspora Jew must be replaced by a very different new Jew. The particulars of the image of this new Jew differed from ideology to ideology, but those aspects of the "old" Diaspora Jew which were to be discarded had remarkable commonality from group to group. In Europe and in the United States, a new image of the Jew was envisioned that would contradict, point by point, the image of the putative physically inept, dependent, passive, impotent, overly intellectual, neurotic Jewish male.

European Jewish religious leaders reacted in a variety of ways to the challenges posed by the new access of Jews to Western scientific and humanistic study, as well as by the pervasively negative attitude toward the most distinctive Jewish lifestyles. Some rabbinical figures attempted to stem the tide by banning secular studies and Western intellectualism outright, agreeing with Rabbi Moses Sofer (the *Hatam Sofer,* 1762–1839) that "everything new is forbidden by the Torah."[9]

However, in contrast to those who saw Jewish and Western education as antithetical to each other, many nineteenth-century European and American thinkers very deliberately worked to harmonize these two traditions of learning. In Germany, modern Orthodox rabbis and intellectuals as well as Reformers sought commonalities between the teachings of Judaism and those of Western wisdom. Such thinkers downplayed rabbinic Judaism's particularistic traditions, and emphasized instead Judaism's "beneficial byproducts," such as a healthful, moderate lifestyle and compassionate, ethical behavior, "the language of *Weltanschauung* rather than religion," as Katz explains: "This attitude was characteristic not of liberal theologians alone, but even of Orthodox rabbis who refused to yield a single iota of traditional doctrine or ritual. Reading their sermons, we find them caring more about the general outlook and attitudes derived from religion than about religion itself."[10]

The most cataclysmic, disruptive Westernizing changes occurred for most Jews after the long physical voyage westward to America. As European Jews emigrated in ever-greater numbers to the United States from the middle of the nineteenth through the first decades of the twentieth century, the educational settings they encountered in America exacerbated day-to-day, real-life conflicts between secular education and Jewish religious practices and folkways.

Jewish immigrants did not begin as an especially literate group; contemporary historians agree that higher levels of secular education among American Jews followed and were a function of upward socio-economic mobility, rather than causing it. Educational achievement was uneven within family units: younger children were far more likely to finish high school and/or attend college than older siblings, and male children received far more years of schooling than female children.[11]

The Yiddish-speaking children of immigrants went to public schools, often receiving from their teachers the English names—and American attitudes—they would carry with them for a lifetime. American Jews took to the public school systems, which seemed to fulfill the emancipation that Europe had promised, with enthusiastic devotion. As Jonathan Sarna describes the attraction:

> Jews perceived them as an entree to America itself and supported them as a patriotic duty. Thus, while the Catholic church looked upon the public school as a symbol of much that was wrong with America, and therefore set up its own system of parochial school education, Jews wholeheartedly supported and even idealized public education as a symbol of America's promise . . . the schools were a synecdoche for America itself.[12]

American public school education became a genuine—and coalesced—American-Jewish value.

On the one hand, many immigrant parents hoped to experience vicarious Americanization through their children's triumphs. As Irving Howe notes, while parents frequently felt themselves "trapped in the limitations of their skills," they looked to their American-educated children to "achieve both collective Jewish fulfillment and individual Jewish success."[13] On the other hand, the public schools not only provided Jewish children with necessary skills to take advantage of American opportunities, they also tended to fill the hearts of Jewish youth with disdain for immigrant mores, and even a repulsion for the behaviors of their Jewish parents. Intergenerational battles often ensued.

Immigrant authors such as Abraham Cahan and Anzia Yezierska describe an intergenerational cultural chasm dramatically exacerbated by the proclivity of the children of immigrants to acquire relatively high levels of secular education. In Yezierska's "Children of Loneliness," for example, a daughter returning from Cornell is repelled by and sharply criticizes her parents in their slovenly tenement kitchen, arousing her father's defensive wrath: "Pfui on all your American colleges. Pfui on the morals of America. No respect for old age. No fear for God. Stepping with your feet on all the laws of the holy Torah. A fire should burn out the whole new generation. They should sink into the earth, like Korah." Yezierska's college daughter reflects on the way education made her aware of her own "natural" affinity for civilized, American ways of life: "How is it possible that I lived with them and like them only four years ago? What is it in me that so quickly gets accustomed to the best? Beauty and cleanliness are as natural to me as if I'd been born on Fifth Avenue instead of the dirt of Essex Street." Yezierska herself, unsurprisingly, was romantically involved with John Dewey, the high priest of secular education.

The association between secular educational/occupational achievement and assimilative weakening of family and Jewish communal ties extended far beyond intellectual issues, and was readily apparent to many observers. Men and women describing elementary and high schools in the interwar period recall much-admired Yankee and Irish school teachers who labored to cleanse the Yiddish inflections from their students' voices and Jewish gestures and affect from their carriage. Jews who aspired to attending colleges or teacher's "normal" institutions were examined and required to demonstrate the pure American quality of their enunciation and presentation.[14]

Despite the conflicts experienced by many Jews during the process of Westernization, a "cult of synthesis" revisioning Jewish culture and Western culture to make them compatible with each other became more and more prevalent both in Europe and America. Jonathan Sarna presents as an example of synthesizing attitudes a graduation message taken from the 1955 Hebrew Educational Alliance of West Colfax (Denver, Colorado) Hebrew School graduation: "We pass to them—to all our sons and daughters—a Judaism and an Americanism which reinforce each other." Suggesting that this cult of synthesis may well be regarded as the birthplace of later coalescence, Sarna recalls Charles Liebman's incisive articulation of the mind-set of synthesizing Jews: "There is nothing incompatible between being a good Jew and a good American, or between Jewish and American standards of behavior. In fact, for a Jew, the better an American one is, the better a Jew one is."[15] The editing of Jewish traditions, downplaying aspects of Jewishness not wholly compatible with American values, was one important acculturation strategy utilized by American Jews.

Another very widespread coping strategy, as Jews dealt with the overt or implicit antisemitism that characterized many American schools and workplaces until well after World War II,[16] was the construction of compartmentalized worlds: Jews behaved as undifferentiated Americans (as middle-class white Protestants) at school or work, and relaxed into their overtly Jewish ethnic identity primarily when they socialized or worshipped with coreligionists. Indeed, as sociologist Herbert Gans discovered, even those acculturated American Jews who sought out largely gentile suburban settings to raise their families in the decades immediately before and after World War II often found themselves longing for the comfort level they found with Jewish friendship circles, and looking for the markers that revealed other Jews in their putatively non-Jewish neighborhoods: Jewish surnames, ritual objects in the home, Yiddish or "Yinglish" phrases punctuating conversation.[17]

A minority of American Jews, motivated perhaps by some combination of ambition, self-loathing, apathy or fearsome memories, opted to minimalize contact with Jews and Judaism to the point of nonexistence. Higher education often played a role in facilitating the entry of aspiring Americans into non-Jewish work and social circles. Small studies conducted at midcentury suggested that extensive secular education tended to alienate individuals from Jewish connections, or at least might be especially sought out by persons striving to become part of the upper echelons of American society. Some studies showed that college professors and professionals, especially psychologists, were usually distant from Jewish life. Symptomatically, such professionals were two to six times more likely to marry non-Jews (depending on location).[18] During a time period when compartmentalization was still at its height, these highly educated persons who wanted to emphasize primarily their American identity often found outmarriage useful on many levels.

Western intellectualism was viewed as antithetical to, and a ticket away from, Jewish associations by some Jewish members of the intelligentsia. One striking example of the American Westernized intellectual Jew was Clement Greenberg, described by an art scholar as "America's most potent and consequential art critic":

> Born in the Bronx in 1909 to Polish Jews of Lithuanian extraction, he attended Syracuse University and not City College, the fabled stamping ground of many other New York intellectuals. . . . In the ideologically troubled and troubling 1930s, he road horses in a Brooklyn park. Yet Greenberg pined for higher social status. All his life, he courted socially elevated women.

Greenberg's enormously influential art theories, articulated first in a 1939 essay in *Partisan Review,* called "Avant Garde and Kitsch," helped him to establish himself as totally removed from his beginnings, according to his biographer. "Like beautiful and well-born women, formalist esthetics seemed to beckon to Greenberg from a higher realm of freedom."[19]

Secular Educational Achievement

In contrast to the often inverse relationship between secular educational achievement and Jewish connectedness in the past, today secular education is pervasive and may enhance Jewish cohesiveness. One reason why secular education is now associated with more, not less, Jewish involvement, is that it has become a source of intergenerational similarities: Jewish families are increasingly characterized by disproportionately high levels of secular education, frequently involving two and three generations of college graduates. While educational opportunities often divide generations and classes among other ethnic and religious groups, among Jews the acquisition of high educational levels often bonds families and social groups together within the community.

This paradigm shift and its significance was explained by Calvin Goldscheider in his 1986 discussion of Boston Jews and non-Jews in *Jewish Continuity and Change: Emerging Patterns in America,* noting that the familial and communal impact of the college education experience changed when college education became widespread among Jewish parents and grandparents as well as children:

> the pattern shifted dramatically for those born between 1916 and 1930 (mostly second-generation) who advanced rapidly beyond high school to college. . . . The bimodal educational pattern characteristic of second-generation Jews has yielded to the greater homogeneity of the third and fourth generations. The growing educational similarity of younger Jews contrasts with the continuing bimodality of both Protestant and Catholic males. Hence, educational differences between Jews and non-Jews has widened, while differences among Jews have narrowed.[20]

Intergenerational educational continuity is no doubt one factor in the "democracy" of Jewish families which Andrew Greeley found in a 1973 study of internal dynamics within white ethnic American families. Greely noted that Jewish parents were far less likely than some others to establish authoritarian hierarchies in the family setting.[21] This, and a cultural bias toward children moving on, out, and up, has meant that Jewish parents have been unlikely to perceive children's educational achievement as threatening; to have a child who exceeded one's own reach is perceived as a badge of honor rather than of shame. Frances Kobrin Goldscheider has shown that Jewish parents have characteristically facilitated their children's separation through education and geographic mobility, while parents in some other ethnic groups have behaved ambivalently or even tried to retain children in familiar educational and employment patterns, for the sake of family and community solidarity. In spite of some ethnic humor that pegs Jewish parents as being more controlling, Jewish parents are most likely to help students apply for college, graduate, and professional schools, to help them look for separate apartments, and to promote independent living in other ways.[22] For Jews, not only higher education, but higher education away from home has become normative.

Among younger cohorts of American Jews, higher education per se does not mitigate against Jewish involvements. Across the denominational spectrum, the coalescence of American and Jewish values is illustrated in the extent to which each segment of the community participates in the American educational dream. Jewishly committed younger Americans, including modern Orthodox Jews, do not substantially differ from the educational patterns characteristic of other Jews in their cohort. Indeed, as Moshe and Harriet Hartman have painstakingly demonstrated in their recent monograph, "the more involved in formal and informal Jewish social circles, the collective celebration of Jewish identity, and the closer to Orthodox affiliation, the higher is the educational achievement." Not only does traditionalism no longer have a negative impact on secular educational levels, but even within individual households, "contrary to popular opinion, Orthodoxy is not associated with more spousal inequality: educational differences are even smaller than among the Conservatives, Reforms, and Reconstructionists." When the narrowed gender gap and the positive relationship between secular education and Jewish connections are considered together, secular education for women emerges as associated with stronger, not weaker, Jewish bonds. As the Hartmans note, "the relationship between Jewishness and education is slightly stronger for women than for men."[23]

The 1990 NJPS data document a pattern of exceptional levels of educational achievement for both men and women. For many decades, Jewish women received more secular education than most non-Jewish women, but less education than Jewish men. The generally high level of secular education among American Jews resulted in an ironic disparity: among most non-Jewish Americans, the majority of men *and* women did not go much beyond high school, so the gender gap in secular education was relatively modest. Among Jews, in contrast, men were far more likely and women somewhat more likely than other Americans to continue their education. Because of their higher levels of secular education in general, the educational gender gap among Jews was more striking. Among Jews ages 55 to 64, for example, "men were twice as likely as women to get any college degree, and four times as likely as women to receive a Ph.D."[24]

An impressive narrowing of the gender gap in secular education is seen in Table 2.1. Among Jews ages 35 to 44, a cohort which is likely to have completed any graduate or professional education, about one-third each of women (32 percent) and men (35 percent) completed college, and an additional 38 percent of women and 41 percent of men had graduate degrees. However, within this highly educated group, there are still significant gender differences, in that men were more than twice as likely as women to have gone on beyond a Master's degree (22 percent compared to 10 percent). Among men ages 55 to 64, levels of secular education are not appreciably different than they are among men ages 35 to 44. Among Jewish women, in contrast, educational levels escalate dramatically from the older to the younger group: for women ages 55 to 64, over half (55 percent) had not gone beyond high school, 20 percent graduated college, and 21 percent had graduate degrees.

Table 2.2 shows that Jewish men and women have nearly identical mean years of secular education, compared to approximately three years less education for all U.S. white males and females ages 25 to 29. For all U.S. white males ages 40 to 44, years of education are three years less than Jewish men in the same cohort; for all U.S. white females ages 40 to 44, the mean years of education are four years less than Jewish women. Thus, in the cohort ages 25 to 44, women's educational achievement before and after the child-bearing years more closely resembles their brothers than their Jewish mothers or non-Jewish sisters. Only during the decade when American-Jewish women today are most likely to bear children, ages 30 to 39, do the Jewish women's mean years of secular education lag by half a year or more below that of Jewish men their age.[25] Among Jewish women ages 35 to 44, 32 percent completed their bachelor's degrees; 28 percent had master's degrees; and ten percent had Ph.D.s or professional degrees.

Levels of higher education tend to differ by geographical location, and when Jews relocate for educational or occupational opportunities, or for other reasons, relocation itself and a variety of geographical factors can have an impact on affiliational patterns.[26] The impact of geography on secular educational levels is also especially pronounced for women. Studies of Jewish populations in a number of cities in the 1980s, show that of Jewish women ages 25 to 34, graduate degrees were earned by 41 percent of women in Boston, compared to 26 percent in MetroWest, New Jersey, 26 percent in Baltimore, 18 percent in Phoenix, 31 percent in San Francisco, 26 percent in Washington, D.C., and 18 percent in Kansas City, Missouri. Thus, normative educational levels can differ quite substantially from community to community, depending to a great extent on the occupational opportunities found in a particular geographical area, and also on the self-selection process through which individuals are attracted to a given area.

Occupational Status and Labor Force Participation

Occupational achievements of American-Jewish men and women today closely follow, and are often built upon—but are not identical with—their educational achievements. Just as dramatic generational change in educational achievement is demonstrated in the 1990 NJPS data, a shift in occupational status for younger Jews, especially women, is evident as well, as seen in Table 2.3. The more striking shift upward in professional status among younger women, as compared to Jewish men, is primarily created by the fact that Jewish men achieved a shift to high-status professions at least a generation earlier than Jewish women. Thus, the percentage of high-status female professionals doubles from those age 45 and over to those age 25 to 44, from 7 percent to 14 percent. Among Jewish men, in contrast, a slight decline occurs, from 26 percent of the older men to 22 percent of the younger men. Within the helping professions, such as teachers below the college level, nurses, librarians, social workers, midlevel technical or scientific work, men showed nearly a 50 percent increase from older to younger groups, with a slightly lower percentage for women. The increased prominence of women among certain professional groups may also be influenced by the possible "feminization" of some fields.

Exploring the leading occupations of American-Jewish men and women 25 years and older, one out of every ten Jewish men in this group works as a manager or administrator, with another 9 percent employed in advertising, insurance, or as real estate agents or consultants, and 8 percent defining themselves as sales clerks. In contrast, about 4 percent each are physicians, lawyers, and accountants, and 3 percent each are engineers and teachers.[27] Anecdotal evidence suggests that Jewish men today, even those with very high levels of educational achievement, are going into business much more frequently than men in their educational cohort did in the 1950s, 1960s, and 1970s. This pro-business trend reverses patterns seen in the decades immediately after World War II, when Jewish men often acquired educational opportunities as part of the GI Bill, and were often eager to leave the family business and to become professionals. Entire families took pride in and facilitated this development—a familial pattern that led to widespread cultural awareness of and numerous jokes about Jewish physicians and attorneys.

The contemporary shift of males into business careers is occurring partially because of new developments in United States public policy and economics, including increased bureaucratic and salary limitations in fields such as medicine, and decreased employment opportunities in many professional capacities, such as engineering and academics. In addition, the businesses that attract contemporary highly educated American-Jewish men often make use of their professional training. Men trained as lawyers or engineers frequently work in business settings that make use of their scientific or legal skills. Finally, it should be noted that the social status of business employment was upgraded throughout middle- and upper-middle-class American society in the 1980s. Journalists and the popular media glamorized successful business entrepreneurs. Thus, some Jewish men may have been partially motivated by status considerations to pursue professional careers in the 1950s and 1960s; their sons may also be affected by status considerations to pursue business careers.

For women, in contrast, the pursuit of higher education and professional careers has the cache of overcoming obstacles and achieving challenging goals. Comparing Jewish and all U.S. women ages 35 to 44 who have gone beyond high school, Table 2.4 shows that well over 40 percent of Jewish women in this age group are employed in professional capacities, including teaching (16 percent), law (9 percent), social work (8 percent), and other professions. Corroborating impressionistic evidence, 1990 NJPS data showed that almost one of ten working Jewish women in the age 35 to 44 cohort is an attorney, compared to only 2 percent of non-Jewish women. On the other hand, 6 percent of non-Jewish women in this age group were nurses, an occupation that attracted few Jewish women. Interestingly, Jewish women are equally likely to work as psychologists as physicians, with 3 percent in each category; non-Jewish women have not become psychologists in substantial enough numbers for this profession to be on their top occupations list. Conversely, non-Jewish women are much more likely than Jewish women in this age group to work as registered nurses and librarians—two professions requiring substantial education and skill but generally less lucrative than some others.

Labor Force Participation among Jewish Women

Like secular education, labor force participation among Jewish women has an interesting relationship with coalescence and Jewish distinctiveness. When asked what defines a "traditional Jewish family," many American Jews talk about the Jewish mother as the paragon of homemaking, the producer of plentiful and flavorful food, the keeper of a spotless house, the (over) concerned mother of carefully cared for children. Indeed, for a good part of the twentieth century, American-Jewish women were distinguished by how readily they dropped out of the labor force and stopped working outside the home for pay as soon as they married or started a family.

But the readiness of American-Jewish women to terminate labor force participation was in itself an accommodation to non-Jewish behavior patterns. Many Eastern European Jewish women worked in business settings, and their marketplace activism was viewed positively within some traditional Jewish communities because it facilitated male devotion to the study of scholarly texts. In the decades before and after the turn of the twentieth century in Imperial Germany, Jews accommodating to German bourgeois values and behaviors "accepted middle class mores for the family and made them their own," as Marion Kaplan has convincingly demonstrated. Devoting themselves to the creation of obedient, soft-spoken, educated children and spotlessly orderly homes, German-Jewish women eschewed the shrillness, slovenliness, garlic, and female labor force participation which they associated with Eastern European households.[28]

When Eastern European women emigrated to the United States such working outside the home for pay among married women was severely discouraged by the German-Jewish Americans[29] who had already become doubly adapted to women being full-time homemakers: first, as German Jews assimilated to the bourgeois German pattern,[30] and second when German Jews adapted to the United States.[31] Eastern European Jewish women also quickly adopted the Americanized pattern of looking askance at outside employment for married women; indeed, when financial necessity forced them to work, they often reinterpreted reality so that they could reply that they were not working outside the home for pay.[32]

The addition of voluntarism to domestic concerns among American-Jewish women followed the Christian-American and German-Jewish pattern as the twentieth century proceeded. Like German Jewish bourgeois homemakers, who acculturated by "adapting to styles of dress and manners of speech, moving out of predominantly Jewish neighborhoods into new ones (often forming new 'enclaves'), and accommodating to contemporary middle-class attitudes toward work and achievement,"[33] American-Jewish women absorbed American middle-class values into their notions of Jewish domesticity. In the United States, as in Germany half a century earlier, "women who did not work outside the home and who focused on the creation of domesticity were the *de facto* symbols of having 'made it' into the bourgeoisie." Focusing on home, children, and communal voluntarism, Jewish women "integrated" the "spirit" of two cultures. Partially because Christian middle-class society both in the United States and in Western Europe had high regard for women who devoted themselves to voluntary efforts on behalf of culture, education, and social welfare, Jewish women, like their Christian sisters "found work, demonstrated competence, and built self-esteem" in Jewish local and national organizations.[34]

Today, dual career Jewish households have become the new normative Jewish family, as seen in Table 2.5. Nationwide, the NJPS data show that among married women with no children, 85 percent work outside the home for pay. Labor force participation falls to 78 percent of Jewish women with one child, 68 percent of mothers with two children, 67 percent of those with three children, and 47 percent of those with four or more children.[35] In many communities, well over half of American-Jewish women with children under six years old are employed outside the home.

The readiness of contemporary American Jewish women to pursue higher education and high-powered careers may be seen as an extremely complicated kind of coalescence, which is built on a rejection of the earlier coalescence, in which Jewish women stayed home and took care of their families in deference to external patterns. After a time, American Jewish women came to believe that they avoided work force participation because it was a Jewish value for married women to be exclusively domestic. Indeed, when they left their homes to go to work, many felt that they were disobeying Jewish norms. In contrast, contemporary Jewish women have been at the forefront of feminist striving, almost universally acquiring higher education and pursuing career goals. Educational accomplishment for women became a coalesced American-Jewish value decades ago, and now occupational accomplishment for women is becoming a coalesced American-Jewish value as well.

New Cultural Contexts for Jewish Lives

Despite these educational and occupational accomplishments, and the realization that there are now few tangible penalties attached to Jewish identification, the American-Jewish love-hate relationship with secular educational and occupational achievement continues. On the one hand, secular education has been the key to Americanization and worldly success: American Jews have been distinguished by their use of public and university education as entrées to socio-economic upward mobility. On the other hand, university education has been blamed for seducing Jews away from associating with other Jews, affiliating with Jewish institutions, and preserving home rituals and other aspects of Jewish domestic and cultural distinctiveness.

Many have assumed that some relationship can be found between widespread secular achievements and disturbing patterns in contemporary Jewish life, such as the fact that the attachment of many Jews to their communal institutions appears to be consumerist, based on perceived needs, rather than on religious commitments or ethnic loyalties. 1990 NJPS data indicate that at any given time, just over one-third of American-Jewish households belong to a synagogue. Just over one-third of American Jews have visited Israel. About one-quarter of American Jews belong to some Jewish organization. Slightly more than one in ten Jewish households belong to a Jewish community center. Marshall Sklare's comment in the 1960s that American Jews were most likely to observe child-centered, yearly rather than daily and weekly rituals is even more true today of the vast majority of American Jews.[36]Some of the National Commission on Jewish Women focus-group participants indicated that even adult Jewish education programs were geared toward generalities and yearly rituals, rather than rigorous and regular involvements with Jewish texts and skill-building activities: as one woman commented, "The rabbi talked about the philosophy of being Jewish and all the spiritual things that were good for me, but there was no ritual or substance in any respect to day-to-day life."[37] Moreover, 1990 NJPS data show that the religious identity of many Jewish homes may be compromised as well: approximately half of recent "Jewish" marriages are outmarriages, that is unions between a Jew and a person who was not born Jewish and does not currently consider himself or herself to be Jewish. Concerns are voiced in public and private about the vibrant continuity of the Diaspora Jewish community. Jewish leaders concerned about low Jewish profiles in many areas of contemporary Jewish life wonder if secular education plays a role in diminishing Jewish connections.

Some observers of the Jewish community (echoing the *Hatam Sofer* in nineteenth-century Hungary) have suggested that the opportunities of the open society are so irresistible that nothing short of total isolation can protect future generations of American Jews from complete assimilation. These fatalistic assessments have come from observers who stand at both ends of the Jewish communal spectrum, and secular and Jewish education have each frequently borne the brunt of these concerns.

Across the ideological spectrum, leaders and laypersons alike have often blamed standard American-Jewish education for its putative "failure" to inoculate American-Jewish children with appropriate levels of Jewish knowledge or loyalty. Left-leaning liberals, stating that Jewish education is minimal and ineffectual for most acculturated American Jews, urge acceptance of the status quo, along with devoting greater communal energies into seducing an assimilated population into newly popularized, more accessible forms of "Judaism" than now exist.[38] Bureaus of Jewish education have conducted evaluations that seem to show that a few years of after-school programming are no better and may be even worse than no school at all.[39] Some leaders have asserted that alternatives to formal Jewish education—sending every teenager to Israel, for example—may be a more effective means of enculturating tomorrow's Jewish adults.

Religious right-wingers opt for isolation from secular intellectual currents, keeping their young people away from college, graduate, and professional schools.[40] Some scholars, looking at patterns which were true in the past, but which are not true today, seemingly agree with this right-wing assessment as they suggest that the higher secular education which is so ubiquitous in American-Jewish life is the "kiss of death" in terms of Jewish identification. Once Jewish young adults leave their homes for college, the secular-education-is-the-culprit theory goes, they will drift, at random and without resistance, into primarily non-Jewish, undifferentiated American attitudes and behaviors, marry out of the faith, and take no steps to raise their children as Jews. Most recently, Seymour Martin Lipset, in his study based on 1990 NJPS data, superimposed the patterns of the past and insisted: "a major source of the extremely high rate of intermarriage is the pattern of attendance by Jews at colleges and universities. Education makes for higher income and status, more culture, and greater influence, but it is also associated ultimately with lesser involvement in the Jewish community."[41]

However, today, as the 1990 NJPS data show, American Jews have entered another stage in the relationship between secular and Jewish education. Earlier patterns have given way to a different set of realities. Contradicting decades of earlier statistical data and folk wisdom, contemporary young American Jews who have extensive secular education are on average somewhat more likely to participate in Jewish activities and establish Jewish homes, while modestly educated young Jews are more often estranged from Jewish organizations and behaviors, married to current non-Jews, and not raising their children as Jews. Among younger cohorts of American Jews, higher secular education does not miligate against Jewish involvements, as it has in the past. Moreover, the semiotic significance of educational and occupational achievement has changed over time, with particularly dramatic changes for contemporary younger Jews.

Several explanations can be suggested for the association of impressive secular education with higher Jewish profiles. First, a positive relationship between secular education and ethnic identification, which contrasts with past impressions, is a characteristic aspect of the larger pattern of white ethnic American identification. Studying middle-class white ethnic Americans in 1990, Richard Alba found that—counterintuitively—those with higher levels of secular education were more, not less, likely to be committed to transmitting ethnic traditions to their children. The status of ethnicity has turned around in the past few decades, and highly educated white ethnics are more likely than their less educated sisters and brothers to seek out the distinct flavors of their own heritages.[42] Second, low achievers are likely to feel uncomfortable and disenfranchised among high-achieving American Jews. Third, outmarriage is no longer a useful route to socio-economic upward mobility for Jews. Fourth, overt antisemitism has declined. Few Jews are denied or lose jobs because of their ethnic/religious identity.

Finally, coalescence is a factor in the higher levels of Jewish connectedness and endogamy among highly educated and successful Jews today. Young American Jews do not perceive their Jewish identity as being in conflict with their potential for high achievement educationally, socially, or professionally. Rather than being an impetus for compartmentalization, outstanding educational and occupational achievements reinforce American-Jewish identity, because achievers perceive other Jews as being similarly highly achieving. Secular education is a coalesced American-Jewish value.

The fact that high levels of secular educational and occupational achievement are not associated with alienation from Jews and Judaism corroborates to some extent the assertions of the "transformationalists," Goldscheider,[43] Cohen,[44] and Silberman.[45] In the 1980s they argued that American Jews had been transformed into a group typified by high-level educational and socio-economic stratification, and that this stratification was in itself an effective new basis for Jewish group cohesiveness. However, transformationalist theory was based on populations for whom Jewish group solidarity was still somewhat reinforced by external boundaries which kept Jews living, working, and socializing together. The transformationalists described a transitional situation that has largely disappeared, in which Jews were consistently thrown together despite their enormous educational and socio-economic advances.

American Jews at the close of the twentieth century face a situation which is unprecedented in Jewish history. As a group, they not only exhibit high levels of secular education and occupational freedom and accomplishment, but can also, with few exceptions, live in any neighborhood and join almost any organization they wish. As Silberman suggested, contemporary American Jews have not been forced to collaborate in the "brutal bargain" of forfeiting their ethnic and religious identities as a condition of their acceptance in wider American society.[46] They can choose to—or not to—participate in public and private Jewish behaviors.

Contemporary American culture eases the difficulties of being a Jew. Jewish names remain unchanged as individuals such as Barbara Boxer, Diane Feinstein, Robert Reich, Neil Rudenstein, William Cohen, and Ruth Bader Ginsburg hold prominent cultural and political positions. Distinctive Jewish behaviors are far more easily accommodated than in the past: Kosher food is available on airlines, in supermarkets deep in the Christian heartland, in major resorts. The *New York Times* announces the suspension of alternate side of the street parking on Shemini Atzeret and other Jewish holidays [of which, ironically, the majority of American Jews are often unaware]. In a new permutation of the Judaization of America, popular writers from other ethnic groups sometimes identify with and emulate Jews; Chinese-American writer Gish Jen, for example, says that she has read American-Jewish writers Bernard Malamud, Philip Roth, Grace Paley, Saul Bellow, and Cynthia Ozick "forward and backward," because "I wanted to become a Jewish intellectual. I wanted to be Isaac Bashevis Singer."[47] African-American General Colin Powell famously declared that he speaks "a bissel" Yiddish.

Permission to be openly Jewish is underscored by the fact that mainstream American culture appears to be "Judaized" in its vernacular expressions. References to Jewish rituals and Yiddish or Hebrew phrases are commonplace. At night, in an HBO-televised live concert in Chicago, comic Adam Sandler chants his wildly popular "Chanuka Song" to an overflow, enthusiastic, mostly non-Jewish crowd, "Veronica, it's time to celebrate Chanuka, put on your yarmulkah, maybe I'll get a harmonica, it's time to celebrate Chanuka." Sandler's song continues with a long litany of Jews in show business, sports, and the public eye—Harrison Ford is one-fourth Jewish.[48] The next morning, on National Public Radio, a political analyst commenting on the rarefied advertising campaign between patrician Massachusetts senatorial candidates William Weld and John Kerry, summarizes the message of the ads: "This one's a no-goodnik, that one's a no-goodnik. If you vote for either one of them, you're a noodnik."[49] Talking to pediatrician T. Perry Brazelton, Katie Couric, the non-Jewish anchor of NBC's Today Show, casually mentions she insists that her young daughter use the word "tush" for the appropriate part of her anatomy.[50] Each year brings new television programs with Jewish characters, often on the most popular series: in the mid-1990s, situation comedies "Seinfeld" and "The Nanny" portrayed ethnic Jewish New York in living rooms across America. On the Jerry Seinfeld show, Jewish and non-Jewish characters frantically search for a "mohel" for the "bris" of a friend's child. "The Nanny" soars upward in the ratings by portraying three generations of loud-mouthed, overdressed, food-obsessed Jewish women. Public television repeatedly airs a musical special featuring Israeli violinist Yitzhak Perlman playing Klezmer music in the streets of Warsaw. Even the alien beings on "Third Rock from the Sun" and the cartoon character Crusty the Clown on "The Simpsons" have Jewish ties.

Because of these profound changes in the cultural contexts of contemporary American life, the structural transformation of the Jewish community into a high educational and occupational status group does not by itself serve to make younger American-Jewish individuals either less or more "Jewish" in any meaningful way. Subsequent chapters will argue that the combination of substantive Jewish education with high levels of secular education is related to higher levels of positive Jewish behaviors, and that minimal levels of Jewish education are related to minimal levels of Jewish affiliation and activity, no matter what the level of secular education.

If secular education has been the key to coalescence over the past century, the coming chapters show that Jewish education may well provide a potential antidote to many negative aspects of coalescence. We turn now to an exploration of Jewish educational patterns in contemporary American-Jewish lives.

Table 2.1 **Secular Educational Levels of Jewish Respondents (1990 NJPS)**
Highest Degree Obtained
Percentages by Age Group and Sex

Level/Degree Attained	Women					Men				
	25–34	*35–44*	*45–54*	*55–64*	*65+*	*25–34*	*25–34*	*45–54*	*55–64*	*65+*
H.S. and Under	26	24	41	55	72	20	19	28	26	56
Some College (A.A.)	6	7	7	5	3	7	5	5	5	9
B.A.	46	32	27	20	16	43	35	32	31	22
M.A.	15	28	20	16	5	16	19	17	17	8
Ph.D. or Prof. Degree	7	10	5	5	4	13	22	18	21	14

Source: 1990 NJPS data, adapted from Hartman & Hartman (1996), p. 42. Percentages have been rounded.

Table 2.2 Mean Years of Education, Jews and U.S. Whites
Percentages by Sex and Age

| | U.S. Jews | | U.S. Whites | |
Age	Males	Females	Males	Females
25–29	16	16	13	13
30–34	16	16	13	13
35–39	17	16	13	13
40–44	17	17	14	13
45–49	17	15	13	13
50–54	16	15	13	13
55–59	17	14	13	13
60–64	16	14	13	12
65+	14	13	12	12

Source: NJPS, 1990; Kominski and Adams, 1991, Table 1. Adapted from Hartman & Hartman, p. 39. Percentages have been rounded.

Table 2.3 Occupational Status Levels of 1990 NJPS Jewish Respondents
Unweighted Percentages by Age Group and Sex

| | Women | | Men | |
Occupational Status Level	25–44	45 and Over	25–44	45 and Over
*Hi-status Professions	14	7	22	26
**Helping Professions	29	18	18	10
Managerial	14	15	16	20
Clerical/Technical	31	52	27	28
Service	9	5	14	14
Other/Refused	3	2	4	3
Total	100	99	101	101

Source: 1990 NJPS data. Percentages have been rounded.

*High professional status: physicians, dentists, attorneys, professors, high-level technical/scientific, high-level executives, etc.
**Helping professions: teachers pre-K through 12, nurses, librarians, social workers, mid-level technical/scientific, etc.

Table 2.4 **Most Prevalent Occupations among Jews and All U.S. Women Percentages of 1990 NJPS Women, Ages 35–44 with Some College**

Occupation	Jewish Women	All US Women
Teachers, all levels	16	25
Managers and administrators	9	6
Attorneys	9	2
Social Workers	8	5
Sales Clerks	5	NA*
Psychologists	3	NA*
Physicians	3	4
Chiropractors	2	NA*
Educational Administrators	2	4

Source: Adapted from Hartman & Hartman, Table Oc-4., p. 4–52, preliminary MS Gender Equality and American Jews. Percentages have been rounded.

*NA These professions were on the top list of prevalent professions among Jewish women but not on the top list of prevalent occupations among all U.S. women ages 35–44 with some college. On the list of all US women—but not of U.S. Jewish women in this age group—were the following professions: registered nurses—6%, and librarians—3%.

Table 2.5 **Labor Force Participation of Jewish Mothers of Children under Six Percentages by City, Jewish Population Surveys (1980s)**

		Full-time	Part-time	Homemaker	Other
Baltimore	(1986)	27	38	35	1
Boston	(1985)	29	36	33	2
Kansas City	(1986)	28	21	44	7
MetroWest	(1986)	22	26	49	4
Milwaukee	(1984)	18	32	36	14
Philadelphia	(1984)	23	14	59	3
Pittsburgh	(1984)	29	25	42	4
Phoenix	(1983)	26	21	50	3
Rochester	(1987)	22	32	42	4
San Francisco	(1988)	36	25	31	8
Washington, D.C.	(1984)	34	30	30	6
Worcester	(1987)	15	34	51	1

Source: Adapted from Gabriel Berger and Lawrence Sternberg, Jewish Child-Care: A Challenge and an Opportunity (Cohen Center for Modern Jewish Studies, Brandeis University, Research Report No. 3, November, 1988). Percentages have been rounded.

Table 2.6 **Labor Force Participation of Jewish Women**
   Percentages of Jewish Female Respondents by Age Group

Labor Force Status	Age 44 and Under	Age 45 and Over
Homemaker	17	19
Student	11	—
Part-time Worker	11	8
Full-time Worker	59	31
Not employed*	4	44
Total**	102	102

Source: 1990 NJPS Data. Percentages have been rounded.

*Includes unemployed seeking work, unemployed not seeking work, and retired.

**Totals shown may be greater than or less than 100% because they are rounded.

THREE

LEARNING ABOUT JEWISH EDUCATION

Education as Liturgical Expression and Social Strategy

Jewish emphasis on study and articulation as means of cultural transmission has deep historical roots. The ubiquitousness of the educational enterprise is expressed in the biblical *Shema Yisrael* (Hear, oh Israel), adapted since ancient times as the central prayer of Jewish liturgy. In its powerful passages, worshipping Jews repeatedly voiced their commitment to provide their children with Jewish education, promising to speak about divine commandments when active or resting, residing at home or walking outside. The prayer presents Jewish education not primarily in an elite or formal classroom situation; rather, ordinary parents are enjoined to be involved in religious matters with passionate intensity, heart and soul, so that these subjects virtually never depart from their lips.

Rabbinical interpretation of these passages, especially *veshinantem levanecha* (and you shall diligently teach your sons/children), focused on the teaching of the oral law and defined the responsibility to teach as applying to fathers and sons.[1] Additionally, assuming that many fathers might not feel themselves capable of fulfilling these educational injunctions, rabbinical law permitted delegation: fathers who cannot teach their sons themselves are expected to hire appropriate teachers. Nevertheless, the expectation was that much education would also take place in the home and other settings.

Historical Jewish societies took quite seriously the responsibility to provide Jewish education for boys and to encourage life-long Judaic study for men. Young boys began their formal education at three to six years old, taught at home by private tutors or attending the community-sponsored *heder*. Boys were often initiated into study of Talmudic texts long before their intellectual development or personal interest would have dictated.[2] Male children were expected to stay in class at least until they passed Bar Mitzvah age, and many communities exerted pressure to keep boys in school through age fifteen, sixteen, or seventeen. Beyond these years, extensive study was the prerogative of those students who had demonstrated intellectual ability. The headmaster (*Rosh Yeshiva*) was often a personage of great spiritual significance and influence within the community as well as the school. Jacob Katz notes, "the *yeshiva* was devoted to educating the masses of the Jewish people; great scholars had always seen it as their special duty to teach publicly and to cultivate large student followings."[3]

In premodern European Jewish communities, the aura of talmudic learning hovered palpably over communal life. First, the legal decisions and text-based discussions of Jewish scholars had widespread influence on the normative behaviors of both male and female members of Jewish folk classes. Second, the world of scholarship in certain ways defined male aspirations from childhood onward.

Female Jews, in contrast, experienced the world of intensive Judaic study vicariously or at one remove. Girls were usually taught practical religious fundamentals at home by their mothers. Many girls were taught to read in their Jewish vernacular but not to read Hebrew; others were taught to read basic Hebrew liturgy in the prayer book. In some families knowledgeable fathers or mothers provided their daughters with text study opportunities or hired tutors for them, and in a few communities young girls also attended school. Except for a scattering of wives and daughters in elite families, who received text education at home from their fathers, brothers, or husbands, the world of talmudic study was largely closed to females.[4] Nevertheless, in European communities women and less-educated men commonly read Yiddish translations of biblical texts and rabbinic commentaries, and participated through these texts in the liturgical activity of ongoing education.

Entry into the elite class of rabbis and their students often gave scholars access to social status and concrete rewards: young scholars might be supported in their studies by communal patrons, and they were prized potential mates for the daughters of rich men. Married into relatively wealthier families, members of the rabbinic elite might enjoy a healthier standard of living and more surviving progeny than the norm. Within such societies, Jewish education thus was often a route to social status and power, and sometimes to physical well-being as well. Once a promising young scholar married into an affluent household, he too might achieve relative financial security; if so, he and his family, possessing both wealth and scholarship, occupied the highest echelons of Jewish society.

Despite this emphasis on the formal classroom, both in European settings and in the early decades of the twentieth century in the United States as well, the formal classroom was not expected to carry the full weight of Jewish education. The classrooms of the European *heder* or the *yeshiva* were engaged primarily in providing intellectual skills and transmitting textual information. The practical, everyday skills and information required to maintain elaborately ritualized Jewish lifestyles, on the other hand, were generally taught in the daily, lived environments of home and synagogue. As Jonathan Sarna points out, Jewish societies assumed that the formal classroom would provide what John Dewey would have called *intentional education,* expecting a wide variety of informal educational activities to take place elsewhere, Dewey's *incidental education.* After emigration to the United States, communities still assumed that schools would have a limited, cognitive purview, as Sarna remarks:

> Not one of the early Jewish schools that we know of, for example, taught classes in "how to be a Jew" or "Jewish holidays" or "Jewish identity." Instead they taught critical skills—like Hebrew reading—just as secular schools taught the rudiments of reading, writing, and arithmetic. The rest was learned outside of school—at home, in synagogue, or through an apprenticeship.[5]

While Jewish education for boys had been widespread in European communities, parents who emigrated to the United States in the late nineteenth and early twentieth century were often too overwhelmed by the demands of earning a livelihood and acculturation to provide their children with extensive formal Jewish education. Jewish enrollment reports around the turn of the century vary widely, but all indicate that enrollment was very far from universal.[6] Public schools, free and ubiquitously available, had the educational pride of place. A few all-day Jewish schools had existed in several American cities during the eighteenth and nineteenth centuries (along with supplementary schools and Sunday schools), but due to a variety of social and economic factors, all-day Jewish schools had closed by the mid-1870s, and would not be available again for decades.[7] Several notable *yeshiva* institutions of higher education had already been established, and limited numbers of young men pursuing rabbinic ordination or desirous of intensive Talmud study attended these schools, often in the afternoon or evening. However, the vast majority of Jewish children of immigrants who received formal Jewish education did so via Sunday school, in after-school classes called *heder* or Talmud Torah, or studies with a private tutor (*melammed*).

Sarna suggests that the historic American-Jewish argument between public schools augmented with supplementary Jewish education, versus all-day Jewish schools, can be categorized as "The Protestant model and the Catholic model":

> The Protestant model held that morality, universal values, patriotism, civics and crucial skills all should be taught in state-funded public schools to a mixed body of religiously diverse students, leaving only the fine points of religious doctrine and practice to be mastered by members of each faith in separate denominationally-sponsored supplementary schools. The Catholic model, by contrast, insisted that such public schools really preached Protestant values and that the only way to maintain a minority (dissenting) religious tradition was through a separate system of religious schooling.[8]

By the time the masses of Eastern European Jewish immigrants started arriving, their American-Jewish predecessors had already decided firmly in favor of the Protestant model, attending public schools and availing themselves of Judaic instruction in after-school or Sunday school settings. These educations differed substantially from educational offerings in traditional European communities. The quality of pedagogy was often problematic. Contemporaneous sources describe Sunday school classes taught by well-meaning amateurs, women and men with little Judaic background, and *heders* and Talmud Torah classes run by pedagogically incompetent immigrant males who could find no other work.[9]

Talmud Torahs were transformed into Hebrew Schools over the first two decades of the twentieth century, due to the energy and dedication of a group of Hebraist educators led by Samson Benderly, a native of Sefad who championed the *ivrit b'ivrit* (Hebrew taught in Hebrew) method developed by educational reformers in Europe and Palestine. Alan Mintz describes their success in transforming the focus of after-school Jewish education:

> . . . sometime around World War I, the incipient Talmud Torah movement was "kidnapped" by young men and women committed to the Hebraist ideol-

ogy. It was they who fanned out over the country and as teachers and principles turned these supplemental Jewish communal schools into *Hebrew* schools.
Working in opposition to the majority of parents and receiving support only
from a few communal leaders, these Hebrew educators forcefully imprinted
their vision.[10]

As afternoon schools became Hebrew schools, the *melammed* was often replaced
by professional instructors trained in the new Hebrew colleges established in diverse
cities. For decades, Hebrew schools devoted themselves to imparting as much Hebrew
fluency as could be accomplished in a few hours a week, along with information about
Jewish history, Sabbaths and holidays, rituals, culture, and customs. The proportion
of children enrolled in Jewish education rose dramatically, as congregations almost
universally sponsored their own schools, requiring Bar Mitzvah boys, and later Bat
Mitzvah girls, to attend a prescribed number of years of classes. However, the actual
number of hours during which students attended Hebrew school decreased. Talmud
Torahs had typically "provided about 400 hours of yearly instruction," while the "average afternoon synagogue school in the 1940s and 1950s" offered "only about 200
hours yearly," and "the Sunday school provided even less, with only 64 aggregate hours
of instruction per year."[11]

Societal Changes and Shifting Jewish Educational Emphases

The years following World War II brought many positive developments to Jewish education in America. First, fertility levels of American Jews, like those of other Americans, "boomed" in the family-oriented ethos of the post-War years. Enrollments of
congregational and community Hebrew schools swelled with suddenly increasing
numbers of Jewish children to educate, creating a sense of success and well-being
within individual congregations and Jewish denominational movements.[12] Second,
about 140,000 Holocaust survivors came to American shores. Some of them came
from richly traditional Jewish societies;[13] their interests and skills served as a cultural
booster shot to acculturated Jewish societies, and intensified the demand for more traditional forms of Jewish education.[14] The all-day Jewish school movement, which had
been relatively limited prior to World War II, began a growth trend, although day
schools were still called—and regarded as—parochial schools, enjoying little popularity outside of the Orthodox community. As Jack Wertheimer notes, the Torah Umesorah movement, established in 1944 as an umbrella movement to link Orthodox day
schools, "oversaw the growth of day schools from approximately 30 before World War
II to over 300 by the mid-1960s."[15]

Third, after the establishment of the State of Israel, Hebrew language, songs
and culture carried the cache of the image of the strong, modern Jew. Journalistic pho-
tos of muscular Israeli men in military uniforms and record albums with pictures of
bronzed female *kibbutzniks* carrying agricultural implements gave American Jews a
new sense of self-esteem.[16] In this environment, attempts to upgrade Hebrew-ori-
ented education found considerable success among elite groups. In some communi-

ties, the availability of Israeli Hebrew teachers facilitated this effort. Indeed, Israeli teachers became commonplace in many communities as the decades passed.

Among the many Jewish day and sleep-away camps proliferating in the 1950s and 1960s along with the increase in Jewish school-age children, Hebrew-speaking summer camps such as Camp Cejwin, Camp Massad, and the Conservative movement's new Camp Ramah flourished. Ramah, initiated in 1947 in a pilot camp serving eighty-nine campers in Wisconsin, grew faster than facilities could be built into seven camps, with an enrollment of 2,833 campers, by 1970.[17] These camps attracted young people who often became deeply committed to Israel, the American-Jewish community, and Judaic studies. Zionist and Jewish denominational youth groups, many of which incorporated educational activities, also attracted enthusiastic participation. Even children and teenagers who received minimal or no formal Jewish schooling often attended such camps and youth groups, and became attached to Jews and Jewishness through them.[18]

However, Jewish communities, like other established American communities, underwent a period of enormous upheaval and social unrest in the late 1960s and 1970s. Among youth, mistrust of authority and alienation from established communal structures were epidemic, emanating from the anti–Vietnam War protests and the Civil Rights movement. Jewish college students were especially active in a variety of protest movements, and a disproportionate number of rebellious student leaders came from middle-class suburban Jewish homes. Many of them regarded Jewish organizations and institutions as manifestations of what they saw as their parents' generations' oppressive, repressed, materialistic bourgeois mentality. At the same time, the Jewish consciousness of many American Jews was galvanized by the shock of the 1967 "Six Day War," in which Israel's existence was perceived as being threatened by massed hostile Arab armies; when Israel won an upset victory, the initial reaction of many American Jews was a surge of attachment to Israel, and an increased sense of Jewish pride. Zionist feeling was stimulated among one segment of the American-Jewish population, and depressed among others.

In this period of unrest, as African-American students asserted that "Black is beautiful," many American Jews became fascinated by the possibility of discovering Jewish "roots." For a time, as Marshall Sklare pointed out in a witty essay on "The Greening of America," Ramah camp administrators and educators were able to co-opt the rebellious spirit of young Jewish Americans to the camp's educational advantage, demonstrating "an unerring ability to utilize age-old symbols and practices in a way that gave them an 'anti-establishment' tone." Counselors and campers alike mortified Americanized parents by wearing colorful knitted *kipot* (head coverings, *yarmulkahs*) on the street, or wearing large, brightly colored prayer shawls (*tallit*) in synagogues.

The solidarity and heady feeling created by such educational camping experiences was a contributing factor to the creation of a diverse Jewish counterculture, including the birth of the *havurah* participatory worship and study movement.[19] The *havurah* movement downplayed the role of paid professional Jewish leaders, and encouraged Jewish laity to educate themselves so that they could serve as prayer leaders, Torah readers, and speakers during worship services. Although the *havurah* movement began with a small, highly educated, and thus idiosyncratic group, it eventually had a profound impact on American-Jewish life. Today, few American synagogues are untouched by havurah-inspired activities and attitudes.

One important educational document of the Jewish counterculture was the *The Jewish Catalogue,* a now much-reprinted "do-it-yourself kit" and layperson's manual for throwing off the "prefabricated" Judaism of the established synagogue and weaving instead a personalized, proactive, do-it-yourself Jewish experience. Sklare disliked *The Jewish Catalogue* intensely because he felt it reflected the "regnant pieties of the youth culture," the self-centered, solipsistic values of the age, and its accompanying fascination with "folk religion and the mystical and the occult," with "handicrafts and cookery."[20] However, it seems clear in hindsight that this publication provided a rich articulation of what we are now calling coalescence. In passage after passage, Jewish behaviors that had traditionally created feelings of communal responsibility within the matrix of the densely ritualized Jewish calendar, were lifted out of their communal context and presented as facilitators of an episodic spiritual experience. The *shofar* (ram's horn), for example, ceased to be the awesome reminder of communal responsibility for sin, and instead became a primitive external symbol of the *id* within:

> Certainly one of the strangest pieces of ritual paraphernalia is the *shofar.* . . .
> The smoothly curved ram's horn has an aura of the primitive about it; for people saturated with sophisticated technology, the *shofar* appears to be a throwback to hoary antiquity. And perhaps this is precisely why the *shofar* is so exciting and stirring—it brings us back to places inside ourselves that are very basic and primitive, very near the root of our being.[21]

Thus, within the pages of *The Jewish Catalogue* the behaviors of traditional Jewish societies were coalesced with the individualistic values of the late 1960s and 1970s.

In yet another aspect of informal Jewish education, an increasing focus on the Jewish heritage as a source of acceptable ethnic identity gave American-Jewish publishers, writers, film-makers, musicians, and comedians a green light to explore the Jewish present and past in their creative endeavors. A burgeoning readership for Judaica meant that American publishers found it profitable to publish the works of Jewishly knowledgeable writers as different as Elie Wiesel, Chaim Potok, and Cynthia Ozick.[22] No longer did Jewish artists find it necessary to encode their exploration of the Jewish experience by hiding it within neutral "American" materials or within the stories of other ethnic groups. Some popular fiction, drama, music, and films served a positive educational function, teaching American Jews about their own past: films such as "Fiddler on the Roof" (1971) and "Hester Street" (1974) were especially noteworthy in this regard.

On the other hand, frequently the "educational" value of Jewish books and films can be considered negative, as Jewish artists poked fun at Jewish behaviors and values. To name just a few artistically outstanding examples, in films such as "The Producers," Mel Brooks's 1968 spoof of Jewish show business would-be tycoons, "Goodbye, Columbus" (1969), a satire on Jewish socio-economic upward mobility, based on the 1959 Philip Roth novella by the same name, and Woody Allen's memorable "Annie Hall," a 1978 film which brilliantly analyzed interfaith romances as an expression of the Jewish inferiority/superiority complex, American Jews learned that Jewishness was comic. Jewish women especially were the butt of denigrating Jewish humor. Readers and viewers often "learned" that Jewish women are the designated Jews, incorporating undesirable Jewish characteristics (and thus themselves undesirable). As noted earlier, recent research suggests that this negative education has played a role in rising rates of exogamy, due to toxic feelings between some Jewish men and women.[23]

Within an environment that legitimated diverse ethnic American heritages, the hegemony of secular Western culture over the American academy began to erode, and Jewish studies departments which had previously struggled to establish themselves developed and grew strong. Numerous universities with relatively large Jewish student populations created Jewish studies programs and departments, and even universities with small Jewish student populations were sometimes funded by the local Jewish community to create one-person chair/departments in Jewish studies. In some schools, such as Brandeis University, a nonsectarian Jewish-sponsored university founded in 1948, the nucleus of the Judaic studies department had been formed around brilliant European-trained scholars, who were now joined by younger American scholars in diverse disciplines.

Ironically, Jewish education was also adversely affected in the 1970s by the fact that antisemitism in the school and workplace was decreasing dramatically, and the world was opening up for Jews in a whole new way. Living in religiously and ethnically diverse neighborhoods, Jewish children often felt the after-school hours were better spent in little league games and ballet lessons than in Hebrew schools. And finally, as Sarna points out, by the 1970s it became apparent that Hebrew schools and the whole Hebrew-speaking movement in the United States had fallen "completely out of touch with the needs of American Jews," and had "ceased to provide young people with the tools to negotiate between the two worlds that governed their identity."[24]

Day school education lost its "parochial" stigma and was strengthened by several juxtaposed cultural trends in the 1970s. Many American-Jewish parents had become disillusioned with the effectiveness of both the public school system and with supplementary style Jewish education. As they perceived the public school system to be "declining," and remembered their own unsatisfactory experiences in afternoon Hebrew schools, the private Jewish school seemed more appealing to many parents.[25] As a result, Orthodox, Conservative, Reform, and community trans-denominational day schools proliferated in large and medium-sized cities. By the early 1980s, of those children currently enrolled in any kind of Jewish education, 28 percent were students in the 449 day schools that had been established across the United States.[26]

Thus, the 1980s and 1990s were, in terms of Jewish education, at once the most promising and the most discouraging of times. Educational institutions were given daunting responsibilities, which they seemed ill-equiped to meet. Jewish supplementary schools had by and large retained early patterns of focusing on cognitive tasks: the teaching of Hebrew and transmission of information about Jewish history and ritual observances. This educational focus was originally based on the assumption that other aspects of Jewish experience would be taught elsewhere, as indeed they were for centuries. However, during the second-half of the twentieth century, informal Jewish experience in neighborhoods, schools, and workplaces faded. Unlike traditional Jewish societies—or even secularized Jewish societies at the turn of the century, which were often steeped in Yiddish or Hebraic culture along with their secularism—American environments provided little in the way of Jewish reinforcement. First settlement American-Jewish neighborhoods, with their Jewish bakeries, fruit stores, fish stores, and butchers heralding the coming of each holiday, their Jewish newspapers and linguistic mix, had largely disappeared, outside of a very few urban areas. Most American Jews were extremely unlikely to hear Jewish languages spoken outside of a synagogue or structured Jewish cultural setting. Jewish homes reported rapidly declining rates of ritual observance. Jewish classrooms had become the primary purveyors of Jewish connections, but were often still operating on assumptions from a previous era.

Contemporary Jewish Education:
Diversity of Jewish Educational Levels

The 1990 NJPS data on Jewish education ratify statistically the paradoxes and contradictions of this picture. These national data document the fact that most American adults and children raised as Jews receive some formal Jewish schooling.[27] The broad parameters of this schooling are easily summarized: Among the 4,360,000 Jewish adults represented by the 1990 NJPS, about three-quarters received some Jewish education. Currently, as well, about three-quarters of American children being raised as Jews acquire some form of Jewish education between the ages of 6 to 18, as do 8 percent of the children of at least one Jewish parent who are not being raised as Jews. The highest levels of current enrollments are found among children ages 10 to 13 who are being raised as Jews.

Despite the large patterns contained in this brief summary, gross, turnstile yes-no figures on Jewish education mean little because formal and informal Jewish education together comprise a multifaceted and complicated spectrum. Communities differ enormously in regard to educational offerings, and even within a single geographical location, educational norms diverge from subgroup to subgroup. In terms of Jewish education, as with other aspects of Jewish life, societal subgroups differ dramatically one from the other. Extensiveness of Jewish education for children is linked to the norms of the subgroup with which the parental household feels aligned. It is also linked to a network of familial Jewish activities, such as Jewish camps and youth groups, home-based ritual observance, and Israel trips. It is difficult to sort out the educational roles played by each of these interwoven activities.

Nevertheless, analysis reveals that formal Jewish education is more powerfully related to adult Jewish behaviors both independently and in combination with other factors than most other single background factors. Formal Jewish education is critical because the great majority of American Jews have access to Jewish texts and cultural traditions primarily through the initial agency of the classroom. The impact of living in an open society, which had already diluted ethnic distinctiveness a quarter century ago, is even more pronounced today, because ever-greater numbers of Jews have moved away from geographical areas that have an ethnic Jewish "presence," and have relocated in the sunbelt and other areas with fewer Jewish cultural resources.[28] Even in more established Jewish areas, the emotional, private, home and neighborhood-based—and often unplanned—informal Jewish education which was significant for earlier Jewish populations has largely given way to a far more public, institutional type of education—an education that requires planning, strategizing, and funding.

1990 National Jewish Population Survey data show that among adults, more men than women have received Jewish education. However, contradicting popular impressions, younger Jews are more likely to have received some formal Jewish education than older Jews, as Table 3.1 indicates. This is especially true for women: over half of women age 65 and older received no formal Jewish education, compared to 28 percent of those ages 18 to 24. Among Jews ages 25 to 44, 28 percent of women and 42 percent of men received one to five years of Jewish education, 23 percent of women and 34 percent of men received over six years, and 34 percent of women but only 14 percent of men did not receive any Jewish education. Nevertheless, despite the increased prominence of formal Jewish education, for most Jews the actual level of Jewish education received is dramatically lower, both in number of years and in hours per week, than their own sophisticated secular educational achievements.

As shown in Table 3.2, among 8 to 12 year olds raised as Jews, girls are somewhat more likely to be enrolled in Jewish classes than boys: 86 percent to 71 percent, respectively. This differential may reflect the impact of team sports in the middle school years. In contrast, among 8 to 12 year olds not raised as Jews only about one in ten had received Jewish schooling. By the time they reached ages 16 to 18, more than three-quarters of Jewish teens raised as Jews had received some formal Jewish education, compared to a mere 2 percent of those not raised as Jews. NJPS data further reveal the fact that among teens ages 16 to 18 who received Jewish education, the average child has received a total of 6.3 years of classes of any type. Those who come from families that define themselves as "Just Jewish" have received only two years of Jewish education, compared to about six years among those self-defined as Reform and about seven years among those self-defined as Orthodox or Conservative.[29]

To some extent Jewish school enrollments reflect the availability of various kinds of programs in different cities and for different age groups. NJPS data indicate that young children ages 6 to 7 are frequently enrolled in one-day programs, such as Sunday school, no doubt because this is the type of program most often available for children of this age outside of a day school setting. Children ages 8 to 15 are most likely to be enrolled in after-school supplementary schools which are usually offered under congregational auspices. One-fifth each of school age children receiving Jewish education are enrolled in all-day programs or in Sunday-only classes. High school students ages 16 to 18 who are still enrolled in Jewish schools include much higher proportions of day school students—44 percent, with the remainder roughly equally divided between after-school supplementary and one-day weekly programs. The high proportion of day school among enrolled high school students is due partially to the fact that many congregations and communities do not offer supplementary programs past age 14 or 15, when confirmation takes place.

As Table 3.3 shows, among adults, the type and years of formal Jewish education previously received are associated with current ethnic/religious self-definition:

persons calling themselves "secular Jews" were more likely than those who said they were "Jewish by religion" not to have received Jewish education—35 percent versus 24 percent. Secular Jews were also much less likely to have received six or more years of supplementary school or day school education than Jews by religion. Denominations of Judaism in parental homes often mirrored the extent of education. Among Jews raised in homes that they identified as Orthodox, only 16 percent received no Jewish education, compared to a high of 61 percent among those raised as "Just Jews."

Among children ages 6 to 18 being raised as Jews, formal Jewish education is reported close to universally by those being raised in Orthodox households and by over three-quarters of those raised in Conservative or Reform households. In contrast, in households considering themselves "Just Jewish," fewer than half (46 percent) received some Jewish education. Among children being raised as non-Jews, fewer than 10 percent of 6 to 12 year olds reported some Jewish education, which may have included enrollment in a Jewish-sponsored early childhood program.

Among children currently enrolled in Jewish schools, the sweeping majority of children raised in Orthodox homes attend full-time schools. Among Conservative families, about 57 percent of children go to part-time programs and about one-fifth attend full-time schools. Nearly half of Reform children (47 percent) are enrolled in one-day programs, 40 percent are in part-time programs, and 8 percent are in full-time programs. It should be noted that these figures connote different types of schools for different age groups involved. The younger children may well have been enrolled in Jewish-sponsored preschools, which have proliferated in recent years and often have a reputation for outstanding programs.

Jewish denominational communities have divergent communal educational norms. Indeed, the disparity in Jewish activism that characterizes various subgroups of American Jews is nowhere more evident than in the levels of Jewish education which they and their children receive. Adding confusion to the Jewish educational picture is the fact that great differences also exist among Jewish parents in their goals for providing their children with Jewish education. The following interchange between two mothers who participated in the National Commission on Jewish Women focus-group discussions illustrates the conflicting goals that may be found even in a single denominational grouping:

> Mother One: I went to Sunday School all those years and I put in the time and I didn't know anything. The only two Jewish words that I knew were bar mitzvah and shalom. I got mad at my relatives who were German Jews. They said Reform Judaism is great because you can choose whether you light candles or not. You can choose whether you keep kosher. They didn't realize that they were choosing for me, because when they chose no, I lost my education. If I didn't know about it, I couldn't even choose. I first had to learn what the holidays were and what the language was like.

> Answering her, Mother Two: The best part about being a Reform Jew is that it stresses the most important part of Judaism. It stresses free choice. Free choice is the basis of Judaism. Who Maimonides was or what little rituals people

choose to perform—these are just small details. You can always pick those up later.[30]

Such differing goals for Jewish education are only one reason for enormous differences in levels of Jewish education. Jewish population density often has a deciding effect on educational opportunities. Perhaps most significant, various subgroups of the American-Jewish community perceive differing types and extents of Jewish education as being normative and "traditional." In some communities, Sunday school programs are the norm; in some, multi-day after-school education; in some, day school for the elementary grades followed by evening Hebrew high school; and in some, all-day Jewish schools pre-kindergarten through high school, followed by a pre-college year studying Judaica full-time at a *yeshiva* in Israel.

The momentum in day school creation and attendance reported in the early 1980s has continued, and the number of American day schools has multiplied exponentially, including the building of increasing numbers of community, Conservative and Reform as well as Orthodox, day schools.[31] Jewish federations are increasingly willing to designate substantial sums toward the operational expenses of local day schools, reflecting the fact that the day school concept has gained relative popularity among committed segments of the American population. Attitudes toward day school are often divided along generational, and to some extent along denominational lines. More than one day school parent has reported being the target of anger from older congregants who fault the day schools for the declining numbers of children enrolled in synagogue after-school programs. To these older Jews, supplementary school programs are the normative form of Jewish education, while all-Jewish schools are still perceived as being un-American, foreign, "too Jewish."

Informal Jewish Education Currently Linked
to Formal Schooling

Many American-Jewish adults have fond memories of youthful participation in Jewish youth groups and camps. Some have speculated that such informal—and often transformative—educational activities may be more effective educationally than formal classes. However, Jewish youth groups and camps do not actually function as alternatives for formal Jewish education today, because nearly two-thirds of children raised as Jews do not participate in organized informal activities. Only those families most Jewishly connected opt to send their children to Jewish camps when so many other alternatives are available, including camps specializing in ballet, baseball, music, and computer sciences. Of those children being raised as Jews, 38 percent are at some time involved with at least one youth group or camp experience. Among those not being raised as Jews, only about 5 percent have ever been to a Jewish camp, and virtually none have participated in a Jewish youth group. The percentage of Jewish children involved in informal educational activities increases with age, from about one-quarter of the youngest children to half of the oldest. Younger children are most likely to attend Jewish camps, of either the day camp or "sleep away" varieties. Older children, in contrast, report many more participating in youth groups than going to Jewish camps.

Likelihood of participating in informal Jewish educational activities is directly linked to formal Jewish schooling, as Table 3.4 illustrates. Well over half of children in supplementary schools (55 percent) and two-thirds of those in all-day schools (66 percent) also participate in informal Jewish education. In contrast, slightly over one-third of those in Sunday schools (35 percent) and only 15 percent of those being tutored participate in organized informal activities. By and large, only those teenagers who have also received at least three years of multi-day formal Jewish education are involved in informal alternatives such as Jewish youth groups and camps. Day school students are the group most likely to be involved in informal Jewish educational settings. Thus, Jewish youth groups, camps, and Israel trips all currently function as complementary educational activities, rather than as complete substitutes for formal Jewish education.

Education from Generation to Generation

"The deeds of the parents are a sign for the children," according to a famous rabbinic dictum, and the validity of intergenerational influence is readily apparent in 1990 NJPS data. As Table 3.6 demonstrates, when both parents have received six or more years of Jewish education, virtually all of their children receive some Jewish education. Indeed, by the time they have reached 16 to 18 years old, the children of parents who received six years of Jewish education have received more than nine years of Jewish education. Day school education is the most sweepingly related to generational, cumulative levels of education. In contrast, when neither parent has received formal Jewish education, only 16 percent of their children receive formal Jewish education. When only father or mother have received Jewish education and the other spouse has not, slightly over half of their children receive Jewish education. Thus, Jewish education is not only cumulative but is often clustered in a particular group of family units.

Familial patterns are important in other ways as well, because the education of children or teens is difficult when their parents do not cooperate. Planners note that American Jews are by and large a very accomplished group of people. They are accustomed to feeling competent in whatever they do. Those adults who lack the Jewish cultural literacy to "do" Jewish home celebrations or rituals frequently retreat from the activity altogether, thus, often unwittingly, creating an environment subversive to Jewish education. Responding to this challenge, many planners have urged a "family education" approach, in which synagogues aim to educate parents and children in parallel and combined educational activities. In some cities, federations have been active in providing partial funding for the establishment of pilot family education programs.

Families Who Say No to Jewish Education

One-quarter of children being raised as Jews, and more than nine out of ten children of Jews who are not, were reported as not receiving a Jewish education, according to

1990 NJPS data. Parents were asked to state the reasons they did not enroll their children in Jewish schools. As Table 3.7 shows, two-thirds of respondents who answered this question said that the children had already received enough Jewish education, or that the children were not interested. One in five responses referred to the putative inferior quality of available schools, and one in ten mentioned the child's age—too young or too old for Jewish education. Interestingly, parental Jewish education—or lack of it—was related to the reasons given for nonenrollment, as well as for nonenrollment itself. Where parents both had received six or more years of Jewish schooling, they almost always mentioned the child's age as a reason for nonenrollment. In contrast, when neither parent received Jewish education, any Jewish education already received by the child was viewed as adequate, or the child's lack of interest was cited.

Clearly, reasons for nonenrollment are as complicated as those for enrollment. In many cases, simple logistics intervene. Single parents are much less likely to enroll their children, for example. Financial considerations and the difficulties of transportation when only one parent is available to drive are almost certainly factors for many. For others, the custodial parent during Jewish school hours may not himself or herself be Jewish. However, beyond these special cases, it is fair to speculate that just as some parents enroll their children in Jewish schools as a form of vicarious Jewish connectedness or activism, others may resist enrolling children in Jewish schools as a form of vicarious ambivalence or outright hostility: what better way to indicate resistance to Jewish connections than by not taking steps to formally connect one's children to the Jewish past, present, and future.

Women's New Roles in Jewish Schooling

Just as the gender gap is closing in secular education, it is closing in Jewish education as well. The Jewish educational profile of American-Jewish women and men shifts across generational lines, with higher overall rates among younger American adults than among the older cohort, because of dramatic increases in the proportion of Jewish women receiving Jewish education. The ubiquitousness of the Bat Mitzvah has had a critical and not always acknowledged side-effect: the celebration of Bat Mitzvah among American-Jewish females over the past two decades has virtually erased the gender gap in Jewish education. Before the Bat Mitzvah became popular, one-third of American-Jewish women used to receive no formal Jewish education whatsoever; today, the fact that girls, like boys, must prepare for Bat Mitzvah has brought them into supplementary schools and day schools at nearly the same rates as their brothers. Thus, Bat Mitzvah is the link to the formal Jewish education which has emerged as the true "Jewish connection" for American-Jewish women today.

NJPS data offer some striking and perhaps surprising information along denominational lines. Table 3.3 shows that among women ages 25 to 44, substantial (six or more years of multi-day schooling) Jewish education was received by 53 percent of Orthodox, compared to 26 percent of Conservative, and 10 percent of Reform women; among men the same age, substantial Jewish education was received by 61 percent of Orthodox, 40 percent of Conservative, and 25 percent of Reform men. In terms of substantial Jewish education, the gender gap is now relatively smallest among the most traditionalist portions of the population. This may be tied to the generally high emphasis put on Jewish education by traditionalist religious groups, and the prevalence of elementary through high school day school education among those populations.

Women's new role in Jewish schooling can be traced back to the Bais Yaakov movement, begun a century ago by Sara Schnirer, a pious Eastern European woman, in a daring response to the challenges of secular modernity. Observing that in enlightened German communities Jewish women who lacked deep knowledge of Judaic texts might more easily drift away from Jewish lifestyles, in 1917 Schnirer opened a school with 25 girls; the school expanded rapidly and new branches were established. In 1937–1938, 35,585 girls were enrolled in 248 Bais Yaakov schools in Poland alone.[32] Although the original Bais Yaakov movement's vitality in Europe was brutally cut off during World War II, along with millions of lives and an irreplaceable, richly diverse cultural heritage, the basic assumptions underlying the formation of the Bais Yaakov schools revolutionized attitudes toward Jewish education for girls. Today, across the American-Jewish day schools spectrum, providing girls with a Jewish education has become a communal norm.

Haredi (right-wing Orthodox) schools, including Lubavitch schools, do not teach Talmudic texts to girls. Ironically the late Lubavitcher Rebbe stated that women should be taught the Gemara in order to preserve the quality of Jewish life, and in order that the tradition should be passed down from generation to generation. In a Hebrew article, he urges that women be taught the oral Torah so that they, who provide the most consistent presence in the home, can supervise and guide their children's religious studies. Rabbi Schneerson asserted that women should study with their husbands subjects even including the "fine, dialectical" points of law which most previous rabbis posited as being inappropriate for women. These study sessions are necessary, says Rabbi Schneerson, because without them women can easily be seduced by the charms of secular studies. He says: "It is human nature for male and female to delight in this kind of study. Through this there will develop in them (the women) the proper sensitivities and talents in the spirit of our Holy Torah."[33]

Women have text-study opportunities, including Talmud, in settings as diverse as the Conservative movement's Jewish Theological Seminary and at the Orthodox Stern College for Women, an undergraduate school of Yeshiva University. The flocking of women to serious adult educational settings goes across the denominational spectrum. Some women endeavor to gain language and cultural skills necessary for the understanding of the Talmud and other rabbinic texts, in schools in Israel or the United States, such as New York's *Drisha* and *Shalhevet* and Boston's *Ma'ayan*. Hadassah formed a new elite educational program called the Leadership Academies in 1998; women compete for participation in these academies, which require them to commit themselves to serious study of Jewish history, culture, and texts. A growing number of synagogues and community adult education settings also provide opportunities for text study.

Even for women who do not have extensive aspirations, adult education has become a vivid fact of the life through the adult Bat Mitzvah phenomenon. Each year many hundreds of adult women learn how to chant the Hebrew liturgy and how to read from the Torah scroll, so that they can participate in adult Bat Mitzvah ceremonies. The meaning of the term Bat Mitzvah, of course, is that one has officially reached the age—twelve for girls—at which one is an individual responsible for one's own religious behavior. However, the vernacular meaning of the Bat Mitzvah in the United States is that one is knowledgeable enough have a ceremonial affirmation—to "be Bat Mitzvah," as in "I was Bat Miztvahed." The opportunity to participate in these events, whether individually or in groups, through synagogues or organizations like Hadassah, is transformative to many women, by their own accounts.

Jewish Women's Scholarship

Jewish women's scholarship has developed into a bona fide field in colleges and universities. Jewish women's studies programs have been established on an undergraduate and graduate level at Brandeis University, where the International Research Institute on Jewish Women was established by Hadassah, the Women's Zionist Organization, in 1997, and on a graduate level at religious institutions such as the Jewish Theological Seminary, the Reconstructionist Rabbinical College, and elsewhere. In Israel, the first Women's Studies Program was established in 1982 at the University of Haifa, and opportunities now exist for Jewish women's studies at the Hebrew University in Jerusalem's Lafer Center for the Study of Women, the Gottesfeld-Heller Center for the Study of Women in Judaism at Bar Ilan University in Tel Aviv, the Schechter Institute established in Jerusalem by the Jewish Theological Seminary, and in many other institutions. Academic women are organized into a Women's Caucus at the Association for Jewish Studies conference, which enables them to more closely attend to each other's works and to supportively share their experiences in the field.

1997 saw the publication of *Jewish Women in America: An Historical Encyclopedia* in two massive volumes, and featuring 800 biographical and 110 topical entries.[34] In the same year, the Jewish Women's Archive was established in Brookline, Massachusetts, for the purpose of retrieving and publicizing the history of Jewish women. Numerous resource books and bibliographies are continually published in areas related to Jewish women's studies, including a critical sourcebook on Jewish American women writers,[35] and many others.

Scholars interested in analyzing the connections between gender, religion, social and historical change, and cultural milieu have explored the history of women in Jewish societies from the Bible onward, and have produced scores of pioneering works in the fields of Bible studies, rabbinics, history, literature, anthropology, sociology, psychology, and popular culture. These scholarly works have had a significant impact on individual departments, on particular fields, and on Judaic Studies as a whole. A 1998 study by the International Research Institute on Jewish Women shows that nearly two thousand students each year take college courses taught by feminist scholars which focus on women in Judaism.[36] Moreover, not only college and university students have been affected by the ground-breaking writing of several generations of Jewish feminist scholars. The insights of female academics are slowly being incorporated into Jewish studies curriculums for children, teenagers, and adults as well.

Adult Education Initiatives Gaining Popularity

In a development that probably would have surprised assimilationists who assumed that American Jewry would gradually lose all distinctive qualities, a largely acculturated segment of the American adult population has recently been seeking Jewish intellectual skills. While in the past years a laity devoted to intensive study was primarily Orthodox, today Conservative, Reform, Reconstructionist, and community opportunities for intensive text study for both men and women have increased. The traditional idea that Jews ought to make it their business to be the people of the sacred books has caught on among a limited but important segment of the population, along with both local and national initiatives to provide adults with intellectual tools and with opportunities to learn. Across the United States, adult education programs have been newly revitalized under the auspices of the Wexner Foundation, the American Jewish Committee, CLAL, and other organizations.

Culturewide shifts are occurring in attitudes toward adult education, and, for all the much-publicized conflicts between American and Israeli Jews, Israel plays a critical role in this American educational process. Conservative and Reform rabbinical candidates are required to spend time studying in Israel, and during the past decade, it has become increasingly popular for observant young women and young men to spend a year of religious study in Israeli *yeshivot* between high school and college.

Women's adult education has undoubtedly served as one important catalyst for adult education in general. All of these developments taken together have created a culture in which Jewish texts are considered appropriate targets for adult concentration. Thus, while the great majority of Jewish adults have little or no relationship to Jewish texts, for a substantial minority, the texts that comprise Jewish cultural history have become a salient part of life. It is important to note that Jewish education is cumulative longitudinally within the life of a Jewish individual. Well over three-quarters of American Jews who attended adult education programs had some previous formal Jewish education.[37]

Is "Being There" Enough?

Author Philip Roth playfully suggests that even a lackluster supplementary school education may light a Jewish spark which comes to fruition decades later. In his novel/confession *Operation Shylock,* (1993) Roth's protagonist (who happens to be named Philip Roth) finds himself inexplicably drawn into deep reading of Jewish sources such as the Chafetz Chaim and later enmeshed in the intricacies of Israeli politics. Sitting in a schoolroom which viscerally brings back to him the discomforts of his childhood Hebrew school experience, the protagonist realizes with surprise the lasting positive impact of long hours of repression and tedium:

... it had all begun back when I'd first taken my seat in that small, ill-ventilated classroom that was the Newark original of this makeshift Jerusalem replica, during those darkening hours when I could barely bring myself to pay attention after a full day in the school where my heart was somehow always light, the public school from which I understood clearly, every day in a thousand ways, my real future was to arise. But how could anything come of going to Hebrew school? The teachers were lonely foreigners, poorly paid refugees, and the students—the best among us along with the worst—were bored, restless American kids, ten, eleven, twelve years old, resentful of being cooped up like this year after year, through the fall, winter, and spring, when everything seasonal was exciting the senses and beckoning us to partake freely of all our American delights. Hebrew school wasn't school at all but a part of the deal that our parents had cut with their parents, the sop to pacify the old generation—who wanted the grandchildren to be Jews the way that they were. . . . What could possibly come of those three or four hundred hours of the worst possible teaching in the worst possible atmosphere for learning: Why, everything—what came of it was everything![38]

Philip Roth's fictional protagonist somehow had a seed of inextinguishable Jewishness planted in his heart, and finds that almost half a century after he languished in Hebrew school he is willing to serve as an espionage agent for the Israeli Mossad. Roth, whose own intellectual and emotional attachment to Jewishness has deepened with passing years, seems to wonder what in his Jewish familial and Hebrew school experiences might make such values and behaviors possible.

Many among the National Commission on Jewish Women focus-group respondents also had positive feelings about their own and their children's Jewish education, despite their vivid memories of boredom and resentment. The women recalled that they resented going to Hebrew school, but learned something and formed emotional bonds, and now their children are resenting going, but are also learning something and forming emotional bonds. To the focus-group mothers, the combination of resentment and Jewish education comprised a kind of American-Jewish tradition. One said: "It is profoundly important to me and my children. Although my son really moans and groans about Hebrew school, there is a love that I see there developing. With the girls too. When I pass our temple, my four-year-old says, 'Mommy, there's my temple.' That makes me feel so good."[39]

Such human contradictions underscore the complexity of analyzing data on the impact and effectiveness of Jewish education. Even after surveying patterns of Jewish education in the United States today, the most important questions remain: What impact does Jewish education have on connections with Jews and Jewishness? Is Jewish education today truly educating for Jewish identity? Is merely being there enough? Although our data cannot answer these questions fully, in the next chapter we work toward an understanding of these critical issues, and we suggest a new typology for the synergy between Jewish and secular education today.

Table 3.1 Formal Jewish Education of Adults
Percentages of NJPS Respondents Born or Raised Jewish
by Age and Gender

Index	18–24		25–44		45–64		65+		All Ages	
	F	M	F	M	F	M	F	M	F	M
None	28	19	34	14	30	12	52	22	36	16
Less than 3 years	4	5	8	8	9	10	8	17	8	10
3–5 Sunday School	6	5	9	6	10	7	6	2	9	5
6+ Sunday School	7	7	15	11	22	7	9	5	14	9
3–5 Supplementary	16	19	10	27	11	24	10	26	11	25
3–5 Day School	9	2	1	1	—	3	1	2	1	2
6+ Supplementary	20	29	17	25	16	27	13	17	16	24
6+ Day School	10	13	6	9	2	9	1	9	4	9
Total Percent	100	99	100	101	100	99	100	100	99	100

Source: 1990 NJPS data. Adapted from Fishman and Goldstein, *When They Are Grown They Will Not Depart,* 1993. Percentages have been rounded.

Note: Data in this and subsequent tables are based on NJPS respondents who were born or raised Jewish, unless otherwise noted.

Table 3.2 Formal Jewish Education of Children
Percentages of All NJPS Children Ever Enrolled
by Age, Gender, and Religious Identity

Age	Raised Jewish			Raised Non-Jewish		
	Male	Female	Total	Male	Female	Total
6–7	59	52	56	9	12	11
8–12	71	86	78	13	8	10
13–15	77	78	77	5	2	4
16–18	77	76	77	2	0	2

Source: 1990 NJPS data. Adapted from Goldstein and Fishman, *Teach Your Children When They Are Young,* 1993. Table includes children with at least one Jewish parent. Percentages have been rounded.

Table 3.3 **Intensity of Jewish Education**
               Percentages by Denomination Raised, Age, and Sex

	Women					Men				
	18–24	*25–44*	*45–64*	*65+*	*All Ages*	*18–24*	*25–44*	*45–64*	*65+*	*All Ages*
					Orthodox					
None	**	30	35	41	34	**	8	3	10	8
Minimal	**	8	12	13	11	**	10	7	9	8
Moderate	**	10	29	20	20	**	21	33	36	31
Substantial	**	53	24	26	35	**	61	58	45	54
Total %	**	101	100	100	100	**	100	101	100	101
					Conservative					
None	20	33	27	62	36	24	11	18	19	15
Minimal	7	13	22	16	15	2	10	17	22	12
Moderate	32	29	33	16	28	25	40	36	48	38
Substantial	42	26	18	5	22	49	40	30	11	35
Total %	101	101	100	99	101	100	101	101	100	100
					Reform					
None	37	30	18	61	31	10	9	3	38	10
Minimal	12	28	24	10	24	21	19	28	24	21
Moderate	37	33	49	29	36	40	49	40	33	45
Substantial	14	10	10	-	10	29	24	29	6	24
Total %	100	101	101	100	101	100	101	100	101	100
					Just Jewish					
None	**	56	54	70	61	**	79	25	53	61
Minimal	**	8	32	10	13	**	7	35	34	21
Moderate	**	7	7	20	11	**	7	33	7	12
Substantial	**	30	8	-	15	**	6	8	6	6
Total %	**	101	101	100	100	**	99	101	100	100

Source: 1990 NJPS data. Adapted from Fishman and Goldstein. Percentages have been rounded.

*Intensity of Jewish Education level: High includes six or more years of supplementary or day school; Medium includes 3–5 years of supplementary or day school and six or more years of Sunday school; Low includes 3–5 years of Sunday school and less than 3 years in any type of formal Jewish education.
**Fewer than 10 unweighted cases in the age/gender/denomination category.

Table 3.4 **Informal Jewish Education of Children**
Percentages of All NJPS Children in Youth Groups and Camp,
by Age and Formal Jewish Education

Age	Youth Group	Camp	Both	None	Percent	Number
6–7	3	23	1	74	100	11033
8–12	14	18	7	61	100	18768
13–15	21	15	8	56	100	10638
16–18	22	14	13	52	101	5867
All Ages	14	18	6	62	100	46306

Type of School of Currently Enrolled

Full-Time	11	40	15	34	100	7166
Part-Time	32	11	11	46	100	9630
Sunday Only	12	17	6	66	101	8017
Tutor	4	10	-	86	100	1550

Source: 1990 NJPS data. Adapted from Goldstein and Fishman. Percentages have been rounded.

Table 3.5 **Type of School Attended by Children Currently Enrolled,**
Percentages of Jewish Children by Age and Sex

	Both Sexes				Boys				Girls			
Age	6–7	8–12	13–15	16–18	6–7	8–12	13–15	16–18	6–7	8–12	13–15	16–18
Type of Schooling												
Full-Time	38	24	16	44	32	29	18	42	46	20	14	48
Part-Time	11	43	54	29	13	43	44	26	8	42	66	32
Sunday Only	52	25	21	27	56	23	25	32	47	27	16	19
Tutor	—	8	9	—	—	5	13	—	—	11	4	—
Total Percent	100	100	100	100	100	100	100	100	100	100	100	100

Source: 1990 NJPS data. Adapted from Goldstein and Fishman, p. 30. Percentages have been rounded.

Table 3.6 Years of Jewish Education Ever Received by Teenagers, Percentages of Jewish Children by Age and Parents' Jewish Education

Parent's Jewish Education*	Children's Years of Jewish Education				Total Percent
	None	1–2 Years	3–5 Years	6+ Years	
Children Ages 13–15					
Both None	64	—	22	14	100
Both 6+ Years	4	—	4	92	100
Father > Mother	15	9	36	41	100
Mother > Father	12	—	41	47	100
Children Ages 16–18					
Both 6+	9	—	6	85	100
Father > Mother	12	3	31	54	100
Mother > Father	35	—	37	38	100

Source: 1990 NJPS data. Adapted from Goldstein and Fishman, p. 37. Percentages have been rounded.

*Only those categories with 10 or more unweighted cases are included in this table.

Table 3.7 Reasons That Children Are Not Enrolled[a] in Jewish Schools, Percentages of Jewish Children by Age

Age	Reasons for Non-Enrollment						Total Percent
	Child Too Old, Too Young	Enough Jewish Ed.	Parents Not Interested	Child Not Interested	Problems With Schools[b]	Child Not Jewish	
6–7	*	*	*	*	*	*	*
8–12	15	24	18	14	29	—	100
13–15	5	26	11	39	16	3	100
16–18	17	23	8	41	11	—	100
All Ages	11	23	14	32	20	1	100

Source: 1990 NJPS data. Adapted from Goldstein and Fishman, p. 41. Percentages have been rounded.

a. For those Jewish children age 6–18 who were not enrolled in a program of Jewish education in the year of the survey. Unspecified reasons omitted from this tabulation.
b. School too expensive, too far away, or of poor quality.
* Fewer than 10 unweighted cases in 6–7 age group.

FOUR

EDUCATING FOR JEWISH LIVING

Diverse Patterns among American-Jewish Subgroups

Living in an open and voluntaristic society, American Jews have discovered that they cannot compel their children to absorb and implement parental values and goals. Individualistic freedoms which enable parents to shape their lives also allow their children to access a seemingly unlimited menu of personal options. Moreover, second and third generation American Jews cannot assume their third, fourth, and fifth generation children and grandchildren will be educated by a matrix of memories and Jewish associations that have been influential in the past. There seems to be no "magic bullet" that can guarantee Jewish identification: everyone knows stories about the offspring of "good Jewish homes" who have few ties to Jews and Jewishness when they become adults, and other stories about the children of unaffiliated Jews who become passionately attached to Jewish life.

However, despite anecdotal examples of the "failure" of Jewish homes and educational systems to enculturate youth, assimilation is far from a random process. Data from the 1990 National Jewish Population Survey, augmented by Jewish population research in several cities, interview, focus-group, and literary materials, suggest a typology of subgroups of American Jews, which is quite different from the simple inverse relationship that used to be assumed between Jewish and secular education.

Contemporary American-Jewish women and men ages 25 to 44 fall into four subgroups or categories, as illustrated in Figure 4.1:

1. high Jewish education and high secular education;
2. low (or no) Jewish education but high secular education;
3. high Jewish education but low secular education; and
4. low (or no) Jewish education and low secular education.

Among younger (ages 25 to 44) Americans raised as Jews who have received some Jewish education, the proportion reporting high levels of both secular and Jewish education is not inconsequential: ten or more years of Jewish schooling are reported by one-quarter of adults ages 25 to 44 with secular degrees beyond the master's level who have also received some formal Jewish education, as seen in Table 4.1. When we separate this group by gender, we see that the correspondence is especially striking for women: over one-third of women ages 25 to 34 who have M.A.s or who have Ph.D.s or professional degrees, and have also received some formal Jewish education, report that they received ten or more years of Jewish education.[1] As this and following chapters will demonstrate, these Jews with high levels of both secular and

HIGH-HIGH

High **Secular** Education
and
High **Jewish** Education

HIGH-LOW

High **Secular** Education
but
Low **Jewish** Education

LOW-HIGH

Low **Secular** Education
but
High **Jewish** Education

LOW-LOW

Low **Secular** Education
and
Low **Jewish** Education

HIGH Jewish Education =
HIGH Jewish Behaviors

LOW Jewish Education =
LOW Jewish Behaviors

Figure 4.1 **TYPOLOGY**

Overlapping Patterns of Secular and Jewish Education

Jewish education have many measurable connections to Jews and Jewishness. While they are decidedly an elite minority, they may be especially important in supplying a leadership cadre to the American Jewish community.

In the category of those who have high levels of secular education but low levels of Jewish education, about half of men and women with high secular and occupational status have average levels of Jewish education (four to nine years), and about one-quarter have minimal Jewish education (three years or less). In the category of those who have low levels of secular education, in contrast, among American Jews ages 25 to 44 who have not completed college, about one-fifth have ten or more years of Jewish education, over half have average levels of Jewish education, and nearly one-third have minimal levels of Jewish education.[1] As Table 4.1 shows, a total of 14 percent of men and 33 percent of women ages 25 to 44 have received no formal Jewish education. Among those whose secular educational level is high school or less, the proportion receiving no Jewish education is strikingly higher.

Jewish and Secular Education Complementary Forces for Continuity

In marked contrast to assimilationists like Clement Greenberg (Chapter 2), for whom intellectualism and cultural excellence were antithetical to Jewish connections, Jewish connectedness among younger Americans (ages 25 to 44) is most prevalent among those with high levels of educational and occupational achievement and high levels of Jewish education. High Jewish education and high secular education coexist for these American Jews with coalesced American-Jewish values, and present a critical new model for the future of American-Jewish life.

This typology contradicts long-standing popular perceptions of a "natural" conflict between secular and sacred education. During the first upward trajectory of American-Jewish socio-economic transformation, as we have noted, Jewish education was widely perceived to exist in antithetical relationship to secular education. However, our typology of a positive synergy between secular and Jewish education is very much in keeping with recent research on ethnic white Americans, and is an illustration of a coalesced value system in which Jewish and secular education have become complementary.

Sociologist Richard Alba argues that the best predictor of interest in transmission of ethnicity among white American ethnics is whether parents have been well enough educated in their ethnic traditions to feel some sense of mastery over their contents. Ethnic Americans with high levels of secular education and also a high ethnic cultural literacy confidence level were the parents most likely to transmit ethnicity to their children on a regular basis.[2] Jews also fit into the pattern found among other white ethnic Americans vis-à-vis the impact of endogamy: endogamously married parents were much more likely to want their children to be very aware of and identify with a single ethnic heritage, while those with mixed ethnic background preferred for their children also to have a mixed identity.[3]

Figure 4.2 presents a new model for looking at the way in which the combina-

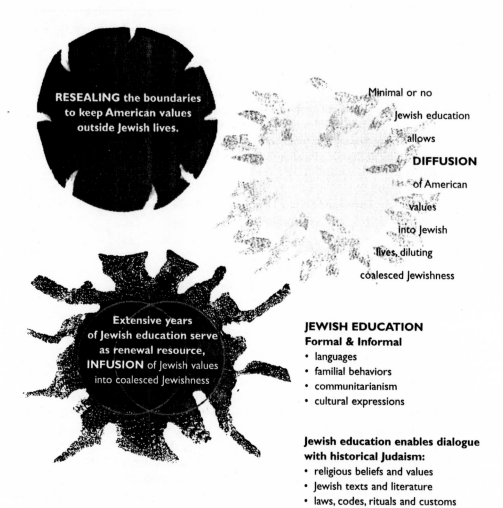

RESEALING the boundaries to keep American values outside Jewish lives.

Minimal or no Jewish education allows DIFFUSION of American values into Jewish lives, diluting coalesced Jewishness

Extensive years of Jewish education serve as renewal resource, INFUSION of Jewish values into coalesced Jewishness

JEWISH EDUCATION
Formal & Informal
- languages
- familial behaviors
- communitarianism
- cultural expressions

Jewish education enables dialogue with historical Judaism:
- religious beliefs and values
- Jewish texts and literature
- laws, codes, rituals and customs

Figure 4.2 **AMERICAN VALUES AND CULTURE SURROUND AND PERVADE AMERICAN JEWISH LIVES: COALESCENCE**

Jewish Education Infuses Jewishness into Jewish Lives

tion of formal and informal Jewish education—in the home and the classroom, in peer groups, camps, and Israel trips—provide an effective strategy for continually reinforcing Jewish distinctiveness despite ongoing coalescence. Barry and Carmel Chiswick, using a parallel economic typology, have aptly suggested that "time-intensive" traditional Jewish societies invested in Jewish adults with strong connections to Jewish culture.[4] Once education has engaged the hearts and minds of individuals, it becomes a gift that keeps on giving. To use a rather homely metaphor, Jewish education develops and enhances an inner cognitive and emotional Jewishness, which serves as a kind of tea bag, continuing to provide Jewish flavor and color to American lives, despite the fact that the surrounding American environment seeps in through permeable boundaries. With extensive Jewish education, and experience with Jewish languages, familial behaviors, communitarianism, and cultural expressions, the individual can engage in a dialogue with historical Judaism, vis-à-vis religious beliefs and values, Jewish texts and literature, and laws, rituals and customs. Without such education, the continual flow of Americanisms dilute Jewish distinctiveness. The only other option is that chosen by the *hareidi* community: resealing the boundaries to keep American values outside Jewish lives.

Partially because secular education and general cultural Americanization are so widespread among almost all segments of the American-Jewish population, coalescence is an important coping mechanism for Jews in each segment of the Jewish identity typology model. However, Jewish cultural literacy levels derived from formal Jewish educational and informal familial and communal experiences are uneven. As a result, the extent and the particular aspects of Judaism that are incorporated into the merged messages differ from one population subgroup to another. Pieces of Jewish history, law, and tradition which get worked into the coalesced value system of an individual who has a high secular education–high Jewish education profile, for example, are often strikingly different from those of an individual with much secular education but minimal or no Jewish education.

Impact of Jewish Education

Statistical analysis attempts to pinpoint phenomena and their causes, but human beings experience their lives in interconnected networks and overlapping contexts. Trying to "prove" that Jewish education "causes" stronger Jewish identification is difficult, because persons who are enrolled in Jewish schools for many years, and persons who sit in Jewish classrooms for many hours each week, are also likely to come from homes in which parents have above-average levels of Jewish behavior. In order to send (and pay for) Jewish education for many years, parents usually have strong Jewish commitments themselves. The household's approach to Jews and Judaism may have a very important impact on children growing up in that environment.

Table 4.2, a regression analysis of factors that influence adult Jewish behavior, isolates each factor and holds the other factors constant, to determine how much impact each factor may have, all other things being equal. This table includes several references to "indexes." Each index was constructed by Goldstein and Fishman to consider clusters of behavior, such as clusters of ritual behavior in the "Ritual Index." The salience of Jewish milieu to patterns of Jewish identification in contemporary American-Jewish life prompted Goldstein and Fishman to construct an index of Jewish milieu and measure its relation to type and duration of Jewish education. This Jewish Milieu Index combines variables on the number of Jewish friends reported, the perceived Jewishness of the neighborhood, and the importance of a neighborhood's perceived Jewishness to the respondent.[5]

Based on the regression analysis seen in Table 4.2, the Fishman and Goldstein study reported that even when socio-demographic background characteristics such as denomination raised and denomination of current household are controlled, a strong positive relation exits between type and duration of Jewish education and every Jewish behavior including Jewish milieu. With all other factors controlled, someone who has had no Jewish education on average scores 3.5 on the index; someone with six or more years of day school education on average will score about 4.0 (out of a possible 6). Longer and more intensive Jewish education is thus associated with lifestyles that strengthen bonds to the Jewish community both directly, through enhancing active participation in a variety of spheres, and indirectly, through fostering informal contacts and networks.

Statistically, both an extensive Jewish education and a high level of Jewishness in the home have a dramatic impact on adult Jewish identification, especially among Jews ages 25 to 44. In the lives of flesh and blood human beings, of course, these factors are seldom separated. However, the interrelatedness of the home and the classroom should not cause us to undervalue their individual significance. Table 4.2 indicates that (1) substantial Jewish education and (2) the Jewishness of the home in which one is raised are each positively related to every behavior measured by the 1990 NJPS that was associated with Jewish identity, including:

- living in a Jewish milieu,
- ritual observance in the home,
- membership in Jewish organizations,
- giving to Jewish philanthropies, and
- opposing mixed marriage.[6]

Jewish education is also related to the actual intermarriage status of respondents: As Tables 4.3 and 4.4 demonstrate, persons who received substantial Jewish education were far more likely to marry another Jew than those who did not. While endogamy should not be used as the exclusive litmus test of Jewish connectedness, it is useful to note that inmarriages are found among 51 percent of Jews ages 25 to 44 who receive six or more years of supplementary school education, 80 percent of those who receive six years of day school, as seen in Table 4.3, and 91 percent of those who receive nine or more years of day school (not on tables). Some reports indicate that 95 percent of those who attend for the full twelve years and graduate day school are married to born Jews.[7] In contrast, Table 4.3 shows that only one-third (34 percent) of Jews ages 25 to 44 who received no Jewish education married another Jew. Inmarriage rates for those receiving one to five years of Jewish education hovered around 40 percent, as seen in Table 4.2. This table also underscored the importance of dividing the data by age. The effects of Jewish education were much less pronounced among middle-aged and older American Jews. For example, inmarriage was found among 58 percent of Jews ages 45 to 64 and 88 percent of Jews over age 65 who received no formal Jewish education.

The impact of Jewish education on the age 25 to 44 population crosses denominational lines. As Table 4.4 demonstrates, inmarriage was reported by virtually all raised-Orthodox respondents and nine out of ten raised-Conservative respondents who received six or more years of supplementary school or day school. Among those who reported being raised in Reform homes, 41 percent were married to Jews, compared to 34 percent raised in Reform homes who had no Jewish education.

The 1990 NJPS data also indicate that the home alone is not enough. For recent marriages, of marriages that included one person who said s/he had been brought up in Orthodox households, 20 percent were marriages to non-Jews. Thus, while the Orthodox inmarriage rate is higher than the Conservative or Reform inmarriage rate when denomination alone is considered, the inmarriage rate is much higher for recent marriages among those who complete nine or more years of day school than it is for those who merely call themselves Orthodox.

Results in this type of table may be somewhat skewed by the fact that calling one's parental home "Orthodox," "Conservative," or "Reform" may in fact reflect code names for a continuum of ritual observance and Jewish involvements, rather than a true indication of denominational affiliation. Thus, responses such as "Oh, we were very Orthodox" are sometimes made about highly affiliated Conservative households, and comments such as, "Well, we were pretty Reform—we didn't do much," may really be code for an unaffiliated household. Needless to say, such responses are frustrating to persons who are ideologically devoted to each of the American-Jewish denominations. However, Jewish population survey research routinely uses religious self-definition in this way. Since denomination is self-defined, a wide variety of behavioral patterns are found within each denominational subgroup.

The 1990 NJPS data reveal that strong Jewish connections are clustered in households in which several members have received substantial levels of Jewish education. Table 4.5 in particular shows that among teenagers ages 16 to 18, those whose mother and father both had six or more years of Jewish education were themselves likely to receive more than nine years of Jewish education. The Jewish education of the mother was in fact slightly more influential than that of the father in the extent of the teenage child's education. When both parents receive adequate levels of Jewish education, they acquire practical Jewish skills—Jewish cultural literacy—which make them feel at home with their own heritage. Parents who have achieved a comfort level with Jewish traditions are far more likely to make the effort to provide their children with formal Jewish education and to create informal Jewish educational experiences in the home.

In terms of denominational identification, Orthodox and Conservative teenagers each had an average of 7.02 years of Jewish education, while those in Reform households received 5.67 years on average. Those whose households were "just Jewish" received a little over two years.

Reports by researchers such as Mordechai Rimor and Elihu Katz,[8] Seymour Martin Lipset,[9] and Alice Goldstein and Sylvia Barack Fishman,[10] have repeatedly indicated the powerful cumulative effect of many hours and many years of Jewish education. These studies based on 1990 NJPS data are further supported by subsequent studies analyzing other data sets, such as articles by Steven M. Cohen on the impact of Jewish education on teenagers and adults,[11] and a recent survey on day school education by Alvin Schiff and Mareleyn Schneider.[12] Each of their studies demonstrates that a powerful positive impact on Jewish identification is connected to a multi-day supplementary or day school education that spans the early childhood, school age, and teenage years.

A recent study by Bruce Phillips argues with these conclusions, but Phillips's study is limited by a failure to consider age as a factor. The significance of age variables is particularly salient in light of Phillips's assertion that "most of the day school graduates were first and second generation Jews [the NJPS survey instrument did not in fact ask about "graduation"] who rarely married non-Jews regardless of the Jewish education they received. Thus, after controlling for generation, Jewish day school education has no more impact on mixed marriage than does two to three day-a-week education." However, presenting his data by generation without considering the age groups involved, Phillips mixes the people he calls "bobbe and zeyde," for whom Jewish education occurred within a densely Jewish cultural context, with younger American Jews whose primary access to both informal and formal Jewish education often takes place outside the home, regardless of their generational status.[13]

When older American Jews are thrown into the statistical mix with those ages 25 to 44, contemporary patterns among younger Americans are obliterated, because the differing age groups cancel each other out. Generation thus cannot be substituted for age, because while there is some overlap, they are not synonymous. The fact is that only 11 percent of today's American-Jewish population were born outside the United States (first generation). When Phillips asserts that generation is more important than education, his evidence is based on a primarily female geriatric population among whom mixed marriage rates were extremely low. First generation data is affected by the fact that most aged female East European immigrants had little formal Jewish education, but were still very attached to Jews and Judaism, because of the intensity of the Jewish environments that shaped their identities. Furthermore, when Phillips writes about first generation day school "graduates," (*sic*) he is describing men whose European "day school" education differed in almost every way imaginable from contemporary American day schools, at least outside the purview of the *hareidi* community.

Prior to analyses of the 1990 NJPS, several pioneering researchers gathered information on limited populations of Jewish students and analyzed the patterns of Jewish behavior that former students exhibit as adults. Himmelfarb (1974),[14] Bock (1976),[15] Ribner (1978),[16] and Cohen (1987)[17] published studies which explore the impact of different types and duration of Jewish education. Both Himmelfarb and Bock[18] suggested that Jewish education must exceed a certain threshold of number of hours and years in order to measurably affect adult attitudes and behavior. Below that threshold, they insisted, Jewish education has no appreciable effect on Jewish identification.

Himmelfarb and Bock suggested that formal Jewish education cannot function independently as a guarantor of adult Jewish identification; informal education and emotional experiences emerge as crucial codeterminants of adult Jewish affiliation. Bock indicated that the lack of affective learning results in a profound impoverishment in the experiential Jewishness of the young, who often feel themselves to be only coincidentally Jewish. Bock distinguished between manifestations of "personal Jewishness," such as "personal religious observances, Jewish self-esteem, participation in informal social networks and cultural perceptions," and "public Jewishness," such as "attendance at services, participation in secular synagogue affairs . . . [and] organizational activities, support for Israel and attitudes about American political issues"; he found that the areas he referred to as personal Jewishness were 1.3 to 2.4 times more influenced by home background than by Jewish schooling, whereas what he called public Jewishness were equally influenced by formal education and home background.[19]

Interestingly, Israeli scholars and educators also wrestle with ways to alleviate the fading of ongoing, unplanned, informal Jewish education even in the Hebrew-speaking Jewish homeland, for many secular young Israelis have little emotional attachment to traditional "Jewishness."[20] In a sense, the ambitions of the European *maskilim* (enlightened intellectuals) and Zionists, who each, in their own way, longed to create a "new Jew," have succeeded too well. Amos Oz remembers the emergence of "a new race": "new Jews who had undergone a certain mutation—heroic Jews, pioneering, bronzed, strong, and stoic. Diametrically opposed to the traditional Jew of the Diaspora. Brave young men and women who had turned the dark night into an intimate friend; young men and women who had advanced past all inhibitions between him and her, past all restraint."

Oz recalls his impression that this new type of Jew in prestate Palestine did not live in Jerusalem:

> On the dark side of the moon, there was also a city called Tel Aviv, a fascinating place of which I knew very little. But I did know that newspapers were printed there, and the theaters were there, and new forms of art and many political parties and stormy debates and, above all, great Jewish athletes. And the sea filled with suntanned muscular Jews who knew how to swim. Swimming was unthinkable in Jerusalem. It required different genes.[21]

The normalization of the Jew, still fresh in Oz's reminiscences, has now proceeded beyond the imagination of Zionist dreamers. Israeli educators worry about preserving awareness of the Jewish historical heritage in the minds of young Israeli Jews, albeit in a differing cultural context than that faced by American-Jewish educators.

Early Childhood Jewish Education

A potential window of educational opportunity occurs when people marry and have children and are looking for Jewish-content child care programs. As Gabriel Berger and Lawrence Sternberg suggest in their analysis of Jewish child care, city studies have indicated that the majority of American-Jewish couples prefer to have their children in Jewish day care, but only a tiny minority do, because the supply of such day care is vastly inadequate to the demand.[22] This paucity of availability is troubling because Ruth Pinkenson Feldman's study of Philadelphia Jewish parents showed that when parents enter their preschool children into Jewish-content child-care programs, the Jewish observance level of the entire household becomes more extensive.[23] This increase in Jewish observance apparently occurred as a passive or second-hand result of the children's early childhood Jewish education. Thus, some research suggests that Jewish education may exercise both a direct and indirect effect on behaviors of individuals and family units.

Educating Jewish Teens and Young Adults

Nine or more years of Jewish education mark an important threshold in the impact of such education on adult Jewish behavior. This impact is arguably intensified by the fact that Jewish education is received during the teen years. The importance of Jewish education during the teen years was suggested by the 1995 Fishman report to the *Al Pi Darko* Conference on North American Jewish Teens,[24] and emphasized by Phillips, who stresses duration of Jewish education continuing "beyond age 13."[25] American-Jewish teenagers are located not only at the crossroads of their own lives, but also at the crossroads of the American-Jewish future. Nevertheless, they comprise not only the most educationally critical but also the most underserved age group.

Despite the proven effectiveness of longer years and longer hours of Jewish education—ideally multi-day education that spans the early childhood, school age, and teenage years, supported by a Jewishly active home life, and complemented by Jewish youth groups, camping experiences, and Israel trips—fewer than one-quarter of American teenagers ages 16 to 18 are involved in Jewish educational programs. Of those who report informal educational experiences, 44 percent are attending all-day schools, 29 percent are attending after-school programs that meet more than once a week, and 27 percent are attending one-day-a-week programs (Table 3.3). In many communities, day school high school programs are only available under Orthodox auspices, if at all.

In many communities, the all-day non-Orthodox Jewish schools come to an end in the eighth grade. Students who have been attending community day schools or Solomon Schechter day schools, for example, often are unable continue with this type of education past the eighth grade. Many communities do not offer supplementary school educational programming on the high school level, to meet the needs of the majority of American Jewish students who attend supplementary rather than day school types of Jewish schools. Numerous communities have a dearth of appropriate programing on any level during the all important teen years .

A type of informal educational experience, the "Israel experience"—of which there are many varieties—has been the subject of great hopes and expectations by many communal leaders. In 1992, over four thousand North American teenagers participated in short-term Israel experiences. The largest numbers of these teens participated in programs sponsored by United Synagogue Youth (USY—13 percent), Massada of the Zionist Organization of America (15 percent), and National Federation of Temple Youth (NFTY—15 percent), with another 7 percent each participating in programs run by the Conservative Camp Ramah and Hadassah's Young Judea. However, only young persons from certain types of communities seem to be attracted to the spectrum of Israel trips. A recent study by Steve M. Cohen on "Geographic Variations in Participation in Israel Experience Youth Programs" finds that "there are wide variations among communities in terms of their Israel program yield," and "those communities with relatively smaller Jewish populations, higher incomes, and higher rates of synagogue affiliation have the highest yields."[26]

Cohen cautions that his study overlooks programs that serve predominantly Orthodox clientele. Orthodox youth—who have very high rates of travel and study in Israel—tend to participate in long-term programs, such as a year of yeshiva study. This tendency reduces the overall level of participation in short-term programs in those areas where Orthodox Jews are highly concentrated, such as parts of New York." With that proviso in mind, Cohen shows that during the 1991–1992 years among youngsters ages 14 to 21, the highest rates of participation were found in Westchester, N.Y., Baltimore, Long Island, and Northern New Jersey; the second tier of participation rates were in Atlanta, Southern New Jersey, Philadelphia, Manhattan, and Chicago. Significantly, despite their large Jewish populations, lower rates of participation were found among teens in Miami–South Florida, Los Angeles, Boston, and the Washington, D.C. suburban areas.[27]

One Israel program that many participants have found moving and transformative is the "March of the Living" trip, which takes young people first to the European death camps and then to Israel, and often includes significant preparatory educational programs. The March of the Living has been in operation since 1988; it has involved thousands of students from forty countries, including twenty-five thousand from North America. A follow-up study of the long-range impact and effects of the March of the Living program by sociologist William Helmreich indicates that most participants stated as their most important goal in participating "to increase their knowledge and understanding of the Holocaust." Working with telephone interviews of three hundred randomly selected participants from the 1988, 1990, and 1992 groups, Helmreich found that the impact of the March was profound. Ninety percent of participants said they would want their spouse to be Jewish, and over 80 percent said that if they married a non-Jew they would want their spouse to convert. More than 90 percent said that the March had significantly affected their lives in the long run, and about half said it had intensified the depth of their Jewish identity and attachment to the Jewish religion. In addition, persons who participate in March of the Living are disproportionately likely to take leadership positions in the Jewish community.[28] Despite these impressive figures, it should be remembered that the available data are not extensive enough to determine how much of the perceived impact of the program can be traced to factors in the original, formative background of participants. Perhaps most important, current research gives us little reliable information about how durable the effects of such programs may be, in terms of influencing the adult Jewish behaviors of participants.

An intriguing analysis of the immediate and one-year after-effects of a variety of programs can be found in Erik H. Cohen's research and evaluation, written for and published by the Youth and Hechalutz Department, the Joint Authority for Jewish Zionist Education. Cohen creates a cognitive map of components and outcomes of short-term Israel experiences. Respondents evaluated many aspects of the success of diverse programs. While respondents varied distinctly according to such factors as extent of Jewish education before the Israel experience, geographical location vis-à-vis population density of Jewish community in country of origin, and the type of program in which they had been enrolled, the overwhelming majority of participants expressed satisfaction with their experiences, and said they would recommend their program to others. Very few students felt the programs should have less Jewish content or be less religious; at the same time, only about one in five felt there should be more Jewish, religious, or Zionist content. One striking finding was that the greatest polarization was expressed among those with no Jewish education and those with six or more years of education: in these two groups at the opposite ends of the educational spectrum, both the greatest satisfaction and the greatest dissatisfaction were found.[29]

What we will not know until we have a large scale, systematic, objective longitudinal study of participants, broken down by age, gender, and religious background, compared to a control group of non-participants, is the permanence of the effects of short-term Israel experiences. Samuel Heilman articulates well-taken caution:

> . . . if the effort of last summer is to have lasting value, the greeting at the airport on the return must be given the same attention as the send off. Institutions and people in the Diaspora must be ready to build upon the good feelings and integrate the returnees in all manner of Jewish life here. From youth group to high school, synagogue to summer camp, community center to Internet, we who care about Jewish continuity must build a network that will capture the fleeting Jewish consciousness of our young people who come flying back from Israel.[30]

Another study by Steven Cohen, based on a 1993 national sample of over fourteen hundred Jewish parents and their 615 teenaged children, who were accessed as a subsample of a Market Facts, Inc., Washington-based Consumer Mail Panel, analyzes the impact of Israel trips, assesses the cumulative and separate impact of Jewish education and parental involvements, and comments on the relative effectiveness of differing types of Jewish schools. Cohen notes that factors such as parental involvement in Jewish activities, age, sex, socio-economic status, geographical region, and Israel experiences all have an impact on the Jewish connectedness of teenagers; however, even after these factors have been controlled, formal Jewish education generally has a moderate impact on the Jewishness of teenagers, and certain types of Jewish education have a pronounced impact. Cohen finds that "the scores of Sunday school students . . . suggest little if any impact of this type of Jewish education upon Jewish identity," while "the part time schools fare somewhat better," the "non-Orthodox day schools score even higher," and finally, "the Orthodox day school alumni substantially outscore the others."[31]

Cohen's analysis is especially important on the subject of "alternative" Jewish education. Israel programs are often touted as a panacea and an alternative to classical educational settings, but both Cohen's and 1990 NJPS figures indicate that the Israel experience is best viewed as a complement to, rather than a substitute for, Jewish schools. The important but limited effectiveness of Israel trips and other types of informal Jewish education is underscored by the fact that 1990 NJPS data also indicate that informal Jewish educational experiences, such as Jewish camps and youth groups, are today accessed almost exclusively by children and teenagers who have more extensive than average years and types of formal Jewish schooling.

Cohen's research indicates that "youth groups and adolescent Israel travel are associated with increments in Jewish involvement, even after controlling for parents' Jewish involvement, Jewish schooling, and youth groups and other factors. . . . The Israel visit of one's youth seems to bring with it a 15 percent increment in the chances of scoring high on Jewish involvement." However, while such trips promote "modest increments in Jewish involvement," this almost exclusively takes the form of high levels of support for Israel. They do not increase levels of other types of Jewish activism in the United States.[32]

For teenagers, especially those who come from dual-career or single-parent families who are concerned about activities during the after-school hours, Jewish community centers are an obvious target locale in which to serve this population. In a Brandeis University report by Amy Sales and Gary Tobin on revitalizing Jewish Community Center youth services, JCC personnel were asked to what extent their institutions engaged in using evaluation, needs assessment, feasibility studies, and marketing studies to guide them as they created programing for teens. They found that most JCCs do not engage in systematic planning to implement youth services. Thus, although teenagers have very definite ideas about what kinds of programing and which locales might be attractive to them, little is being done systematically to access their ideas and put them into play. The authors come to the conclusion that "teens are often a lower priority in JCCs than are seniors, pre-schoolers, and other groups. Their low status is reflected in the Youth Departments' budgets, in the low level of staff time allocated to teens, in the limited availability of Center resources for teen services, and in the lack of available and/or appropriate space for teen activities." They comment wryly, "JCC leadership may claim that youth are a priority for the Center, but their actions frequently belie this assertion."[33]

Jewish education for teenagers is also affected by personal home factors. Almost one-third of American-Jewish children live in homes that have been affected by divorce. Blended families, even more than single-parent families, have been proliferating in the Jewish community, with about one-fifth of Jewish children living in such households. For both parents and children in single-parent and blended families, Jewish life cycle events can present stressful situations.[34] Planning for celebrations can pull children in two directions. They often have difficulty dealing with the Jewish emphasis on family, especially around Sabbaths, holiday time, and life cycle events. Jews in all subgroups of the Jewish population and all Jewish denominations experience divorce. Rates of divorce are far lower among Jews who call themselves Orthodox or who have a high rate of ritual observance; they are twice as high as average among Jews who are married to non-Jews. Nevertheless, children in each family type or denomination experience their own set of problems.

Some educators believe that many of the emotional problems generated by synagogues, Jewish schools, and Jewish community centers can be minimized if Jewish educators adopt the attitude that Jewish customs and ceremonies are not pegged to gender divisions and to stereotypical images of the normative family, but are the birthright of all Jews. For example, references to Sabbath and holiday celebrations can make it clear that rituals such as candle lighting and kiddush over wine are not the "property" of the two-parent family, but can appropriately be part of the repertoire of the single person, single gender, or single-parent household as well. Since this is the approach of rabbinic law as well, this is an example of an instance where coalesced individualistic values and *halakhah* can coexist usefully.

While a high correlation between years and extent of Jewish studies and Jewish identification is strongly suggested by the 1990 NJPS data, no study has yet systematically analyzed the role of curriculum in these relations or the effect of "successful" or "unsuccessful" programs of study on the Jewish identification of adults. Some have speculated that being in a "Jewish place" during certain key periods of life has an educational impact as defining as any specific curriculum elements. In particular, the teenage years have been identified as potentially critical years for the tasks of enculturation. Although the 1990 NJPS survey instrument did not ask adult respondents at what age they began and ended their formal Jewish education, those who had been enrolled in Jewish schools for the most years were, in simple arithmetic terms, almost certain to have been in Jewish educational settings during part or all of their teen years. Phillips's 1993 Survey on Mixed Marriage, which asked specifically about the duration of Jewish education, found that "respondents who continued past age 13 in even a one day-a-week school" married non-Jews less often than those in more intensive schools who terminated their Jewish education at age 13.[35] This is an extremely important finding, and one that suggests the critical importance of further research.

University environments are quite diverse in their Jewish offerings, and college-level educational experiences can differ dramatically in terms of their effect on Jewish identification. Those students who attend colleges that offer vibrant and appealing Jewish environments, such as excellent Jewish studies programs or popular Hillel-type extra-curricular activities, may actually be drawn closer to Jews and Judaism during their college years. Conversely, those who find themselves in settings where it is considered strange or odd to be Jewish may be increasingly alienated. College friendship groups can also have a powerful impact on feelings about being Jewish, although it should be remembered that the NJSP data cannot provide information on the relative importance of contemporaneous Jewish education or friendship circles, since the data reflect friendship circles at the time that the study was made, not at the time during which individuals attended school. Additionally, as Sidney and Alice Goldstein have shown in their 1996 study of *Jews on the Move*, migration itself—including migration for educational purposes—is associated with lower levels of Jewish identification and activism, where there are no intervening factors.[36] Some college students are motivated to seek out Jewish activities and persons and will do so no matter how unfamiliar or unpromising the setting, while many more appear to be quite influenced by the perceived attractiveness and accessibility of new Jewish ties—or lack thereof—and by the often happenstance vagaries of school and work settings and friendship circles.

What students bring to the university setting also has a profound impact on what they get out of it. Students appear to be influenced not only by the Jewish offerings of the university, but also by the positive or negative nature of their previous Jewish educational experiences and by the extent to which the values and behaviors of their parental homes had seemed to support or contradict what they were taught in Jewish schools. Indeed, one student study of Orthodox day school graduates on the Brandeis University campus suggested that the behavior even of this very selective group was extremely diverse: students whose parents' behavior had reinforced day school curriculum were far more likely to continue independently to observe Jewish rituals than were students whose parents' lack of Jewish observance had seemed subversive to day school policy.[37]

Education and the Future of the American-Jewish Community

The strong relationship between formal Jewish education and later Jewish behaviors is disputed by some. Although statistical data indicate that extended Jewish education matters, Jewish communal analysts and leaders still disagree about the ramifications of the evidence. While many urge countrywide educational interventions designed to move children and their parents along the road "from assimilation to the dream of universal Jewish literacy," such as those suggested by Boston federation executive Barry Shrage,[38] others argue that focusing communal energies on Jewish education ignores half of American-Jewish children, namely those who are receiving no formal Jewish education.

CUNY Professor Egon Mayer acerbicly notes that communal monies expended on Jewish education have generally increased, despite the fact that enrollment numbers have decreased because of "the dramatic decline in the numbers of children born to two Jewish parents, and a parallel increase in the numbers of children born to interfaith parents," which in his view render attention to "traditional forms of Jewish education" far less relevant in the larger picture.[39] In opposition to this view, taking strong exception to what they see as communal leaders whose attention "has been riveted on the unaffiliated" as they create "well-meaning efforts to reach individuals on the margins," Jack Wertheimer, Charles Liebman, and Steven M. Cohen argue instead that attention should be devoted to "the key institutions requiring support," such as "synagogues, day schools, summer camps, youth groups, campus programs, and religious and cultural institutions of higher learning": "That is to say, institutions which emphasize Jewish particularism and foster strong identification within the group. These settings for natural and intense social interaction also teach the lesson that there is a distinctive Jewish world view, and that being Jewish means, to some degree, being different."[40]

It will probably be true for the foreseeable future that the majority of American Jews will receive a few short years of Jewish education. Nevertheless, the elite population which receives more substantial Jewish education is critical to American-Jewish life, because it comprises the potential future intellectual, organizational, and religious leadership of the community. Moreover, Jewish education appears to have a relationship with even the most personal of lifestyle decisions, affecting Jewish households and family life. Without communal support for intensive and extensive Jewish education, there seems little hope for Jewish vitality in the United States. Attitudes toward Jewish education have become the symbol of American-Jewish willingness or unwillingness to consciously resist coalescence and live in partial dissonance with American mores and values. How the American Jewish community chooses to interpret and react to educational options will have great impact on communal direction during the opening decades of the twenty-first century.

Table 4.1 **Levels of Secular and Jewish Education Received**
       Percentages of Jews Ages 25–44

Highest Secular Degree Obtained	Some Received: Years of Jewish Education												None received: No Jewish Education		Total
	1–3 years			4–6 years			7–9 years			10+ years					
	All	*M*	*F*	*All*	*M*	*F*	*All*	*M*	*F*	*All*	*M*	*F*	*M*	*F*	
High school or less	29	30	27	33	36	29	18	17	19	20	17	25	20	43	100
Some college (or A.A.)	21	19	23	33	30	36	22	24	20	24	27	21	7	30	100
Bachelors degree	19	17	23	37	42	31	23	22	24	21	19	22	13	28	100
Masters or nursing degree	17	22	13	41	45	38	14	12	16	28	22	34	6	21	100
Other professional and graduate degrees	20	15	30	30	36	18	25	28	18	25	22	34	13	30	100
Total	22	22	23	36	39	31	20	20	20	22	20	26	14	33	100

Source: 1990 NJPS data. Percentages have been rounded.

Table 4.2 **Background Factors which Influence Adult Jewish Behavior**
Regression Analysis for Selected Variables

Independent Variables	Ritual Index	No. Jewish Orgs.	Contribute Jewish Causes	Jewish Milieu	Attitude to Intermarriage	Intermarriage Status
			Dependent Variables			
Index of Jewish Education	*	*	*	*	*	*
Age	*	*	*	0	0	*
Education	*	*	*	0	0	0
Gender (D)	*	*	*	*	*	0
Marital Status (D)	*	0	*	*	*	—
Foreign Birth (D)	*	0	0	*	*	—
Denomination Raised (D)	*	*	*	*	*	*
Jewish Friends (D)	*	*	*	—	*	—
Jewishness of Home	*	*	*	*	*	—
Region of Residence	*	0	0	*	*	—

Source: 1990 NJPS data. Adapted from Fishman and Goldstein.

R²   .412   .167   .306   .234   .160   .146

Key:
(D).....Dummy Variable
*.....Significant at <.05
0.....Not Significant
—.....Not in Model
1. Dummy variable with more than two components; if any one of the components was significant in relation to the reference group, we have given that variable an *.
2. Refers to whether all household members were Jewish.
Note: For ease of presentation and interpretation, we have not provided all the regression coefficients in this table. They are available from the authors on request.

Table 4.3 **Respondents Who Married Born Jews**
Percentages by Index of Jewish Education and Age

Index	Age Group		
	25–44	45–64	65 + over
None	34	58	88
Less than 3 years	42	58	71
3–5 Sunday School	40	41	*
6+ Sunday School	45	59	81
3–5 Supplementary	38	82	87
3–5 Day School	*	*	*
6+ Supplementary	51	65	85
6+ Day School	80	79	*

Source: 1990 NJPS data. Adapted from Fishman and Goldstein. Percentages have been rounded.

*Fewer than 10 unweighted cases.

Table 4.4 Respondents Ages 25–44 Married to Born Jews Percentages by Level of Jewish Education and Denomination Raised

Level of Jewish Education	Denomination Raised			
	Orthodox	Conservative	Reform	"Just Jewish"
None	*	53	34	14
Minimal	*	47	39	23
Moderate	*	45	45	11
Substantial	100	91	41	58

Source: 1990 NJPS data. Adapted from Fishman and Goldstein. Percentages have been rounded.

Key:

*................Fewer than 10 unweighted cases.

Minimal.........Less than 3 years of Jewish education of any kind and 3–5 years of Sunday school.

Moderate........6 or more years of Sunday school, 3–5 years of supplementary or day school.

Substantial......6 or more years of supplementary or day school.

Table 4.5 Years of Jewish Children's Jewish Education: A Multiple Classification Analysis by Denomination Raised, Ritual Scale, and Parents' Jewish Education

	All Ages	Ages 16–18
Grand Mean	4.17	6.33
Denomination		
Orthodox	4.91	7.02
Conservative	4.13	7.02
Reform	4.20	5.67
Just Jewish	2.04	2.01
Ritual Scale		
Low	2.94	6.23
Medium	3.94	5.95
High	4.94	6.76
Parents' Jewish Education		
Both None	2.77	3.70
Both 1–5 Years	3.48	4.97
Both 6+ Years	5.39	9.12
Father > Mother	3.78	4.84
Mother > Father	3.98	5.02

Source: 1990 NJPS data. Adapted from Goldstein and Fishman.

FIVE

FORMING JEWISH HOUSEHOLDS
AND FAMILIES

Family Values in Traditional Jewish Societies

American-Jewish households have often been portrayed as the epitome of traditional middle-class family values. Whether satirized by novelists and screenwriters for obsessively nurturing, close-knit, and sober family groupings or extolled by clergymen for the same attributes, Jewish families have seemed to exemplify normative middle-class virtues.

This picture of Jews as unusually oriented to marriage and the family had a realistic basis in many historical traditional Jewish communities. In previous Jewish societies, a congruence of religious values, economic necessities, and cultural and societal pressures often worked together to encourage Jewish individuals to marry. Within traditional Jewish culture, marriage was seen as sacred, the only salutary and productive state for adult human beings, and specific behaviors for all members of the family unit were prescribed by Jewish law. Gender role divisions were pronounced, with societal and devotional behaviors for women and men clearly demarcated. Male and female piety and male text study were adult activities, and children were raised to emulate adult behavior as soon as possible. Few Jewish couples admitted to remaining deliberately childless; infertility was the source of anguish when it occurred, and couples often took whatever heroic efforts were available to them in an effort to have children.

Jewish societies provided no comfortable cultural niche for an adult without spouse and children: there was no celibate clergy, no tradition of a son or daughter remaining unmarried to care for a widowed father or mother. On the contrary, rabbinical literature warned Jewish congregations to avoid hiring an unmarried rabbi or religious teacher. A child who remained unmarried was often regarded by parents as a source of shame, and by the community with suspicion. While the synagogue and study hall were critical locations for male religious activities, the family was the basic building block of society, and it was within the family unit that ritual piety was structured and transmitted.

War, disease, or economic depressions, and possibly the occasional influence of surrounding ascetic civilizations, may have caused episodic increases in the proportion of unmarried adults in some Jewish societies.[1] Extended family units, while never as ubiquitous as some observers have nostalgically imagined, were not uncommon in many communities. In some societies, a young husband and wife might share living quarters for short or extended periods with the parents of the husband or, more commonly, the wife. Similarly, it was not uncommon for aging or widowed parents to share living quarters with their middle-aged children. In some communities family members lived in separate quarters around a common courtyard. In times of migration especially, other relatives, such as siblings, aunts, uncles, and cousins, were often accommodated by nuclear family units, until they were in an economic position to establish their own households.[2]

Conversely, periods of migration, often necessitated by persecution and/or poverty, were also times of geographic disruption, during which family units were subjected to special physical and emotional stresses, increasing the rupture and dissolution of nuclear family units. During times of migration and other historical stresses, many ruptured family units reformed into new "blended" families with stepchildren from prior marriages sharing quarters with younger children from the new biological and matrimonial unions.[3]

Although economic factors were certainly a prime consideration in many arranged matches, most parents were concerned to guarantee the financial security of the young couple, rather than to acquire fortunes for themselves. Research by David Biale and others has shown that while ascetic attitudes were not unknown in historical Judaisms, a positive attitude toward the—controlled and domesticated—appetites of the flesh was a more prominent Judaic posture. Certainly by the nineteenth century the expectation (if not always the reality) of European parents and professional matchmakers who arranged marriages was that affection would follow betrothal and marriage.[4]

Premarital sex was socially discouraged, although not precisely prohibited by Jewish law. Extramarital affairs were severely prohibited, however, and much legal and cultural effort was devoted to preventing situations that might encourage adultery. The offspring of an extramarital sexual encounter between a married woman and a male to whom she was not married was considered a *mamzer,* a bastard (unlike the child of premarital encounters, who had the rights of any other Jewish child), and was forbidden to marry into the legitimate Jewish community for ten generations.

Within marriage, a woman had the legal right to sexual fulfillment. Husbands were instructed by rabbinic texts to concern themselves with their wives' sexual needs, and never to force sexual advances on an unwilling spouse. Judith Hauptman argues that although talmudic texts sometimes articulate attitudes toward women and sexuality which are offensively sexist or even grotesque by contemporary standards, rabbinic law often developed in the direction of increased awareness of and sensitivity to women and their needs.[5] In addition the biblical texts read in synagogues on a weekly and holiday basis were often "suffused with eroticism," as Rachel Adler notes, affecting the outlook of Jewish cultures as well as forming a basis upon which rabbinic law wove "the sights and smells and textures of the created world into ritual."[6] Indeed, as Daniel Boyarin demonstrates, rabbinic texts on the whole express the view that marriage is valuable because it promotes companionship and a domesticated but ongoing erotic sexual expression, over and above reproductive needs.[7] Significantly, widowed and divorced persons well past reproductive age were encouraged to remarry, and within marriage to resume sexual activity.[8]

Although children were cherished, traditional Jewish cultures focused on adults and adult activities, and were not, in the contemporary sense, child-centered. Age rather than youth was respected, and childhood was regarded as the training ground for adulthood. Elderly parents were the responsibility of their middle-aged children, who were expected to provide not only for the physical needs but even more for the emotional and social well-being of their aging parents, ensuring that they maintained their dignity and communal status in social situations.[9]

Within nineteenth-century American-Jewish communities as well, familism and domesticity were paramount considerations, despite the fact that many aspects of traditional religious home-based ritual had not been retained. Whether descended from wealthy, aristocratic Sephardic families who had participated in the formative decades of the country or from German-Jewish families who had more recently come to the United States and worked to establish themselves financially and socially during the eighteenth and nineteenth centuries, American-Jewish men and women aspired to the bourgeois lifestyles of the American middle and upper-middle classes. In a popular synthesis of Christian and Jewish ideals of gender role divisions in the family, both religious cultures were perceived as placing women firmly in the domestic realm and in the extended domesticity of communal good works. Acculturated Jewish women were much influenced by the reigning cultural Christian myth of true womanhood, and sought to promote the image of Jewish women as the equals of their Christian sisters in familial devotion, piety, spirituality, and literary sensitivity.[10] The role of the father departed significantly from Jewish traditions; in the United States fathers were far more likely to be valued for their entrepreneurial skills than for their personal piety or learning.

The years of mass immigration of European Jews and other ethnic groups into the United States from 1880 to 1924 were often deeply disruptive to the families and family values of emigres. Immigrant journalism and literature are replete with tales of familial rupture: Husbands sometimes came to the United States before their wives, became acculturated, and lost interest in their European families either left behind in Europe or eventually brought to the United States, only to be abandoned. Adolescent boys and girls sometimes boarded steerage to travel alone, and had to make their way unprotected in the New World. In crowded American tenements, married couples were faced with enormous financial and emotional stress, which sometimes contributed to alienation and divorce. Children, who quickly learned the language and mores of America through the public school system and rough street cultures, were often filled with disdain for their immigrant parents.[11]

As discussed earlier, secular education was for many Jews the key to socio-economic advancement and acculturation, while Jewish learning was for most immigrants and their children not a salient value during the first half of the twentieth century. For most immigrants, Jewish learning moved from the center of ideal Jewish family life to the periphery. Familiar economic patterns were disrupted as well. Those European women who had been wage earners in their communities of origin learned that in America it was acceptable for unmarried girls and women, but not married women, to be perceived as working outside the home for pay.[12] Jewish men almost

universally took on the American ideal of the husband as successful breadwinner. Ironically, even some households that counted themselves as socialists often worked extraordinarily hard to establish themselves financially.

Nevertheless, to a remarkable extent, Jewish family life rallied and reestablished
itself in America during the first half of the twentieth century. During the great economic Depression, Jews, like other Americans, tended to marry late and have small
families, but most of them married eventually; singleness continued to be considered
unusual behavior in Jewish families and communities. Many aspects of the traditional
Jewish family were still salient.

Following the Second World War, American society put a strong emphasis on
marriage and family life, an emphasis that highly traditional religious groups such as
Catholics, Mormons, and Jews each experienced as supportive of their own particular religious-societal vision of "family values."[13] American Jews, like other religious-
social groups, frequently viewed the societywide American emphasis on the family
unit as specifically legitimating their own idealized visions of home and family. This
American cultural emphasis on marriage and the family reinforced established Jewish
values. Jewish men and women, many of whom were extensively Americanized by the
middle of the twentieth century, often adopted both the external and the internal prescriptions of this American/Jewish domestic image.

In 1946 more than half of American-Jewish women were married by age 22 and
over 80 percent were married by age 25, and in 1953 almost two-thirds of Jewish
women were married by age 22 and more than three-quarters were married by age 25.
In the 1950s and 1960s, American Jews were the most universally married of all American populations. Both a 1957 census and the 1970 National Jewish Population Survey reveal 95 percent of Jewish adults married by the time they reached ages 35 to 45,
and the 1970 NJPS shows four out of five (78 percent) of all Jewish adults as married.[14]

The post-War baby boom facilitated by these early marriages temporarily reversed what had been a century-long trend toward smaller Jewish families. Working
with statistics going at least as far back as Prussia in the middle of the nineteenth century, Steven Cohen and Paul Ritterband note that with the loosening of the hold of
religion and the introduction of family planning, birthrates for Protestants, Catholics,
and Jews all declined, but the Jewish birthrate declined far more than the other two.[15]
Even during this family-hungry period, more than any other ethnic group, Jewish
couples planned their families carefully, having their children a little later, providing
space between siblings, and concluding their childbearing a little earlier than other
women—with the result that their families were somewhat smaller. The 1970 National
Jewish Population Study revealed that married Jewish women had 2.8 children per
family, although their fertility rate still lagged behind the American non-Jewish average of 3.5, as seen in Table 5.1.[16]

Contemporary Jewish Marriage and Fertility

To many people, the phrase "Jewish family" evokes a picture of a married-with-children household. To a large extent, popular stereotypes about the solidity of the Amer-

ican-Jewish family remain intact. The "Jewish mother" is a well-known symbol of relentless family cohesion, projected in vehicles like Woody Allen's 1988 film, "New York Stories: Oedipus Wrecks," in which a nagging Jewish mother's huge, omniscient head floats over New York streets, loudly advising her middle-aged son to dress properly, eat right, and get married. The Allen protagonist, ultimately listening to Mama and dissolving his relationship with a tall, blond, gentile divorcee with three children, finds serenity and ecstatic happiness in the plain and plump arms of a Jewish woman who knows how to boil chicken just like his mother.

In real life, however, contemporary Jewish family life has been profoundly transformed—as has family life for American households in general. Jewish households in the 1990s do not look or behave as they did in traditional Jewish societies or in post–World War II American communities. Survey research dramatically demonstrates, and anecdotal materials underline the fact that in terms of their family formation, American Jews today resemble other middle- and upper-middle-class white Americans much more than they resemble American Jews who preceded them in the decades after World War II. The proportions of married Jews have shifted downward, and the age of marriage has shifted upward in 1990 NJPS data. Jewish women and men marry slightly later than other white Americans—and all Americans marry later now than they did forty years ago.

1990 NJPS data show that 65 percent of Jews are married, as seen in Table 5.1. Table 5.2 further demonstrates that 62 percent of women and 46 percent of men are married in the ages 25 to 34 group, as are almost three-quarters of women and men ages 35 to 54. Thus, a perhaps startling figure of 25 percent of Jewish women and men ages 35 to 44 are not currently married. In the midlife decades, as might be expected, the percentage of divorces increases as well, so that the proportion of currently married Jews never exceeds four-fifths of the population at any age. After age 35, Jewish men are consistently "less divorced" than Jewish women—indicating that divorced Jewish men remarry more often than divorced Jewish women, frequently to non-Jewish women or to Jewish women who fall into a younger age category. The "most married" Jewish cohort is comprised of men ages 55 to 64, at 87 percent married.

Table 5.1 also indicates the relationship between geographical location and marital status. In cities like Boston with large proportions of young adults, often students or professionals beginning their careers, percentages of Jewish singles are dramatically higher (29 percent single) than they are in cities with many retired persons like Miami (7 percent single), or midwestern communities, whose singles tend to go elsewhere in pursuit of career opportunities or social life, such as Cleveland (11 percent single) or St. Louis (9 percent single).

Tables 5.3 and 5.4 illustrate changing patterns in childbearing among American-Jewish women. Among 1990 NJPS respondents, more than half of women ages 25 to 34 (55 percent) had no children, as seen in Table 5.3. In comparison, among Jewish women ages 35 to 44, one out of four (24 percent) had no children; in that age group, 11 percent of women had never married and 14 percent were divorced or separated. Given their currently predominantly unmarried state, it is not clear that all or even most of the 24 percent of childless women in the age 35 to 44 group will in fact achieve the status of motherhood. Thus, while nine out of ten American Jewish women ages 45 or over reported having children, either biological or adopted, we cannot assume that when the current group of childless women age 35 to 44 are a decade older, they also will have become mothers.

Postponed marriage and childbirth are now phenomena that have been in place for several decades. Some demographers predicted early on that these trends would result in smaller families. Since the mid-1980s, demographers have estimated the completed size of the contemporary Jewish family at well under two children per household.[17] Moreover, in addition to other factors that affect delayed childbearing, some states have age limits for adoption, so that adoptive as well as biological birth becomes more difficult for older mothers.

American-Jewish women are currently most likely to have their children during the fifteen-year period between ages 27 to 42; their mothers were most likely to have their children during the fifteen-year period between ages 20 to 35. For women currently ages 55 to 64, the average age of marriage was 22 and the average age of first childbirth was 24. In contrast, among married, fertile 1990 NJPS respondents ages 35 to 44, the average age of marriage was 25 and the average age of first childbirth was 27. (Women who have not yet married and had children were excluded from these percentages.)[18]

The anomalous fertility level of the 1950s "baby boom" is evident in Table 5.4: Women married in the 1950s were the group most likely to have three or more children; indeed, at 55 percent with three or more children, they are by far the most fertile Jewish group in the 1990 NJPS data. In contrast, among women who married during the years of massive immigration and the economic Depression (1900 to 1939), almost three-quarters had two or fewer children, with only 26 percent reporting three or more children. It is worth noting that 28 percent of women who married during the 1970s report three or more children—a slightly higher rate of larger families than reported among those who married prior to 1940! This is an important fact to remember as an antidote to nostalgic pictures of "cheaper by the dozen" Jewish families. While such families have always existed—and still do—they do not represent the American-Jewish norm at any time during the twentieth century.

American Jews have been shown to be highly committed to family planning, and being impeccably reliable in the matter of expected family size. Family planning is probably one of the first and most profound aspects of coalescence, American Jewish couples, who have slightly fewer children than other white Americans, have long been distinguished by the accuracy with which they plan their families and use contraceptive devices to implement their plans.[19] Among activists on behalf of birth control and women's suffrage in twentieth-century America were women who lectured eloquently in Yiddish and probably felt that they were rebelling against Jewish culture. However, for their daughters and granddaughters, birth control is an axiom of American-Jewish culture. Contemporary American Jews are vigorously in favor of family planning, both on a personal and on a communal level. Studies indicate that even among ultra-Orthodox Jewish women, contraceptive usage is the norm; however, women in that environment often do not begin using birth control until after they have had five children, do not always tell their husbands they are using it, and typically describe their motivation as being medical, rather than personal.[20]

Despite the ubiquitousness of Jewish family planning, the likelihood of a woman's having born children and the number of children in her completed family is correlated with the strength of a woman's Jewish connections. Looking at fertility levels by years of Jewish education reveals modest patterns, as seen in Table 5.5. Among women ages 30 to 49, having seven or more years of Jewish education was somewhat associated with having four or more children. Among women over age 50, in contrast, no such association exists. This association between Jewish education and fertility probably does not indicate that Jewish education causes higher fertility levels, but instead reflects the recent greatly increased likelihood that women from highly committed families will receive extended Jewish education. This explains differences by age as well: for older women, the family was often a more important source of enculturation than the classroom, whereas for younger women the classroom assumes increasing importance.

Not surprisingly, women who call themselves Orthodox are more likely than others in the same age group to be married and have children; as a group, Orthodox women alone are currently having children above replacement (replacement = 2.1 children per family) levels. Conservative women expect to have more children than Reform women, but among 35 to 44 year old Conservative and Reform women few differences in actual family size exist.[21]

Data on women ages 35 to 44 also show that women who identify themselves as "Jewish by religion" are much more likely to have children than women who consider themselves to be secular Jews. Being a Jewish mother is strongly associated with belonging to a synagogue, belonging to and working for Jewish organizations, making donations to Jewish charitable causes, having mostly Jewish friends, observing Jewish holidays, and seeing Judaism as a "very important" aspect of one's life.

Just as they have in the recent past, American Jewish women today are likely to give birth to their first child somewhat later than non-Jewish women: currently, larger proportions of non-Jewish white women have children in their early twenties than do Jewish women. This is probably tied both to the elevated socio-economic ambitions of Jewish men and women, who often chose to schedule childbearing after given career goals are attained, and to the related disproportionate tendency of Jewish women to finish college and to earn graduate degrees. In other ways, however, patterns of childbearing among Jewish and non-Jewish women are similar, with total completed childbearing for both groups having diminished over the past three decades.[22]

Despite their low fertility the vast majority of Jewish women still place an enormous value on having children. Jewish women are less likely than any other religious or ethnic group to state that they wish to remain childless. Most American-Jewish couples hope to have children "some day." Unlike women of other ethnic groups, where higher education is associated with lower expectations of childbearing, the more highly educated a Jewish woman is, the more children she expects to have. Calvin Goldscheider and Frances Kobrin Goldscheider report that "Jews with doctorates expect 2.2 children and only 11 percent expect to be childless; Jews with 'only' college degrees expect only 1.8 children and 21 percent expect to be childless." In contrast, the reverse pattern is true of highly educated Protestants and Catholic women.[23]

However, 1990 NJPS data reveal that highly educated Jewish women do not actually have as many children as they once expected to. Although Jewish career women are more committed to the idea of having families than any other group of career women, they are at least as likely as other white middle class women to postpone the onset of childbearing until they have reached what they consider to be an appropriate level of financial or occupational achievement. Expectations do not always conform to reality. On the contrary, "as education increases among both Jewish men and women, the proportion with no children increases." Indeed, "among those with a masters degree . . . Jews have significantly higher levels of childlessness than non-Jews."[24] Working with the 1970 NJPS and the 1990 NJPS, Frank Mott and Joyce Abma point out that Jewish women ages 16 to 26 years old who were interviewed in a national study in 1969–1970 expected to have an average of 2.5 children; that cohort, today ages 35 to 44, have in fact born an average of only 1.5 children and expect an average of 1.7 children completed family size.[25]

Dual-Career Jewish Households

A contemporary transformation of labor force participation patterns among Jewish women has meant, in practical terms, that most American Jewish women work outside the home for pay for most of their adult lives. Contrary to popular misconception, the dual-career household is not "non-normative," it is the new normative American-Jewish family. This transformation goes across denominational lines, and is influenced in every denomination by economic factors. Within the right-wing Orthodox world, the presence of working mothers of young children is eased by that community's adherence to the East European precedent of working women and scholarly husbands. Above all, the new prominence of the working Jewish mother reflects not assimilation but coalescence, the blending of American and Jewish values and behaviors (as detailed in chapter 2).

National Commission on Jewish Women focus-group participants spoke eloquently about the ways in which they balanced personal, professional, and Jewish concerns. For women who identified religiously as Orthodox, Conservative, Reform, Reconstructionist, or secular, the occupational-family formation profiles were remarkably similar. All described hectic days and complicated time-management schemes. Those who were married described jigsaw puzzle type arrangements with spouses. Working mothers tried hard to find quality time for all family members and wanted space for both children and husbands in their lives. Typical was the following detailed outline by an Orthodox mother:

> I get up at six—the baby wakes me up. I shower and get myself together and make the baby's lunch. Around 6:30 my husband gets up and the other child gets up. I take care of the baby and he takes care of my other son. I feed him, make his lunch, make my own lunch, and get dressed. My husband takes our son to school so everyone is out of the kitchen by about 8:15. I take my son to the babysitter and go to work. I am a guidance counselor in a high school. I have 90 emotionally disturbed children on my case load. I see each one once a

week for a few minutes. . . . I've heard it all and a lot of it is very sad. Then I pick up my older son from school at 4:00 and bring him home and pick up my younger son right after that at 4:30. I play with them for about an hour and get supper at 5:30. Then they get baths and my husband comes home at 6:30 and everyone is happy. We run around and play for another hour. I put the one kid to bed at about 7:30 and other one will stay up till 9:30. Then my husband and I get a chance to talk.

A common thread among the focus-group participants who were working mothers was the necessity for carving out specific times for specific activities and people. They were impatient and angry when people they interacted with didn't respect these time blocks, and came late or were otherwise unreliable. In general, the working mothers exhibited a clear sense of being in control of their own time and their own lives. They struggled to accomplish this goal, but they seemed indeed to be accomplishing it, and many conveyed an impression of vibrant self-actualization. Perhaps surprisingly for women with so many demands on their time, the working mothers were very likely to volunteer some time for Jewish organizations, but they chose their volunteer activities very carefully. Many said they demand clearly defined goals and they "can't just come and chit chat," preferring activities with "a beginning, a middle, and an end . . . a specific task within a time frame." Almost universal was a preference for activities that make use of their own particular talents, and are carefully orchestrated. The causes that attracted focusgroup participants tended to be oriented around their children, or local disadvantaged persons, Jewish causes, or feminist causes, and more of them said they are willing to donate money than volunteer time.

Divorced Individuals and Family Units

The American-Jewish family is not only formed later than in the recent past, but is also often less durable as well. Rates of divorce, once far lower in the Jewish community than among non-Jews, are climbing and, while still slightly lower, are close to the national average. Jews also retain the propensity to remarry; in examining rates of divorce, it should be kept in mind that they include currently divorced individuals only, not those who have been divorced and remarried. The rate of currently divorced Jewish males rises from 4 percent among those ages 25 to 34 to 9 percent among those ages 35 to 64, falling to 3 percent among those ages 65 and older. The overall rate of currently divorced Jewish males is 6 percent, compared to 7 percent of all white American males. Rates of currently divorced women double from 7 percent among ages 25 to 34, to 14 percent among ages 35 to 44, and 15 percent ages 45 to 64. The disparity in currently divorced status for women and men illustrates the fact that divorced men remarry more quickly than women, and that many second wives are not Jewish.

Divorce has increased in all segments of the Jewish community, although there is an inverse relationship between the traditionalism of the household and the likelihood of divorce, with households strongly connected to Jewish behaviors and community showing lower rates of divorce than those with weak connections. Divorce is twice as likely to terminate a mixed married relationship as an inmarried Jewish house-hold; conversely, once a Jewish-Jewish couple has divorced, the ex-spouses are twice as likely to marry non-Jews the second time around than they were when entering into a first marriage.

The Jewish divorce, or *get*, is a legal proceeding terminating the conditions set forth upon the signing of the *ketubah*, the legal contracts entered into at the time of the couple's wedding. Jewish divorce proceedings may only be initiated by the hus-band, except under the most extraordinary circumstances, but theoretically should not be performed without the wife's acquiescence. One of the most distinctively "Jewish" problems associated with divorce is that of the *agunah*, the woman whose husband has obtained a civil divorce but who will not cooperate in providing her with a *get*. (An *agunah* may also be a woman whose husband has disappeared and cannot be proved dead, but that definition is not applicable to this discussion.) In the absence of a *get*, under the terms of Jewish law a husband is free to remarry, while his wife is not. If a Jewish woman remarries without a *get*, her children are considered to be *mamzerim*, while her husband may remarry without stigmatizing his progeny.

The Conservative movement has long urged the insertion of clauses in the wed-ding contract that would make sure a woman can receive a religious divorce even if her husband is uncooperative. Within the Orthodox world there have also been sev-eral initiatives for including clauses that would accomplish the same purpose, but they have not been widely used.

Advocacy organizations for women being denied a *get* have been formed in sev-eral cities and on a nationwide basis.[26] Still, many activists in the Jewish community have expressed frustration or outrage because thousands of women are trapped in sit-uations in which husbands and lawyers use the obtaining of a Jewish divorce as a tool for blackmail or wreaking vengeance.[27]

The proliferation of such "chained women" is in many ways a product of the hyphenated position of American Jews. The freedom of choice that many American Jews take as their birthright, together with the inequity of Jewish divorce law regard-ing women, combine to make the position of Jewish women vis-à-vis divorce even more unequal than it has been in historical Jewish communities, because American-Jewish men have the option of obtaining a civil divorce and remarrying. Indeed, the position of the Reform movement has been that civil divorce is the appropriate method of dissolving an American-Jewish marriage, and that the *get* is unnecessary, as spelled out in a Union of American Hebrew Congregations *Guide for Jewish Couples Contemplating Divorce*: "Reform Judaism in the United States has interpreted divorce as a purely civil action to be dealt with in the secular courts. It eliminated the *Get* as anachronistic and therefore unnecessary. The divorce rituals that some Reform rabbis have introduced have no halachic validity and have not been intended for that pur-pose."[28]

The Reform elimination of the *get* is considered by some to be anti-Jewish woman. Together with its espousal of patrilineal descent, the movement's dismissal of *get* can be seen to ease the way for male outmarriage, removing the privileged sta-tus that Jewish law gave to Jewish women as potential marital partners. Most impor-tant, since American Jews move back and forth through very porous denominational boundaries, previously married women who find themselves wishing to marry Conservative or Orthodox men, or to marry any Jew in Israel, are put into a situation in which rabbis require a halakhic divorce before a new marriage can be implemented.[29]

The Orthodox world has had its own specialized problems with divorce. Understanding all too well the desperate need of Orthodox women for a religious divorce, some lawyers servicing traditional communities have allegedly deliberately specialized in "encouraging husbands to extort large settlements from their wives in return for granting a *get.*" One male attorney combating a policy of "absolute blackmail" on the part of such colleagues initiated a "Get Project" in the *New York Law Journal* for the purpose of collecting data in the form of cases and complaints—affidavits, bank books, correspondence between litigants—concerning lawyers who encourage *get* extortion.[30]

Increased divorce has produced increased numbers of blended and single-parent families. Almost one-third of American-Jewish children live in homes that have been affected by divorce: about one-fifth of Jewish children live in two-parent households in which at least one parent has been divorced, and one-tenth of them live in single-parent households. The number of Jewish single-parent families seems deceptively small when compared to all Jewish households. However, when only households with children are considered, because of the generally low Jewish birthrate, single-parent households comprise about 10 percent. In single-parent households—usually headed by women—annual income is in general severely diminished, when compared with the income of both divorced men and married couples. In Boston, for example, twice as many divorced women as divorced men reported annual incomes of under $15,000 a year in 1985.[31] Thus, single Jewish mothers and their children comprise the new poor in American-Jewish society, rivaled only by certain segments of the elderly and the newest immigrants.

Not surprisingly, older children are more likely to be step-children in blended households than are younger children, with the commensurate rise in divorce and remarriage rates among adults. Thus, the number of step-children doubles from the newborn through five-year-old group to the age-six though nine-year-old group, almost doubles again from the six through nine year olds to the ten to thirteen-year-old group, and becomes 50 percent larger during the teen years. From the youngest to the oldest pre-college age group, the numbers of step-children become five times as large.

Interestingly, the presence of step-children in Jewish households is not a new phenomenon, although it was less prevalent among American Jews in the 1950s and 1960s than it was in many earlier epochs of Jewish history. Because of the Jewish propensity for remarriage, in Jewish societies in which men and women were frequently widowed by disease and disaster, a not inconsiderable number of Jewish children were raised by one biological parent and one step-parent, who often then went on to have another biological family together. Jewish memoirs and literature frequently recount the adventures of older children growing up in such situations. Today's step-children, however, are far more likely to arrive at their "blended" living arrangements because of parental divorce, rather than bereavement.

As sociologist Nathalie Friedman has pointed out, blended families vary widely in their composition. Her study of Jewish families touched by divorce included "six different family constellations," with an even greater number of custodial arrangements. Add to this mix the various permutations of religious affiliations or lack thereof, and the possibilities are diverse indeed. One commonality among Friedman's respondents, however, was their desire for increased sensitivity to their and their children's life situation.[32]

Unmarried Jews and Their Households

The most striking transformation in the adult population of American Jews is that historically unprecedented numbers are unmarried, as seen in Table 5.1. The large proportion of unmarried American Jews—about one-third of the population—is due primarily to delayed marriage and secondarily to rising rates of divorce. These unmarried individuals are, as a group, the Jews about whom the least information has been available prior to the 1990 NJPS. For example, information about the household arrangements of unrelated unmarried individuals who share living quarters has often been ignored in studies of specific metropolitan Jewish populations. In many cases, the numerous men and women who lived together either before marriage or in lieu of marriage have not been adequately reported to be analyzed in these surveys; they appear as "single" adults. The 1990 NJPS data to some extent begin to fill this gap and provide some interesting insights into patterns of single life.

Among the entire group of individuals about whom information was gathered in the 1990 NJPS, 36 percent were described as unmarried by the respondents, including 23 percent who had never married, 8 percent who were currently divorced or separated, and 5 percent who were currently widowed. Among currently unmarried individuals, 32 percent were ages 18 to 24, 26 percent were ages 25 to 34, 16 percent were ages 35 to 44, 9 percent were ages 45 to 54, 6 percent were ages 55 to 64, and 12 percent were age 65 and over. While all of these populations are "unmarried," their life situations may differ significantly.

Five percent of all singles reported living with roommates, and surprisingly, given anecdotal impressions, only 1.2 percent said they were living with "partners" or "lovers." One can only assume that romantic living arrangements between singles have been underreported. As might be expected, the youngest unmarried adult populations were the most likely to include "roommate" living arrangements. As age increased, cohorts of unmarried individuals were less and less likely to include persons described as "roommates" and more and more likely to include persons described as "lovers" or unmarried romantic partners.

Elderly Jews

One important population of Jewish households which often does not fit into and/or is not serviced by the nuclear family unit are elderly Jews. As Acklesberg notes, "Many elderly people . . . now live alone; their isolation makes it difficult for them to cope with illness, the death of loved ones, and the responsibilities of household management."[33] Indeed, elderly Jews comprise a numerous population and often endure problems of isolation and marginalization. Persons over age 65 account for more than one of every eight adults in the 1990 NJPS. A large proportion of Jews by religion are found in this older population. This fact, combined with the fact that a large proportion of elderly Jews live alone, makes single-person households particularly numerous among persons identifying themselves as Jews by religion.

Among all U.S. white respondents in the 1990 U.S. Census, 13 percent were age 65 or over. Because of their relatively lower birthrate, Jews, in comparison, averaged 17 percent age 65 or over. Broken down by religious profiles, individuals age 65 or over accounted for 20 percent of Jews by religion, 7 percent of secular Jews, 10 percent of Jews by choice, 12 percent of Jewish apostates, and 8 percent of non-Jews living in Jewish households.

The proportion of elderly Jews varies dramatically from community to community. In some areas, such as San Francisco, the percentage of Jews age 65 and over has actually declined from 16 percent in 1959 to 14 percent in 1987.[34] In other sunbelt areas, however, the percentage of older Jews is quite high. Jews over age 60 accounted for 67 percent in Palm Beach, Florida, for example, compared to 44 percent in Miami, and 35 percent in Atlantic City.[35] Aside from sunbelt migrations, communities with relatively high proportions of older Jews may arise because of very stable social arrangements, so that older Jews tend to remain in the community after retirement, or may have few economic opportunities for younger Jews, giving the elderly a more prominent profile.

Among the oldest age groups, unmarried individuals do not often report the presence of either lovers or roommates. Indeed, unmarried elderly Jews tend to be more polarized demographically, financially, and geographically than members of any other age group.[36] Despite the high rate of Jewish mobility, a significant proportion of elderly Jews live in the same geographical area as at least some of their children. But large numbers of elderly Jews live in single-person households far from family. Some live close enough to persons similar to themselves to form family-like support networks. They may live in nearby apartment buildings or may find a congenial spot in a local library or Jewish community center to socialize. Although affluent older unmarried Jews, most often women, may be as likely as less affluent persons to feel isolated because of changes in the world around them, they have more flexibility: they are able to relocate to the more desirable sections of the urban areas they have always lived in, or to spend part or all of the year in communities in the sunbelt which are more amenable to the needs of the elderly.

Later Childbirth, Longer Lives Equal More Sandwich-Generation Jews

The children of elderly Jews are, today more than ever, part of a sandwich generation. American Jews, like other middle- and upper-middle-class Americans, are living longer, and passing through young-old, middle-old, and frail-elderly categories. At the same time, their middle-aged children have increasingly followed the national patterns of postponing marriage and childbirth and working throughout their own child-raising years. These middle-aged children are frequently in the position of trying to meet the needs of school-age children, household expenses, and aging parents at the same time. Sometimes the "children" have themselves entered their retirement years. The dual-pronged nature of these responsibilities ranges from emotional pressures to simple physical demands for time. When the middle-aged "child" caring for children and aging parents is a divorced or widowed person, the emotional and physical demands are exacerbated. As American Jews continue to postpone marriage and childbirth and as the American-Jewish population as a whole continues to "gray," the prevalence of Jewish sandwich households will continue to increase.

The life situation of sandwiched women and men is often invisible from a statistical standpoint. It differs from Jewish societies in the past, in which relatively young grandparents frequently helped to raise grandchildren, and older grandchildren helped to meet the needs of their aging grandparents, often living in physical proximity to each other. While such intergenerational support systems were never universal—as some Jews nostalgically imagine—they were fairly common, and still are in many non-Western cultures. Among contemporary American Jews, however, an intergenerational shared domicile is uncommon enough (fewer than 5 percent of American-Jewish households) to be almost considered an "alternative lifestyle," especially when placed in juxtaposition with the typical small American nuclear family.

Jewish Gay and Lesbian Households

The increased permeability of gender boundaries and an increasingly tolerant social environment has raised the consciousness of the Jewish community about Jewish gay and lesbian individuals and households, just as American society in general has become more aware of homosexual Americans. Little statistical information has been gathered on American Jews with a homosexual orientation, except in cities with high population density such as San Francisco. Gary Tobin and Sharon Sassler's *Bay Area Jewish Community Study* interviewed 463 homosexual respondents, representing about eighteen thousand Jews in the Bay area. Their profile of the gay and lesbian population indicates that they are predominantly between the ages of 25 and 44, that 55 percent are female and 45 percent male, and that almost two-thirds migrated into the Bay area after 1970. In terms of religious and organizational involvements, one-quarter of San Francisco's homosexual Jews belong to synagogues, compared to one-third of the heterosexual Jewish population.

In terms of denominational identification, the most striking difference between the Bay area's homosexual and heterosexual Jews is their unexpectedly lower proportion of Reform Jews: Reform homosexual Jews comprised 24 percent, compared to 44 percent of heterosexual Jews; in comparison, homosexual Jews calling themselves "just Jewish" comprised 27 percent, compared to 17 percent of heterosexual Jews.[37]

Most observers assume that nationwide proportions of homosexual Jews are about the same as those in the general population, despite the popular impression of greater numbers due to the publicized prominence of accomplished homosexual Jews in theater and the arts. As explored in anthologies such as Christie Balka and Andy

Rose's *Twice Blessed: On Being Lesbian or Gay and Jewish,* Evelyn Torten Beck's *Nice Jewish Girls,* and Melanie Kaye/Kantrowitz and Irena Klepfisz's *The Tribe of Dina,* the homosexual population is as diverse as any other Jewish population, and includes Jews of all ages and Jewish denominations, from Orthodox through completely secular.[38] Some have always been single, some are married with children, and some are divorced, with or without children. Some are open about their sexual orientation, some closeted. Essays, memoirs, and fiction by and about gay and lesbian Jews is increasingly available and provides important insights into their lifestyles, concerns, and challenges.

A few small qualitative studies have looked at particular populations of homosexual Jews. A fascinating study by Jonathan Krasner on the attempt to exclude the Jewish Young Gays and Lesbians (JYGL) organization from marching in the 1993 Manhattan Israel Day Parade[39] explored the conflict between New York area homosexual Jews and certain segments of the New York Orthodox community, some of whom declared that "The very idea of an organization of Jews who are, unfortunately, gay is antithetical to everything Judaism stands for."[40] Krasner notes that whereas in the past homosexual Jews were likely to agree with the assumption that they must choose between being actively gay or actively Jewish, contemporary American Jews are much more likely to assert as their birthright both their religious ethnicity and their sexual orientation. He cites a leaflet entitled "Jewish, Gay, Proud and Angry!! We Support Israel," which was distributed during the communal conflict over the Israel Day Parade: "We hope that before too long, all elements of the Jewish community will accept us as we are . . . *Hiney may tov u'manayim, shevet achim ve'achot gam yachad.*"[41]

Gay and lesbian Jews have much in common with other American-Jewish men and women. Like heterosexual Jews, homosexual Jews coalesce American and Jewish values and behaviors, although they have some very specific concerns that sometimes diverge from those of other American Jews, located around family issues, involvement with synagogues and other public Jewish arenas, and Judaism as a culture and theology.

Family ties are always complex, but for homosexual Jews the complexities often have a special edge. Memoirs, essays, fiction, drama, and film by Jewish homosexuals suggest that in terms of relationships with family of origin, the romantic choices of homosexual children may be perceived as transgressive behavior, as a rebuke to parents, or as a rejection of Jewish law and tradition, which are widely perceived to outlaw male homosexual behavior and to disapprove of lesbian activities. Harvey Fierstein's autobiographical play and film, *Torchsong Trilogy,* for example, deftly portrays the mutual guilt and resentment and deep family love felt by a Jewish mother and her gay son. Mourning rituals are a frequent motif in Jewish gay and lesbian fiction, because they provide such a rich opportunity to explore family relationships. As Douglas Sadownick observes in his novel *Sacred Lips of the Bronx,* "The Jewish custom of sitting *shiva* to mourn for the departed—coupled with the chore of feeding all the sitters dying from hunger and heartbreak—provided our family with a project big enough to distract us. . . . Jewish mourning is a sit-down affair. The suddenly observant family convenes on cardboard boxes for a week."[42]

It may be that because of their political and sexual liberalism, Jewish families are more accepting than average of gay and lesbian family members; nevertheless, many Jewish homosexuals recount familial disappointment when informed of their sexual preference. In his collection of stories, *Dancing on Tisha B'Av,* for example, Lev Raphael's newly Orthodox protagonist burns with dual passions for Orthodox ritual and for men, likes to have his sister sitting in the women's section as he reads the Torah, but suspects that her liberal attitude toward homosexuals in general is based on a demand that he not force her to acknowledge that her own brother is gay.[43]

In Sarah Schulman's novel, *Empathy,* a daughter emerges from her own lengthy soul searching to be able to reassure her father at the end of an interactive family seder that her sexual orientation is not a weapon against him: "I just want to tell you that, despite what Freud says, the reason I am a lesbian is not because of wanting to hurt you. It's not about you in any way. I really love you, Pop, and I'm a lot like you and being a lesbian is about me. Okay?"[44]

Whatever the problems of heterosexual Jews in finding romantic partners, marrying, and establishing a Jewish household, they know that these enterprises have society's support. For homosexual Jews, in contrast, the search for a "nice Jewish boy" or a "nice Jewish girl" may evoke unsupportive comments or behaviors in others.

Involvements with Jews and Judaism are extremely important to many homosexual Jews. Among a growing list, Jyl Lynn Felman's collection of short stories, *Hot Chicken Wings,* features a concluding glossary of Hebrew and Yiddish terms.[45] For gay and lesbian Jews with a strong Zionist consciousness, the relatively homophobic Israeli environment provides a particular challenge, as described in Marcia Freedman's memoir, *Exile in the Promised Land,* and fictionalized in Alice Bloch's novel, *The Law of Return.*[46] Judith Plaskow's theological essay, *Standing again at Sinai* is a well-written indictment of the otherness of women from the Bible onward; Plaskow argues for a fundamental reworking of Judaism, including a new theology of sexuality.[47]

The position of gay and lesbian Jews vis-à-vis contemporary American-Jewish communities has frequently galvanized Jewish feelings about broad aspects of social change. Jews with conservative attitudes toward changes in the Jewish family often see gay and lesbian Jews as the epitome of individualistic—and thus antifamily—lifestyles. Reuven Kimelman charges in his discussion of "Homosexuality and Family-Centered Judaism" that according societal and religious approval to Jewish homosexuals will further devalue procreative sex, and will prove the final insult to the Jewish family:

> Without commitments of time, money and emotions, there will be no family to speak of. The creation of families is a major investment. . . . It is clear that Jewish continuity is already threatened by too many singles not marrying and too many couples declining to invest in the future by replenishing themselves. . . . Religious legitimation of extra-normative sexual relationships threatens to undermine the privileged position of normative marriage. Such legitimation tends to equalize the status of the two, especially in the eyes of children. Instead of being a social ideal, family-centered marriage would become simply another alternative. Already a besieged institution, it is questionable whether its protective walls can withstand much more battering. Thus, Jewish family ad-

vocates should reserve sanctification ceremonies for rites of marriage between men and women.[48]

Conversely, Martha Acklesberg argues that the rich potential of non-normative households to participate in and contribute to the Jewish community exposes the manifold weaknesses of traditional, normative family units. Acklesberg insists that the goals of societies which prefer marriage—"for companionship and emotional intimacy, for mutual economic support, for generativity (child-bearing and child-rearing), and, particularly within the Jewish community, for preserving tradition and contributing to the continuity of the community"—are now and have always been met outside the nuclear family unit. Ackelsberg claims that giving the nuclear family first-class status makes everyone else second class. Ackelsberg takes the stance that exclusion of individual Jews from full participation in Jewish life because of their marital status is both immoral and dishonest, because so many contemporary Jews cannot fit into the normative family model.[49]

Kimelman agrees that numerous Jews do not fit into traditional family units, but sees their non-normative status as a voluntary defection, and argues that more individuals would be encouraged to defect by legitimating their single lot. Not surprisingly, Kimelman stands near one end of the *halakhah* versus egalitarianism sacredness continuum presented in chapter 1, and Acklesberg stands near the other. For Kimelman, the hegemony of halakhic considerations preordains the outcome of arguments, whereas for Ackelsberg, the hegemony of equality is axiomatic "in a truly egalitarian, inclusive community" out of which she hopes to create "a new Jewish family ethics."[50]

Abusive Households

Families with acute problems, including abusive households, once mistakenly thought to be almost nonexistent within Jewish communities, are now openly acknowledged to occur across denominational lines. Substance abuse, wife abuse, and child abuse are now recognized phenomena in Jewish households.[51] No doubt, there was always some incidence of these problems in traditional Jewish societies and in the United States, even when communal leaders were resistant to recognize them and unwilling to deal with them. Today, all segments of the Jewish community have begun to work to meet the needs of problem families. Dr. Samuel Klagsbrun, executive director of Four Winds Hospital, a private psychiatric hospital in Katonah, New York, has been working with abusive situations in Jewish households for many years, including high profile situations such as the notorious case of Hedda Nussbaum, who allowed her daughter Lisa to be beaten to death by her husband, Joel Steinberg.

Dr. Klagbrun says that the situations he treats in Jewish homes often run counter to information about abuse taught in medical schools: battered Jewish women have usually not grown up in battering households, have no prior indication that a potential spouse has violent tendencies, and are not themselves masochistic and "getting something" out of a sick relationship. Women with few economic options and little life experience are often "cornered" in abusive situations after an apparently normal courtship, and are very fearful about their ability to successfully negotiate a separation. Couples counseling often exacerbates the vulnerability of such women, because husbands promise change, wives believe them and let down their guard—and are battered even more severely than before. Klagsbrun believes that resistance to dealing with violent family dysfunctions has, ironically, been based on attempts to preserve traditional family values such as *shalom bayis,* the Jewish ideal of the serene and orderly household. In addition, loathing of women's liberation makes some in the right-wing Orthodox community skeptical about battered women's assertions and unsympathetic to women who come to them for aid: "these women don't feel safe going to rabbis who will tell them they've been contaminated by women's rights." When women finally work up the courage to leave, husbands frequently respond with escalated violence. As Klagbrun notes: "Seventy-five percent of murders of women who are abused occur at the time of, or shortly after, the time the woman leaves. Their fear is real."[52]

Communal efforts on behalf of battered Jewish women may be due partially to the unpleasant glare of media publicity surrounding some rather notorious cases, such as that of a dysfunctional Hasidic family, in which Blima Zitrenbaum was brutally attacked on the Sabbath of February 10, 1996, allegedly by her bearded, traditionally-garbed husband. As one reporter explained:

> The case is being watched closely by advocates of *agunot,* women whose husbands refuse to grant them a Jewish divorce. They say Blima Zitrenbaum, 34, is an agunah—Hebrew for chained woman. And Joseph Zitrenbaum, in a recent phone interview with *The Jewish Week* from the Rockland County Jail, confirmed that he does not want to grant his wife a *get,* or Jewish divorce. . . .
>
> "She didn't want to go back to him because of the drugs," said a man who identified himself only as Jacob, a member of the synagogue where he said Joseph Zitrenbaum would pray or seek shelter.
>
> "He used to come to synagogue all stabbed with drugs," said Jacob, who sat in on the trial one day. "A few people are scared to testify. They are afraid he will be free and he would come after them."
>
> . . . . "After Mrs. Zitrenbaum was beaten [in February] we called for the rabbis to declare that when women are almost murdered by their husbands, the rabbis should have their marriage annulled," said Rifka Haut, co-founder of Agunah, Inc., the Brooklyn-based organization that helps agunot.
>
> "There was no response," said Haut, who said Blima Zitrenbaum had called her several times for advice before the February beating but never since.[53]

Many communities have established kosher facilities for battered women and their children. As one example of contemporary communal responses to Jewish dysfunctional family units, Ohel, a division of Brooklyn Children's Home and Family Services, offers Sabbath observant foster care for children and a community residence and supportive apartment program for Jewish young adults with emotional disabilities. The organization distributes literature to alert teachers and neighbors to the "10 warning signs of child abuse," which range unflinchingly from physical evidence such as "bruises, welts, burns, bites, fractures, and lacerations" to "inappropriate sexual knowledge or behavior for age or cultural environment."[54] Other programming for problem households include efforts to locate Jewish homeless individuals and families, and to meet their needs in kosher, Jewishly aware facilities.

Relocating Gender and Ethnic Boundaries

American-Jewish culture has adapted its norms of gender role construction and has relocated its ethnic boundaries vis-à-vis many gender issues so completely, that it can arguably be said to have reached a postfeminist state. During the last quarter of the twentieth century, the lives of American Jews as individuals, in family groups, and in communal settings have undergone sweeping changes vis-à-vis gender role construction. However, many of these changes are so thoroughly coalesced and have come to seem so commonplace that their revolutionary status and flavor has been virtually lost. As a result, feminism and its impact on American-Jewish life seem to some observers limited to those few women who combine fervid Jewish and feminist concerns. Indeed, in a recent *Portrait of American Jews* by a preeminent ethnographer of American-Jewish communities, the author dismisses Jewish feminism as affecting only "the minority of those American Jews who chose to be actively Jewish."[55]

Despite the camouflage of coalesced familiarity, feminisms continue to produce change across the spectrum of mainstream environments. The most completely coalesced changes in American-Jewish gender role construction focus on personal aspects of life: women's health issues, friendship circles, erotic liaisons, marriage, family relationships, child-bearing and childrearing. The attitude of American Jews toward women has been sweepingly more liberal than that of other American ethnic groups and than that of Jews in some other areas of the world, such as Israel and Latin America. American Jews, for example, are overwhelmingly committed to equal educational and occupational opportunity for women, and to reproductive choice. Thus, in the realm of personal choice, marriage, and family planning, the American community that has by and large relocated its ethnic boundaries. Rather than being defined as a community that is highly prescriptive in its gender role construction, American-Jewish men and women today, especially outside of Orthodox communities, tend to be characterized by more permeable gender role constructions than those found in many other groups.[56]

Jewish women have changed in the area of professional development: education, vocational choice, and career advancement, as we have seen. While these are areas of feminist impact, which Jewish women share with other American women, they are also examples of coalescence, because Jewish women's attitudes are influenced by Jewish communal norms and values. For example, in their feminist enterprises Jewish women can draw on the cultural biases toward competence, articulateness, and assertiveness in women, which were common in traditional Jewish societies. Jewish cultural biases favoring women who blend marketplace activism with familial passion may be reflected in the fact that among Jewish women, unlike women in other religious and cultural subgroups, higher levels of education and occupational achievement are accompanied by higher levels of expected—albeit unfulfilled—fertility.[57]

Observing large Jewish organizations and the cultural artifacts they produce can provide useful demonstrations of both the diversity and the grassroots nature of coalescing transformation in the United States. The national president of Hadassah, the Women's Zionist Organization of America, proudly declares that Hadassah women have "returned to our Jewish feminist roots."[58] The June/July 1996 issue of *Hadassah* magazine features the feminist-influenced political, cultural, and religiously-oriented articles: "Letter from Washington: Synergy & Harmony," by Hanita Blumfield, describes how "Jewish women are finding that the strength they give to the women's movement can provide benefits for the Jewish agenda as well"; "Nice Jewish Girls," by feminist journalist Marlene Adler Marks, describes how, "Cultural stereotypes run about two generations behind, but the images of American Jewish women are catching up with a new reality"; "World of Our Mothers," by Rahel Musleah, is an illustrated essay on Jewish women painters who "defied the stereotypes of their generation"; and "Late Mitzvas," by Barbara Trainin Blank," is about geriatric female prayer leaders and *b'not mitzvah*. Among the subjects discussed in this most middle-class, middle-brow publication are the Jewish Caucus in Beijing, the importance of grooming a new generation of Jewish feminist leaders, the resentments of nursing home residents toward traditional Jewish restrictions on women, wife abuse in Jewish homes, and the spiritual fantasies of pre–Bat Mitzvah girls. The articles search for "heroines . . . who go beyond the boundaries life sets up for them."[59] The publication unequivocally states: "Hadassah has a place at the feminist table."[60]

These changes have taken place throughout mainstream populations and across denominational lines. For example, one recent issue of *The Jewish Parent Connection*, a publication of the Orthodox Torah Umesorah National Society for Hebrew Day Schools, features articles such as "Babysitter or Day Care Center: That Is the Question"—which makes the assumption that "Due to today's high cost of living . . . it is frequently necessary for both Jewish parents to pursue careers." The pediatrician/author considers the "pros and cons" of "nanny, au pair, babysitter, or day care center," without ever once trying to instill guilt in the working mother or assuming that she should remain at home until her children are in school all day long.[61] Two other articles considering ways for women with small children to find time for their spiritual lives suggest a proactive approach, including studying the High Holiday liturgy well before the holidays, determining which prayers are most meaningful and important, and hiring a babysitter or negotiating with family members who can facilitate participation during those parts of the service; during this process, the authors urge mothers to establish "channels for communication without recrimination" with the children's father, presumably to engage him in the task of enabling spiritual time for his wife.[62]

Despite the fact that American-Jewish women, like many other middle- and upper-middle-class women, are likely to begin sentences with "I'm not a feminist, but . . . " the personal lives of both women and men have been transformed by feminism according to virtually every sociological measure. Ironically, it is the very domestication of feminist values and their coalescence into the lives of millions of male and female American Jews that accounts for feminism's perceived invisibility. Feminism has become a de facto, highly coalesced American-Jewish family value.

Contemporary Jewish Family Values

It is important to place perceived threats to the Jewish family in the context of wider societal change. American society as a whole currently struggles to provide physical and psychological support to households that it recognizes as normative family units while at the same time avoiding delegitimization of persons who live in non-normative households or choose alternative lifestyles. The conflict between those who wish to place most emphasis on societal support for normative family units, versus those who wish to place most emphasis on overcoming societal prejudices against persons who choose alternative lifestyles or alternative households, rages fiercely, among scholars and within the popular press and media as a potent political issue.

Among the "new familists,"[63] professors and policy analysts such as Mary Jo Bane,[64] Steven Bayme, David Blankenhorne,[65] Jean Bethke Elshtain, Sylvia Ann Hewlitt,[66] Christopher Lash,[67] and Mary Ann Glendon,[68] have mourned shifting trends in American marital status, and have warned that these trends accompany social and moral decline and perhaps even the decline of Western civilization as we know it. To these observers, the normative two-parent, monogamous, fertile family unit requires and instills the qualities of character that are necessary to the physical and moral vitality of individuals, households, communities, and states. Blankenhorn summarizes the six social functions of the family as procreation, socialization, affection, sexuality, cooperation, and pluralism, and posits that normative family units are best designed to provide the context for balancing larger social needs with individual diversity.[69]

Familists of many faiths believe that contemporary preoccupations with the rights and material success of individuals have undermined a more productive emphasis on social groupings and their interwoven responsibilities. Bruce Hafen, for example, argues:

> In familistic relationships, shared commitments and mutual attachments transcend individual self-interest. These relationships are rooted in *unlimited* personal commitment—not merely to another person, but to the good of the relationship and to the family entity as a larger order. Because of the unlimited nature of such commitments, detailed lists of rights and duties can neither describe nor prescribe a familistic relationship. . . .
>
> Contractual relationships, by contrast, combine solidaristic and antagonistic elements. By definition, these relationships are *always limited* in both scope and intensity. Parties enter a contractual relationship primarily because of self-interest. They weigh their commitment to the relationship, calculating the return of profit, pleasure, or service.[70]

Profamily sentiments are brought to a broader audience by conservative media figures such as Dr. Laura Schlessinger, arguably "the most successful radio therapist in

America," described as "an intense 49-year-old size 2 with permed hair, a jeweled Star of David around her neck, red-lacquered nails and the unmistakable air of someone who is always sure she's right." Schlessinger urges callers to think about spouses, children, and other family members—and about the family as a whole—rather than to focus on their own narrow needs; she asserts that religious guidance is a healthier influence on people than psychological counseling: "Modern therapy promotes self-centeredness. Everything is rational or relative. I'm not. My morality is based on the Old Testament and the Talmud. Whenever I can, I try and push people toward religion."[71]

However, other policy analysts and writers refute the familist vision of history and society. They insist that the mid-twentieth-century notion of the family is neither ancient nor universal, but instead was shaped by modern economic, political, and social transformations.[72] Moreover, they point out that unlimited personal commitment was expected only of women/wives/mothers in most traditional societies; women—not men—were expected to sacrifice personal goals for the good of the family unit. In contrast, American men prided themselves on rugged individualism in the supposed heyday of family values, Barbara Ehrenreich suggests, and frequently neglected families and abandoned relationships as the spirit moved them; Ehrenreich charges that it was men's "flight from commitment" in the 1950s and 1960s that provided fertile ground for feminist growth in the 1970s.[73] Male infidelity still seems to be a factor in marital dissolution: Judith Wallerstein and Sandra Blakeslee, themselves supporters of the traditional family unit because of the corrosive effect that divorce often has on children, observed that the men they studied who initiated divorce proceedings always had extramarital romantic involvements, whereas the women they studied who initiated divorce almost never did, but instead were unhappy with the quality of the marital relationship.[74]

While more marriages may fail today because women are less likely to be trapped socially and economically than they were in the past, marriages that succeed have been shown to incorporate much more fulfilling roles and choices for women. Marital stability between certain kinds of people can arguably be strengthened rather than disrupted by feminist social change. Indeed, when Wallerstein and Blakeslee studied *The Good Marriage,* they found that egalitarianism enhanced marital relationships:

> Their marriages had benefited from the new emphasis in our society on equality in relationships between men and women. However they divided up the chores of the household and of raising the children, the couples agreed that men and women had equal rights and responsibilities within the family. Women have taken many casualties in the long fight to achieve equality, and many good men have felt beleaguered, confused, and angry about this contest. But important goals have been achieved: marriages today allow for greater flexibility and greater choice. Relationships are more mature on both sides and more mutually respectful. A couple's sex life can be freer and more pleasurable. Today's men and women meet on a playing field that is more level than ever before.[75]

Their observations complement a study of *Equal Partners: Successful Women in Marriage*, in which Dana Vannoy-Hiller and William W. Philliber found that husbands who were perceived as sharing familial responsibilities were participants in extraordinarily satisfying relationships.[76] These self-perceived successful egalitarian relationships must be placed in the larger context of troubling findings on the general emotional status of women in married households: married women report 20 percent more depression than single women, more nervous breakdowns, and more physical symptoms of somatized mental disease, according to Walter Grove. In contrast, married men enjoy far better mental health than single men.[77]

Households that differ from popular perceptions of past families have shouldered the blame for many developments which precede and extend far beyond them, suggest some social historians. Stephanie Coontz warns that familists hearken back to dangerously mythologized households of *The Way We Never Were*, and cautions today's American families to avoid "the nostalgia trap" which can blind them to the truths of past and present.[78] The soul-numbing consumerist materialism which currently appalls many familists is not a new, alien growth fostered by antifamily individualists, argues Elaine Tyler May, but was already a prime component of and perhaps even the economic rationale for family-oriented society in the post-War years. May asserts that "the sexually charged, child-centered family" which "took its place at the center of the postwar American dream" was a kind of centerfold for the economic agenda of business and government: "By stimulating . . . suburban housing developments and providing subsidies to homeowners, the federal government effectively underwrote the baby boom, in addition to the lifestyle and community arrangements which fostered traditional gender roles in the home."[79] Today, according to Susan Faludi, a rose-colored distortion of the nature of families in the past and concomitant scare tactics in looking at present trends are part of a *Backlash* against new opportunities for women and less restrictive gender-role constructions in contemporary society.[80]

The American-Jewish community faces similar challenges as other white Americans, especially white ethnic Americans. However, because of a shrinking proportion of Jews in the American population, Jews sometimes experience these changes not only as a threat to the normative family unit, but also as a threat to Jewish continuity. Communal responses to the current diversity of Jewish households have hardly been dispassionate. Not only is there active disagreement about how best to achieve the goals of Jewish communal continuity and vitality, but also about how these goals should best be defined. Like many traditional communities, Jewish societies in the past used communal sanctions to encourage marriage and remarriage. In contrast to this traditional approach some contemporary observers have expressed the view that hostility to existing non-normative Jewish households is not only "politically incorrect" but is also likely to be perceived as destructive and alienating by the large numbers of Jewish individuals who live in those households. Others have taken a neoconservative viewpoint, urging a "triage" approach, and recommending that Jewish communal attention and resources be focused directly upon those households that most closely fit traditional models of Jewish family life.

While transformed patterns of family formation have been seen by many as evidence of declining Jewish family values, accuracy demands acknowledging that the earlier familism of American Jews was just as much in keeping with American mores as postponed marriage and family formation are today. When American Jews married early and had their children early in the 1950s, they were following American patterns which happened to coincide in many ways with Jewish attitudes toward the primacy of marriage and family life. Today, when they postpone marriage to acquire higher education and establish their careers, they are following patterns that are part the middle- and upper-middle-class white American cohort to which they now belong.

Despite communal anxiety, changing lifestyles of Jewish mothers and fathers have not led to a waning of interest in Jewish "family values." Quite the contrary, adjusted lifestyles have given rise to a new version of the normative Jewish parent. Thus, as mentioned in our discussion of education and occupation, Jews are more likely than other parents to facilitate the independent lifestyles of their children. Anecdotal evidence indicates that today's Jewish parents often consciously aspire to avoid using guilt as a manipulative device, as sociologist Marshall Sklare described Jewish parents making personal sacrifices to provide children with, "the best of everything"—and requiring of the child, in return, that mix of personal affection and stellar accomplishments that could guarantee parental "*nachas*, a Hebrew term for pleasure or gratification," absorbed into Yiddish and Judaized English:

> While it is possible to receive *nachas* in many ways, there is only one true and abiding source of *nachas:* that which is received from children. Or put another way, if one does not have *nachas fun kinder* all other pleasures and gratifications are empty. [The parent] . . . offers the child what are sometimes termed the "advantages," or in common American-Jewish parlance, "everything," as in the expression, "they gave their son everything." . . . By being open-handed, by sacrificing for the child, the parent reduces his vulnerability. After all, only an ingrate would withhold *nachas* from a generous parent."[81]

No study has as yet measured the extent to which American Jewish parents today have abandoned the "guilt trip" as a method for socializing their children.

One positive change that has occurred partially as a result of the working mother syndrome, American-Jewish fathers have reportedly become more involved with the detailed daily raising of their young children. Teachers at Maimonides Day School in Brookline, Massachusetts, for example, report that they are almost as likely to see working fathers as working mothers of young children at midday programs such as plays, ceremonies, and special parties—a situation that differs markedly from parental gender-role divisions in the past. Presumably, the fact that both parents have to juggle work and home responsibilities and make a special effort to be available for such programming means that female parents are not uniquely designated within the family unit for events that disrupt the work week. Significantly, while paternal sharing of child rearing can be perceived as contemporary, gender neutral, sensitive, etc., it actually is more in keeping with the traditional role of the Jewish father as moral educator of his family, which was abandoned by many American-Jewish immigrants and second generation males in their economic strivings earlier in the century.

The American-Jewish community faces the daunting task of supporting Jewish family life without resorting to hostility toward less traditional family units. It seems likely that Jewish communal vitality in the future will not be linked to the formation of particular types of households, but will instead have to depend more directly on the commitments of individual Jews.

Equally important, Jews living in married-with-children households will also probably continue to have attitudes and expectations of marriage and parenthood that differ from those of Jewish spouses and parents in other historical eras and societies. As Norman Linzer suggests, "in a heavily institutionalized, traditional society, institutions narrow choices for decision-making." With the institutions of Jewish law and communal approbation in place, "clarity of roles" and "consistency of behavior" were reinforced; the authority of family, community, and Jewish tradition discouraged individualistic, transgressive behavior.[82] When such external forces cease effectively to reinforce familism and communalism, connections to Jewish and Jewishness are more likely to grow out of personal considerations.

Individualism may well be historically antithetical to traditional Jewish family and communal values, but American Jews, for better and for worse, have coalesced the individualistic ethos into their concept of Judaism. Judaism is perceived by many American Jews as a possible source of personal, spiritual renewal, rather than as a social construct. In an atomized community, religion is atomized as well. Because the cohesiveness of the Jewish community has diminished, the impetus to make one's household into a Jewish home—regardless of marital status—now more than ever before arises from within the individual. Once the Jewish household is established, it reinforces the Jewish connections of the individuals who created it, as both quantitative and qualitative data indicate.

American-Jewish families today can be seen as a microcosm of the challenges besetting middle-class America. Once perhaps the most predictably normative of American family types, contemporary American-Jewish families now seem to be the epitome of change. In reality, American Jewish families today are, as they have been for decades, amalgams of American and Jewish values; as American families change, Jewish families change as well. As a result, strategies that proved relatively effective for preserving Jewish lifestyles in the past may require a shift of emphasis if they are to meet American Jews, quite literally, where they live.

Table 5.1 Marital Status of American Jews and All Americans
Percentages 1990 and 1970 NJPS and Selected City Studies
1970 and 1990 U.S. Census

Location	Year Study Completed	Married	Single	Widowed	Divorced
Baltimore	1985	68	19	9	5
Boston	1985	61	29	4	5
Cleveland	1981	69	11	13	8
Denver	1981	64	23	4	9
Kansas City	1985	70	17	7	5
Los Angeles	1979	57	17	12	14
Miami	1982	61	7	23	8
Milwaukee	1983	67	14	9	10
Minneapolis	1981	66	22	7	5
Nashville	1982	70	17	8	5
New York	1981	65	15	11	9
Phoenix	1983	63	18	9	10
Rochester	1987	68	23	6	3
St. Louis	1982	68	9	17	6
St. Paul	1981	66	20	11	3
San Francisco	1988	69	19	4	7
Washington, D.C.	1983	61	27	4	7
Worcester	1987	69	14	18	18
*NJPS	1990	65	17	10	9
U.S. Census	1990	64	21	8	8
NJPS	1970	78	6	10	5
U.S. Census	1970	72	16	9	3

*Source: 1990 NJPS respondents, born or raised Jewish. City data based on population studies. See endnote 16 of this chapter.

Table 5.2 Marital Status of American Jews
Percentages by Age and Gender
Compared to All Americans, 1990 Census

Marital Status	18–24 F	18–24 M	25–34 F	25–34 M	35–44 F	35–44 M	45–54 F	45–54 M	55–64 F	55–64 M	65+ F	65+ M
Married	12	2	62	46	74	73	75	77	77	87	57	82
Never Married	88	96	30	50	11	17	7	9	2	6	2	3
Divorced (or separated)	1	1	7	3	14	10	14	11	14	6	4	3
Widowed	—	—	1	—	1	1	4	3	8	1	38	12
Total	101	99	100	99	100	101	100	100	101	100	101	100

Source: 1990 NJPS data. Percentages have been rounded.

	20–24 F	20–24 M	25–29 F	25–29 M	30–34 F	30–34 M	35–39 F	35–39 M	40–44 F	40–44 M	45–54 F	45–54 M	55–64 F	55–64 M
Married	35	21	29	49	72	66	76	74	75	80	75	81	68	83
Never Married	63	77	62	46	17	26	10	15	6	8	5	7	4	6
Divorced	3	1	8	5	11	8	13	11	16	12	14	11	18	8
Widowed	—	—	—	—	1	—	1	—	3	1	6	1	9	3
Total	101	99	99	100	101	100	100	100	100	101	100	100	99	100

Source: 1990 U.S. Census, Bureau of the Census, *Current Population Reports,* series P-20, no. 445. Percentages have been rounded.

Table 5.3 Family Formation Status of Jewish Female Respondents
Percentages by Age of Respondents and Age of Children

Ages of Jewish Female Respondents	No Children	Children 18 or Under	Children 19 or Over	Total
18–24	93	8	—	101
25–34	55	45	—	100
35–44	24	71	5	100
45–54	—	40	60	100
55–64	—	3	97	100
65+	—	—	100	100

Source: 1990 NJPS data. Percentages have been rounded.

Table 5.4 Number of Children Born to Jewish Women
Percentages by Decade of (First) Marriage

Decade of Marriage	Number of Children					Total
	1	2	3	4–5	6 or more	
1900–1939	13	60	15	8	3	100
1940–1949	18	38	34	11		100
1950–1959	7	38	47	8		100
1960–1969	13	55	22	10		100
1970–1979	23	50	19	7	2	100
1980–1989	41	42	14	3		100
Total	22	46	24	7	1	100

Source: 1990 NJPS data. Percentages have been rounded.

Table 5.5 **Fertility Levels and Jewish Education of Women**
Unweighted Percentages of 1990 NJPS Females
Who Have Children
Number of Children by Years of Jewish Education

Years of Jewish Education by Age	Number of Children					n=
	1	2	3	4–5	6–10	
0–3 years						
30–49	30	47	20	3	—	74
50–64	3	36	41	17	2	58
65–74	7	48	31	14	—	29
75+	23	38	23	15	—	13
TOTAL	17	43	29	10	.6	177
4–6 years						
30–49	20	56	22	2	—	88
50–64	14	43	32	10	—	69
65–74	14	51	28	7	—	43
75+	14	71	7	7	—	14
TOTAL	19	51	24	6	—	223
7–9 years						
30–49	14	60	16	10	—	58
50–64	—	49	44	7	—	43
65–74	13	20	53	7	7	15
75+	36	55	9	—	—	11
TOTAL	12	51	29	8	.8	128
10–12 years						
30–49	23	50	21	5	1	92
50–64	3	42	39	15	—	33
65–74	15	65	5	15	—	20
*75+	—	—	—	—	—	4
TOTAL	19	49	22	8	.6	156
13 and over						
30–49	17	27	27	13	17	30
*50–64	—	—	—	—	—	7
*65–74	—	—	—	—	—	0
*75+	—	—	—	—	—	1
TOTAL	18	36	22	13	11	45

Source: 1990 NJPS Data. Percentages have been rounded.
*Fewer than 10 cases.

SIX

OBSERVING RELIGIOUS ENVIRONMENTS IN JEWISH HOMES

Religious Observances in Traditional Jewish Households

Family life was characterized by an interwoven Jewish texture in most historical Jewish societies. The language spoken in the home was often a Jewish dialect such as Yiddish, Ladino, or Judeo-Arabic, each of which incorporates many Hebrew words and phrases. In devout homes, religious law dictated every aspect of life. Children were taught to recite prayers and blessings numerous times each day as soon as they started to speak. Clothing for men and women conformed to a complex fabric of requirements. Husbands and wives adjusted their sexual encounters to the intricacies of Jewish family law. Men aspired to lifelong study of Jewish texts, either as a full-time or—for most—a part-time enterprise. Even in the less devout and scholarly families which may have comprised the majority of households, religious socialization and familiarity produced an environment in which each day, week, month, and season were marked by Jewish rituals, sights, sounds, and smells.

At the end of each week, the odors of baking *challah* (Sabbath bread) and special foods permeated dwelling places, and Sabbath observances required the family's best clothing, along with candles, wine, prayers, and songs. On the last Sabbath of each Hebrew month, women made a special effort to attend the synagogue to pray for good health and happiness during the coming weeks; as the festival of the New Moon (*rosh hodesh*) began, groups of men spilled from synagogues into night's darkness to locate the thin, bright crescent in the sky. The cycles of the year were punctuated by religious occasions: midfall season was celebrated with the building of a *Succah* (ritual branch-roofed hut) and prayers over exotic oriental plants; the dark days of winter with *Hanukkah* lights and gifts of coins; the early spring with the frantic cleaning, restricted diet, and liturgical pageantry of Passover; early summer with the sweet dairy foods and all-night study of *Shavuot;* and midsummer with a three-week period of intensifying self-abnegation, culminating in the twenty-four-hour fast, the harrowing text of *Lamentations,* and the mournful chants of *Tisha B'Av* dirges. In this context, the daily sound of the *shofar* (ram's horn) echoing from the synagogue after morning services in late August and the High Holy Days of early fall did not stand alone as the religious monoliths of the year (as they do for many American Jews), and the aura of deep moral seriousness which surrounded Rosh Hashanah and Yom Kippur are remembered by many as being suffused with genuine awe.

Internal and external boundaries reinforced the bonds between Jewish families and Jewish communities and separated them from the non-Jewish families and communities around them before the impact of political emancipation and modern social movements such as socialism, nationalism, secularism, and individualism. Even as modern ideas and movements began to dissolve the tightly woven Jewish character of Jewish family life, many Jewish family behaviors were retained for some time, according to memoirs and fiction by secular nineteenth- and twentieth-century Jews. Thus, Sholem Asch describes his early twentieth-century "emancipated" heroine, Rachel Leah Hurvitz, who "followed her husband into apostasy" when they fled from shtetl life to secular, intellectually liberated Warsaw—and yet emphasizes the"warmth and festal splendor" of their Friday night table. Despite their loudly asserted agnosticism, the Hurvitzes and their friends, similarly emancipated secular Jewish Polish nationalists, Zionists, and socialists, all crave a Sabbath environment on Friday nights; characteristically, they sit around the traditional foods of the Sabbath table reading very untraditional Polish epic poetry and arguing politics.

> . . . the table was covered with a white cloth on which stood two candles burning in polished brass candlesticks. Two cakes were on the table, covered with muslin, nor was the silver sugar bowl lacking. . . . For although Frau Hurvitz regarded herself as a progressive woman, and although her husband was notorious in Warsaw as a "renegade" who seduced pious Jewish youths from the straight path, Rachel-Leah could not bring herself to deny her own upbringing and to ignore the Jewish feast-days. . . . "Why don't you know that it's Friday evening? We're anything but pious and yet we always light candles on Friday evening. It's just a habit," she concluded shamefacedly, as if to excuse herself. "I'm glad you've come tonight. You'll have your share of the fish."
>
> . . . Hurvitz the teacher was a freethinker and notorious in the small Jewish towns of Poland as a seducer of pious youth, but whenever Friday evening came he felt impelled to bathe and change his underwear as he had been accustomed to do from childhood. The blood of his forbearers cried aloud in him, and however sternly he called to mind the rationalistic explanations of how the Sabbath and other festivals had come into being, he could not help himself: whenever a holy day approached the ancient customs resumed their sway over his blood, and he was filled with the obscure mystical feeling that is evoked by the Sabbath.
>
> As soon as he set foot in the big living-room after his last lesson on Friday evening, he felt the Sabbath peace that his wife had spread over the house like a fair linen cloth. . . . [1]

Secularized adaptations of Jewish family behaviors often traveled across the ocean with Jewish immigrants in the nineteenth and early twentieth century. For example, Alfred Kazin describes his socialist parents, cousins and friends enjoying the festive Friday night serenity which pervaded the immigrant American home of his childhood:

> Afterwards we went into the dining room, and since we were not particularly Orthodox, allowed ourselves little pleasures outside the Sabbath rule. . . . The evening was particularly good for me whenever the unmarried cousin who

boarded with us had her two closest friends in after supper. . . . They were all dressmakers, like my mother; had worked with my mother in the same East Side sweatshops; were all passionately loyal members of the International Ladies Garment Workers Union. . . . As they sat around the cut-glass bowl on the table—cracking walnuts, expertly peeling the skin off an apple in long even strips, cozily sipping at a glass of tea—they crossed their legs in comfort. . . .

I was suddenly glad to be a Jew, as these women were Jews—simply and naturally glad of these Jewish dressmakers who spoke with enthusiastic familiarity of Sholem Aleichem and Peretz, Gorky and Tolstoy, who glowed at every reminiscence of Nijinsky, of Nazimova in *The Cherry Orchard*, of Pavlova in "The Swan."[2]

Ritual Observance in Contemporary Pluralistic Jewish Households

As Asch and Kazin suggest, secularized Jews with vivid memories of intense Jewish environments often maintained aspects of traditional Jewish family behaviors, albeit in a "not particularly Orthodox" mode.

The observance of familial and social elements of Jewish Sabbath and festival traditions as a kind of nonideological default mode diminished, however, with the demands of six-day workplaces, the dimming of immigrant memories, the migration of Jews away from densely populated centers of Jewish life, and the adoption of American norms which made Sunday, not Saturday, the day of leisure and renewal. Some Reform temples officially transferred their worship or study sessions to Sundays. Perhaps most important, for many second generation Americans, the more frequent demands of Jewish observances seemed antithetical to modern American life, and they opted for more streamlined modes of observance which emphasized yearly festivities such as the High Holidays, Hanukkah, and Passover. As Marshall Sklare commented about Jews at midcentury in America's suburban heartlands:

> The highest degree of retention will occur when a ritual: (1) is capable of effective redefinition in modern terms; (2) does not demand social isolation or the adoption of a unique life style; (3) accords with the religious culture of the larger community while providing a "Jewish" alternative when such is felt to be needed; (4) is centered on the child; and (5) is performed annually or infrequently.[3]

Sklare's observations have been borne out over the passage of time. For many American Jews, Rosh Hashanah and Yom Kippur have held an element of spiritual poignance and solidarity with historical Judaism; for some, the yearly Yom Kippur fast has been a kind of endurance test testifying to enduring Jewish identity, and perhaps also legitimating self-perceived laxness vis-à-vis other observances. Hanukkah has been celebrated as the Jewish winter festival of lights which may partially insulate children from the pervasive Christmas presence in American culture. The Passover seder service-meal has emerged as the family holiday par excellence, with the additional benefit that its official rationale is a celebration of freedom, which most Americans value. In contrast, Sabbath and kashruth observances—which were widely considered the defining behaviors of Jewish identity in traditional communities—are ignored by the majority of American Jews partially because they are socially intrusive, requiring behavioral restrictions and separation from mainstream American activities on a regular basis.

Overviews of ritual observances in American-Jewish households drawn from the 1990 NJPS data reveal certain large patterns and also striking diversity between subgroups: Passover is the most widely observed ritual for all American Jews, Hanukkah candles are most widely lit in homes with school-age children, and Yom Kippur fasting is still widespread, especially in Eastern Seaboard communities with dense Jewish populations. Regular Sabbath and holiday observances characterize fewer than one-third, and home-based kashruth (two sets of dishes) is found in only one out of seven American Jewish households. Respondents identifying as Jewish by religion have a dramatically higher level of observance than those calling themselves secular Jews. Conversionary households have a somewhat higher level of general ritual observance than inmarried households, and Jews who affiliate by paying dues to synagogues or temples have a much higher level of observance than Jews who merely cite a denominational preference without joining. Jews with higher levels of secular education have higher levels of ritual observance; those with high levels of Jewish education far outdistance all others in their cohort.

In certain types of households having a Christmas tree is more common than any Jewish ritual: Four out of five mixed-married households (one spouse not Jewish) have a Christmas tree, compared to fewer than three percent of inmarried Jews who affiliate with some kind of temple.

Analyzing the meaning of changing ritual observances is complicated because of divergent semiotics of ritual behaviors: various American denominations of Judaism assign different meanings to particular behaviors. Not participating in a ritual may signify alienation or rupture in one religious environment, and nothing at all in another environment.

Within the Reform movement, for example, the dietary restrictions of traditional kashruth were for decades not considered salient to exemplary religious behavior. A person might be an active, fully committed Reform Jew, attend temple regularly and celebrate the Jewish festivals, visit and support Israel, read Jewish newspapers and books, and never give religious dietary restrictions a thought except when planning a community-wide Jewish event which involves Conservative or Orthodox Jews. Similarly, non-Orthodox activists might well light candles religiously every Friday night, but not be concerned about lighting them before sundown. Activist Conservative Jews might have two sets of dishes and be punctilious about not eating biblically prohibited foods, but could in good religious conscience drive to synagogue worship each Sabbath. Thus, it is rather simple to measure the presence or absence of certain behaviors in the home, but much more complicated to ascertain and compare what these behaviors mean in terms of Jewish connections and commitments.

It seems clear as well that certain behaviors develop new meanings as the broader

American culture changes. Influences from inside and outside the Jewish world can invest activities with very different significance. Two general trends have contributed to the changing status of aspects of Jewish culture, (1) the rise of ethnic difference as a desirable characteristic of American families; and (2) the search for spiritual experience as a benefit of religious identification.

As ethnic difference has become celebrated in American society, distinctive customs and rituals have lost the negative coloration that seemed to disfigure them in the eyes of many Jews earlier in the twentieth century. For example, the strikingly European Klezmer music which many sophisticated older American Jews avoided for years in favor of whatever was popular on the American musical scene has now acquired a new cache as ethnic music, and has been legitimated by mainstream radio and television. Jews can enjoy Klezmer music because it fits into a non-Jewish notion of what music is currently supposed to be. Similarly, large groups of older non-Orthodox Jews regarded the dietary laws as evidence of Jewish ignorance, superstition, and social isolation; for some younger non-Orthodox Jews, in contrast, kashruth may appear to be the prototype for today's health and social-consciousness based concerns about diet, and may be combined with vegetarianism or some ecologically friendly regimen. It is fair to say that in the 1980s and 1990s the American cultural obsession with dietary "rules"—concerns about heart disease, cholesterol, fiber, osteoporosis, insecticides, antibiotics, cruelty to animals, oppression of migrant workers—may have enhanced the new legitimacy of kashruth in some circles. Consumers of kosher products certainly include non-Jewish buyers, judging by current marketing, which places kosher products in supermarkets far from sizable Jewish populations. Kashruth observance may thus seem anachronistic to some Jews, but trendy to others.

Along the same lines, specialized behaviors such as building a *succah,* going in groups to a body of water on *Rosh HaShanah* afternoon to symbolically dispose of sins through the custom of *Tashlich,* or even dressing in costume and attending the Purim reading of *Megilat Esther* (The Book of Esther) were for many years primarily adhered to by consistently observant Jews; in contemporary activist Jewish communities, these rituals seem colorful, spiritual, and/or good indoctrinators of children, and they have acquired popularity as a spiritually significant "Jewish experience," appropriate for families who may not be consistently observant in other ways.

Denomination Shifts and Current Ritual Observance

A full-page supplement of the Jewish newspaper *Forward* may well wonder, "Jewish Food—The Kosher Revival: Is It Health or Is It Religion?" in a special section which explores "Meat-Free Fare, God's Ideal Menu" and features "Asher Lazar, the Macrobiotic Guru of Borough Park."[4] However, despite the perceived prevalence of both trendy and traditional Orthodox behaviors in some communities, 1990 NJPS statistics show that well under 10 percent of American Jews are Orthodox. As Table 6.1 shows, a much higher percentage of Jews report being raised Orthodox than are currently Orthodox. Moreover, Table 6.2 demonstrates that the vast majority in each denomination were groomed for that lifestyle—especially among Orthodox Jews. Nine out of ten Jews who currently call themselves Orthodox grew up in Orthodox homes; 5 percent of currently Orthodox Jews were raised as Conservative, 5 percent as "just Jewish," fewer than one percent as Reform, and one percent as non-Jewish. Anecdotal evidence aside, the vast majority of Jews who grow up in non-observant environments do not choose to follow the strictures of rabbinic law. Perhaps newly Orthodox Jews, or *ba'alei teshuva* (masters of return) as they are often referred to, seem more numerous because they contradict the assimilationist expectations created by the larger pattern in Jewish communities.

While certain types of ritual observance have enjoyed a revival among limited groups of American Jews, the far more pervasive American pattern is that the flow of Jewish ritual observance is downward. This downward movement is related to the general demographics of the Jewish community. First, 20 percent of American Jews currently say they are not Jewish by religion, but are instead "secular or unaffiliated" Jews.[5] Of the Jews by religion, as seem in Table 5.1, 10 percent say they are "just Jewish." Each of these categories has much lower levels of ritual observance than any denominationally affiliated group. Of those persons who are currently "just Jewish," 16 percent were raised in Orthodox homes, 18 percent in Conservative homes, 15 percent in Reform and homes, 47 percent in "just Jewish" homes, and five percent in non-Jewish homes, as seen in Table 5.2. Thus, according to these respondent data, it would appear that twice as many Jews are currently Just Jewish as were raised that way.

Second, affiliations have shifted towards less ritually observant denominations: 1990 NJPS respondents reported that 27 percent of them were raised as Orthodox Jews, for example, but that currently only 6 percent are Orthodox, as seen in Table 6.2. In the 1970s the dominant denomination among affiliated younger American Jews was Conservative Judaism; in the 1990s the largest number of younger American Jews identify themselves as Reform. While 26 percent of American Jews say they were raised as Reform, 38 percent are currently Reform, and Reform Jews as a group, not unexpectedly, have lower levels of ritual observance than Orthodox or Conservative Jews because Reform ideology places religious emphasis elsewhere. Thus, the largest number of affiliated American Jews are now associated with the denomination whose norm is low ritual observance levels. Among persons who are currently Conservative, 60 percent report being raised in Conservative homes, 32 percent in Orthodox homes, 4 percent in Reform homes, and 2 percent each in "just Jewish" or non-Jewish homes. Among those who are currently Reform, 59 percent were raised in Reform homes, 12 percent were raised in Orthodox homes, 26 percent in Conservative homes, 6 percent in "just Jewish" homes, and 2 percent in non-Jewish homes.

No doubt some of the impact on denominational level and ritual observances in Jewish homes can be traced to outmarriage and the subsequent mixture of religious backgrounds of persons residing in Jewish households. As Tables 6.4 and 6.5 show, the households studied in the 1990 NJPS included a substantial number of persons who were not born Jews or who were not raised as Jews or who do not currently consider themselves to be Jewish. When all the individuals living in qualified households are considered, slightly over half (51 percent) are persons who are born Jews and currently consider their religion Jewish; 2 percent were not born Jewish but are currently Jews by choice; 14 percent were born Jews but now consider themselves secular or to have no religion; 3 percent are persons who were born or raised Jewish but have converted out into another religion; 5 percent are adults who had at least one Jewish parent but who now consider themselves to be something other, such as nothing, mixed, or non-Jews; 9 percent are children under age 18 who are being raised into another religion; and 16 percent are persons who were not born Jews and are not now Jewish.[6]

When only persons who had some tangible connection to Jewish identification are considered, about two-thirds of individuals in Jewish households consider themselves to be Jews by religion; 16 percent are born Jews with no current religion; 9 percent had childhood connections to Judaism but are currently identified with another religion. Of the children in these households, one out of ten children under age 18 were being raised within some other religion, 16 percent were identified as "secular Jews," 46 percent were considered to be Jewish by religion, and 31 percent had no religion.

Taken as an undifferentiated group, Jews keep fewer rituals today than in the past, and younger American Jews appear to keep fewer rituals than older Jews. Table 6.3 shows that 62 percent of all Jews consistently attend a Passover seder, 60 percent light Hanukkah candles, 49 percent fast on Yom Kippur, 17 percent light Shabbat candles, and only 13 percent have two sets of dishes for the purpose of keeping a kosher home.

However, when Jews are divided into specific groups, it becomes evident that rituals are not uniformly disappearing among all groups of younger American Jews. Younger does not necessarily mean less observant. As examined in detail below, Table 6.6 shows that younger Orthodox Jews are more observant than their elders, younger Conservative Jews as a whole are slightly less observant than their elders, and younger Reform Jews observe at roughly the same levels as middle-aged and older Reform Jews.

Synagogue membership is associated with higher levels of ritual observance; within this general observation, ritual observance is higher among Orthodox than non-Orthodox Jews, and higher among Conservative than Reform synagogue members.[7]

Geographical location is also related to ritual observance; one "factoid" from city studies in the 1980s which dramatically illustrates this phenomenon is that the non-Jewish spouse of a Jew in Baltimore was more likely to fast on Yom Kippur than a born Jew in San Francisco. Whether the product of peer pressure, communal norms, or geographical self-selection, Jews who choose to live in areas with higher Jewish population density, a vigorously interactive Jewish population, and a strong traditional presence have a much higher level of ritual observance than those who live in areas where Jews are spread out and Jewish communal structures reach limited segments of the area's Jews.

Perhaps most heartening to those who would like to bolster levels of ritual observance, Jews ages 30 to 49 with high levels of secular education have higher levels of observance, and ritual observance among those with both high levels of secular and Jewish education increases dramatically. Thus, among persons with seven to nine years of Jewish education, those with master's degrees are ten times more likely to light candles than those with only a high school education: only 4 percent of persons with seven to nine years of Jewish education but not more than a high school education light Sabbath candles, compared to 40 percent of those with seven to nine years of Jewish education and master's degrees. Among those with seven to nine years of Jewish education, 36 percent of those with a high school education fast on Yom Kippur, compared to 82 percent of those with graduate or professional degrees. These data demonstrate that Jews have little to fear from high levels of secular education, provided they also ensure the availability and attractiveness of high levels of Jewish education as well.

Parameters of Sabbath Observance in Jewish Homes

It is worthwhile to pay special attention to the status of Sabbath and kashruth observance in contemporary American-Jewish society, because these two behaviors were the trademark of Jewish identity for much of Jewish history; both Jewish and non-Jewish writings, for example, presented the forcing of Jews to violate kashruth observance (compelling Jews to eat pork, typically) as the epitome of communal humiliation and an occasion of deep despair. Sabbath observance was regarded from Leviticus through the Hebrew prophets and the rabbis who shaped Jewish laws and communal observances as the great moral and behavioral pillar of Judaism.

Interwoven into the dense fabric of Sabbath prescriptions and prohibitions are prescient laws of social responsibility: limits to the demands which can be made on servants and domestic animals, for example, and boundaries to activities spurred by ambition and avarice. As with other areas of human existence, rabbinic codes dealing with the Sabbath have held that human beings require prescriptive guidelines: if Jewish law does not make heads of households give their working persons and cattle a day of rest, most would not do so; if the law does not demand that Jews abandon business talk and activities for twenty-four hours in order to devote time to spiritual renewal, their strivings would be incessant.[8] An appropriate contemporary comparison can be found in the rhetoric of Americans who work for laws that guarantee parental leave or equal rights for minority groups; political activitists assume that employers will be motivated by greed and prejudice, unless they are forced by American law to be compassionate, fair, and even-handed.

Historically, great emphasis was placed on Sabbath observance, which according to rabbinic law was to be set aside only in life-threatening situations. Numerous, detailed rabbinic behavioral "fences" were created around thirty-nine prohibited activities (*melakhot*), in order to prevent inadvertent desecration of the Sabbath's formula for a day that differed in almost every regard from the work week. While such prescriptions have often seemed onerous to outside observers, twentieth-century American-Jewish thinkers as different as Abba Hillel Silver[9] and Abraham Joshua Heschel,[10] leading Reform and Conservative rabbis, have argued that the Sabbath's power to transform the lives of Jewish households and communities derived not from ascetic denial but from the peculiar elevated environment, blending sensual and spiritual celebration, which Sabbath observance was capable of creating. Such assessments of the importance of Sabbath observance are aptly summed up in Ahad HaAm's famous aphorism: "More than Israel kept the Sabbath, the Sabbath has kept Israel." (Ahad HaAm, *Hashiloah*, 1898, iii, 6)

Paeans to the Sabbath's potential for psychological transcendence, of course, are not the same thing as sociological, measurable observance of the Sabbath in specific Jewish communities. Historical sources such as responsa literature, letters, memoirs, and stories indicate that some level of Sabbath observance was fairly standard in Jewish homes until political emancipation and the Jewish Enlightenment offered other behavioral options. Sabbath observance had been officially moderated by the Reform movement in Germany in the eighteenth and nineteenth centuries, and the majority of non-Orthodox households streamlined ritual behaviors. Responding to secular movements and ideologies, by the turn of the twentieth century many urban East European Jews had abandoned strict observance; memoir literature indicates that behind closed doors, observance levels varied widely even in more secluded *shtetl* surroundings.

Home-based Sabbath observance was jettisoned in a wholesale fashion by many American-Jewish immigrants, although candle lighting and occasional synagogue attendance were retained by a significant population. Some American Jews were motivated to retain such Sabbath rituals as candle lighting out of loyalty or nostalgia: several urban respondents remembered mothers leaving the family store to light candles—and then returning to work in the store, often with some muttered ironic comment about necessity. Synagogue attendance had an additional motivation—it seemed like an American thing to do; in a country whose currency claimed "in God we trust," attendance at a Jewish church once a week put worshipers in the mainstream, especially if the house of worship was Americanized, quiet and orderly, with plenty of English prayers.

Jews who insisted on strict Sabbath observance on American shores were always in a minority, and their numbers declined with suburbanization. Skare and Greenblum's study of *Jewish Identity on the Suburban Frontier* in the 1950s demonstrated a dramatic drop in Sabbath and kashruth observance between respondents and their parents. About half of parental homes were reported to have some form of Sabbath observance and kosher homes, specifically lighting candles and having a special Sabbath meal, and buying only kosher meat for the household; in contrast, among the Lakeville respondents about one-third reported Sabbath candle lighting and special meals, and fewer than 10 percent avoided pork or bought kosher meat. It should be noted, that even among their parents, only 29 percent recited the Sabbath *kiddush* blessing over wine on a regular basis; among respondents, 16 percent recited *kiddush*, indicating an Americanized familial, rather than traditional ritualistic, approach to Sabbath behaviors, a tendency which Sklare and Greeblum call "declining sacramentalism."[11] Indeed, before the incremental buildup of Jewish educational systems, dramatically nourished at midcentury by the infusion of a more religiously intense, post-Holocaust immigrant population, it seemed to some observers that Sabbath and other regular traditional observances were destined to quietly flicker out.

More than thirty years after the Lakeville study, American Jews nationwide have followed this trend toward declining sacramentalism, with 19 percent of Jews by religion and three percent of secular Jews lighting Sabbath candles on a regular basis. Using 1990 NJPS data, contemporary Sabbath consciousness in Jewish homes can be roughly measured by looking at questions about lighting candles and not handling money, which are, on a theoretical level, less denominationally biased than some other questions. The inquiry about whether "someone in the household lights candles" does not refer to time of candle lighting, (strictly observant Jews light candles 18 minutes before sundown, while more liberal Jews light candles at a time they deem appropriate) and is thus useful for tracing the most basic Sabbath observance, common to all wings of Judaism, as well as one that visibly signals some sort of demarcation to children and other household members. In contrast, asking the respondent if s/he "refrains from handling money" on the Sabbath is a useful way to look at mainstream *shomer Shabbat* (Sabbath observant) behaviors; no religious denomination specifically advocates mercantile activity on the Sabbath; at least theoretically, Jews who do not feel it is religiously incumbent upon them to avoid telephones, electricity, or automobiles on the Sabbath might still try to avoid handling money.

Contrary to the stereotyped relationship between elderly Jews and piety, increasing age does not necessary imply increasing levels of Sabbath observance. On the contrary, among Orthodox households, younger respondents indicate more rigorous levels of Sabbath observance than middle-aged or elderly respondents. For example, 70 percent of Orthodox Jews ages 30 to 49 said they didn't handle money on the Sabbath, compared to 55 percent of those ages 50 to 64 and 49 percent of those ages 65 to 74.

Higher levels of Sabbath observance among younger Orthodox Jews is due to three interrelated factors: (1) Older American Jews perceive denominational identification to be institution based, whereas younger American Jews perceive it to be behavior based—older American Jews are more likely to indicate that they are "Orthodox" if they belong (or belonged) to an Orthodox synagogue, and they are more likely to have belonged to an Orthodox synagogue because of ties to immigrant-generation relatives; younger respondents tend to perceive that an "Orthodox" response indicates relatively high levels of ritual observance. (2) Younger Orthodox Jews are much more likely to have received an extensive Jewish education, and thus to be more intellectually aware of the requirements and rationale of rabbinical law. (3) Older respondents may suffer from physical, psychological, social, or financial limitations which they perceive as justifying deviations from their ritual observances.

It is also entirely likely that increased Sabbath observance among younger Orthodox Jews is linked to decreased economic privations in Orthodox households. Secular educational and occupational patterns among younger Orthodox Jews resemble the non-Orthodox population. Given the pro-ethnic environment in the United States in the 1970s, 1980s, and 1990s, and given the normativeness of the five-day work week, it has been easier than ever before in American-Jewish life for Jews who wish to make arrangements—such as working on Sundays and Christian/secular holidays—so that they can observe Jewish Sabbaths and holidays. Added to the relative ease of Sabbath observance may be a resistance to American corporate mores. St. Louis raised Israeli novelist Allen Hoffman has his characters deride the American-Jewish work ethic and neglect of Sabbath observance:

> . . . And most tragically, there was no Sabbath in America. How could there be? It was too busy, almost everyone worked on Saturday. The Jews of Krimsk had not come to America to rest; they had come to improve their lives. Through

hard work anyone could become a Rockefeller, a Vanderbilt, or a Morgan. . . . opportunity for those with ingenuity, intelligence, and no fear of hard work—especially on Saturday. No one worked harder on the Sabbath than the ex-Krimskers did. . . . The Jews in America seem possessed.[12]

Despite their clear statistical decline, family-based Sabbath observances are intensely significant to an activist minority of the population in every wing of Judaism. One Reform businesswoman in her 50s, proudly commenting that her grown children who are "still very Jewish" join her every Friday night for a Sabbath meal with candles and *kiddush,* said that the Friday night family encounter was part of her general strategy of involving her children with all aspects of her life, business, social, and religious (Interview, May 1990). Orthodox feminist Blu Greenberg, (Interview, Oct. 1990), declared that she would not have "given up one moment of our wonderful family Shabbat meals for any feminist goal," although she has struggled with certain details of the interface between feminism and traditional Sabbath observances:

> It wasn't always easy on Shabbat. Getting ready for Shabbat, I took on 90 percent of the housework, chauffeuring, etc., and I was aware I was always preparing, cooking, cleaning—and worrying that we weren't presenting good role models for our kids. Choosing one particular role is never satisfying. On the other hand, I do feel that we need an anchor at the Shabbat table. So we all say *kiddush* together, and sometimes I make the *motzi* [prayer over bread]. . . . Increasingly I want to affirm the distinctiveness of gender; I feel this is something the feminist movement can learn from Judaism. Blurring all the lines leads to chaos, not to harmonious relations. If you take feminism to its logical conclusions, the task of lighting Shabbat candles is up for grabs. That makes me feel emotionally ill at ease.

Many households devise their own American Sabbath combinations, sometimes based more than they realize on what they observed in their parental homes. For example, a National Commission on Jewish Women Focus Group participant compared Sabbath observances when she was a child in her parents' home, commenting, "It wasn't so much the religious aspect of it as their way of life," with that of her own five and eight year old daughters:

> I grew up in a very Jewish home and I think I'm still growing up in a very Jewish home, but it's very different than the way it was at my parents. My parents are both very active and still are in the synagogue. When my sister and I were growing up, you went to synagogue on Friday night with your parents and then you could go out afterwards. On Saturday morning my father went to synagogue, but then they shopped on Saturday afternoon. . . . I think it is different for us. . . . We don't really go to synagogue that often. I still keep a kosher house; I want my grandmother to be able to eat at my house and feel comfortable. I light candles on Friday night before we go out. My kids go to synagogue with my father.

Although she insists that her home is "very different" than her parents' home, her two daughters are in fact receiving a very similar Jewish experience as she received—Sabbath means candles, synagogue, then the mall!—albeit some of their experience is with grandparents rather than parents.

Among activist non-Orthodox Jews a familial or communal "warm" experience is often a very appealing element of ritual observance, while punctilious observance of ritual detail is perceived as irrelevant or conformist, as another focus-group participant suggested:

> Religion for me is twofold. Part of it is spiritual and part of it is community. To me, community matters more than conformity. It is not about going to synagogue every week or whether you light candles every Friday night at sunset, because that would never happen in my house. Sometimes we light candles on Saturday, because we never got to it on Friday. Our intention is still there. I think our kids are growing up absolutely knowing they are Jewish, and delighted they are Jewish. We spend a lot of time at the JCC. My kids love their Hebrew school—our Hebrew school is wonderful. Our rabbis are so warm and loving, they make it a really nice place to be. We don't always go to Shabbat services; we don't get there all the time, but when we do it is not a have-to-go. I think their Jewishness is good and positive even though we don't conform to all the rituals.

Perhaps most poignant, another young working mother among the National Commission focus-group participants talked about her aspirations for a family Sabbath experience, and her difficulties in attaining it on an ongoing basis; she said that starting Friday morning she would think about lighting the candles and having a family meal, and she would hope she could do it during the day, but that often she wasn't able to get home on time to make it happen: "I always think about lighting candles when it's candle-lighting time, though," she sighed.

Kashruth Observance in Jewish Households

Observance of the Jewish dietary laws, colloquially "keeping kosher," involves three basic components: (1) restricting consumption of animal products to creatures not prohibited by biblical law, (2) eating only meat or poultry that has been slaughtered according to Jewish ritual specifications and has been soaked and salted to remove most of the blood, and (3) avoiding the mixing of milk and meat products. Rabbinical law created around these basic precepts is complex; among the requirements are separate dishes and utensils for foods with dairy or meat ingredients.

Statistics from the 1990 NJPS suggest that, ironically, at a time when the word "kosher" is a frequently used expression in the general American lexicon, actual observance of the dietary laws in Jewish homes is extremely limited. Nationwide, two sets of dishes are reported by 14 percent of all current Jews (born Jews and Jewish by choice), 16 percent of those who say they are Jewish by religion, five percent of secular Jews, and 20 percent of converts into Judaism. As with Sabbath rituals, keeping two sets of dishes in the home is more consistent among Orthodox Jews under age 65 than among any other group: four out of five Orthodox Jews ages 30 to 64 have two sets of dishes (or are vegetarians), compared to 70 percent of Orthodox Jews age 65 or older. Among Jews ages 30 to 49, kosher households are reported by 82 percent of Orthodox, 33 percent of Traditional, 21 percent of Conservative, 4 percent of Reform, 21 percent of Reconstructionist, and fewer than one percent of "just Jewish" respondents.

In contemporary American-Jewish communities, kashruth observance is not accepted by all Jewish denominations as a normative religious behavior. It is described by leaders of the Orthodox, Traditional, and Conservative movements as a critical observance, but Reform Judaism until recently did not suggest the dietary laws as a normative behavior, and the valuation which Reconstructionist leaders place on traditional kashruth varies from community to community. The extent of home-based kashruth observance is often related to geographical availability and to communal norms: Eastern, urban Jews living in neighborhoods with a strong traditional presence have always been more likely to include many kosher households, while Sklare and Greenblum, as indicated earlier, found that fewer than 10 percent of midwestern suburban Jews at midcentury made a point of purchasing kosher meat for their homes. Some American Jews have opted for vegetarianism as an alternative (and to their minds superior) form of kashruth,[13] a phenomenon which will be discussed later in this chapter.

Religiously observant Jewish societies are characterized by careful attention to guarding against importing nonkosher food elements into the home. As with all contemporary ritual observances, "keeping kosher" actually occupies an observance continuum. On the left are respondents who say they have kosher homes even though they do not have two sets of dishes or purchase their meats from a reliable kosher butcher; in their eyes, avoiding pork or shellfish in the home makes their household kosher. Some respondents purchase kosher meat, have two sets of dishes and do not eat milk and meat at the same time, but will purchase non-meat food items after checking the labels to exclude items with nonkosher ingredients, such as animal-based shortening or emulsifiers. Within the Orthodox community, official standards of kashruth involve rejecting prepared food items in cans and packages that are not marked certified by a recognized rabbinical authority [such as Ⓤ, k, etc.]. Even fresh produce can be suspect in some communities. The most stringent contemporary practitioners maintain or have revived the practice of obtaining milk only from Jewish or other reliable sources (*cholev Yisrael,* or Jewish milk), because some non-Jewish European farmers were known to mix pig's milk into cow's milk in order to stretch their profits. *Cholev Yisrael* advocates were given an unexpected boost in Boston in 1996, when one milk manufacturer claiming an "all natural" product was discovered to be adding shark oil to milk as a "natural" source of vitamin D, rather than "artificial" vitamins and minerals. Similarly, in some communities, leafy vegetables growing near the ground were and are carefully checked, leaf by leaf (*bodek*), for insects, and are sold in specialized markets.

Persons reporting that they observe kashruth outside the home, like those who say they have kosher homes, have variant notions of what "keeping kosher out" really means. Ideally, an Orthodox Jew is expected to maintain the same standards of kashruth outside the home as inside the home, eating only in certified kosher restaurants and thus avoiding all foods that are cooked or served in utensils that are also used for nonkosher items. In practice, the majority of kashruth-observant Jews in the United States today make at least slight compromises in kashruth observance outside the home.[14] More liberal observant Jewish households and communities set more flexible parameters.

However, for the vast majority of American Jews kashruth observance outside the home has been lax to nonexistent for decades. By the middle of the twentieth century Jews in the United States evolved a de facto communal norm of dual standards for kashruth observance. The majority of individuals in kosher households monitored foods that were brought into the home far more carefully than those they ate outside the home, leading to the oft-noted proliferation of Chinese restaurants even in Jewish neighborhoods where most housewives prided themselves on their own kosher kitchens. In households such as these, the kashruth standard was shifted away from what individuals ingested, and projected instead onto the pots, plates, and tables of the household. This dual standard—strictly kosher at home, anything goes outside the home—sometimes led to some rather humorous problems of defining what comprised "home." Thus, one midwestern woman reports that in the 1950s synagogue-affiliated Conservative teenagers in her community were allowed to eat nonkosher hot dog outside, but not in the family automobile, because it was considered to be part of the home "and they weren't allowed to *traife up* (render nonkosher) the car." Similarly, Letty Cottin Pogebrin writes that her mother secretly prepared bacon strips in a special, nonkosher pan in their putatively "strictly kosher" home, but served the bacon on paper plates and called it "lamb chops on paper," presumably to preserve the innocence of both her dishes and her daughter's standards, as well as a kosher grandmother's peace of mind.[15]

Pogebrin's responses to this "slippery," elaborate but inconsistent web of "codes and symbols," was representative of many in her generation:

> In my family, kashruth was one of those realities with many layers. At home, my mother obeyed the Jewish dietary laws; she bought her meat from the kosher butcher and maintained separate sets of dishes and cookware for meat and dairy meals. However, in the homes of people who did not keep kosher, we ate meat with milk—Chicken a la King, for instance—and in restaurants we ate trayf, ritually unclean foods like pork or shellfish. . . . but then, after going to all that trouble, why did Mommy cheat on her own rules? At the end of a meat meal, if no outsiders were present, she served my father evaporated milk in his coffee, the way he liked it. And because I was so skinny, she fed me baked potatoes with butter and sour cream along-side my flanken. . . . My mother's kashruth fraud is part of a category of family secrets I think of as "cheating on Judaism."
>
> . . . Jews are also not allowed to carry money, cook, work, or shop on the Sabbath. But it was okay for Daddy to go into his office on Saturday because he had a heavy case load. It was okay for us to carry money to buy some bagels or

coffee cake on the way home from shul. It was okay for Mommy to cook on Saturday if she hadn't prepared enough food in advance of the Sabbath. It was okay for me to go to the movies on Saturday if I was bored stiff and was getting on my parents' nerves. Exceptions were made but never exactly acknowledged. They were our secret.[16]

Finding kashruth observance—like Sabbath observance—cumbersome in American social settings, especially in communities that were not otherwise grounded in ongoing ritual observance, and perhaps perceiving dual standards as adult hypocrisy and self-deception, many children who grew up with middle-American kosher/nonkosher behaviors abandoned kashruth observance altogether. Nevertheless, some currently retain, at least in vestigial form, the sociologically normative American-Jewish division between inside and outside cuisine, as one focus-group participant formulated it: "I am not kosher. I love seafood. I don't bring it into the house. I eat it out. I don't bring ham into the house. I don't do any of that sort of thing. I try to make it as kosher as I can without being kosher."

Affiliation with synagogues is strongly related to higher levels of ritual observance. For example, a study of Conservative Jews also based on 1990 NJPS data notes that households that are currently affiliated with Conservative synagogues are four times more likely to report kashruth observance than those not holding memberships—24 percent, compared to 6 percent. The higher level of Conservative kashruth observance was part of a pattern, with members of Conservative synagogues reporting 37 percent Shabbat candle lighting, compared to 11 percent among nonmembers, and 90 percent seder attendance, compared to 60 percent among non-members. Still, this study shows that even among members only one-quarter of Conservative Jews report kosher homes, a dramatic attrition of home-based kashruth as a communal norm. Clearly institutional affiliation, rather than behavior, is predominant in their religious self-perception. Even at public religious events, such as Bar/Bat Mitzvah celebrations, kashruth observance is far from universal in Conservative families: about half of families, whether composed of two born Jews, a born Jew and a Jew by choice, or a Jew and a non-Jew, reported that their children's Bar/Bat Mitzvah receptions were kosher.[17] It is, of course, quite possible that the synagogue itself required kosher catering as a condition for the event.

While the vast majority of American-Jewish households are not kosher, in many communities considerable care is taken to ensure that official functions and institutions maintain kashruth standards. This disparity between actual communal household norms and official behaviors is partially due to the attempt to make official functions as inclusive as possible, open to the entire spectrum of Jews from the most to the least observant; some also aim to maintain kashruth as an official communal norm. It should be noted that this concern for inclusive communal kashruth is far more conscious and consistent now than it was several decades ago. Federation functions, for example, not infrequently violated Sabbath and/or kashruth restrictions in the 1950s and 1960s; in contrast, the Council of Jewish Federations (CJF) General Assembly, attended by thousands of lay and professional leaders, during the 1980s and 1990s was distinguished by the prevalence of lively and well-attended Sabbath sacramental and worship opportunities, and the lack of any official functions that violated the letter of Sabbath laws.

Revival of Traditionalist Behaviors

Public attention has sometimes been focused on the putative religious revival of American Jews via the *ba'al teshuva* movement, in which previously less ritually observant Jews become more observant, usually in an Orthodox context and sometimes within right-wing communities. This movement has received much attention partially because it seems counterintuitive; among Jews who assumed that assimilation was the prevalent direction of Jewish life, it was startling to see young Jews deliberately choosing to become strictly observant of restrictive rituals such as dress codes, Sabbath and holiday observance, dietary laws, and the laws of family purity (*taharat ha'mishpakhah*). Promoted by religious movements such as Chabad/Lubavitch and institutions such as the Jewish Outreach Movement in the United States and Israel, *ba'al teshuva* efforts have changed many lives.

Systematic studies of newly Orthodox American-Jewish women by Lynn Davidman and Debra Renee Kaufman suggest that Jews with high levels of secular education are most likely to be attracted to modern Orthodox settings, in which secular education and occupational achievement are mainstream, whereas Jews with less education, especially those who experimented with drugs, Eastern religions, or "new age" types of spirituality, are most likely to find their way into right-wing Orthodox or Hasidic settings.[18] This general observation is probably equally true of men and women. A finding specific to women is that disillusionment with sexual freedom can lead some women to seek out the definitive, structured gender role construction of traditional Orthodox societies.

In true coalesced style, their search for sexual limitations is often articulated in terms of feminist self-esteem; the seemingly restrictive constellation of laws surrounding *niddah* (menstrual impurity) and Jewish family values as incarnated in *taharat ha'mishpakhah* are viewed as liberating:

> I am a child of the liberated generation. Since we are talking about *niddah* now I will refer to sexual liberation although I think what I am saying applies to many areas of liberation. . . . For all the sexual freedom I felt in my late adolescence and early adulthood, I can tell you it was more like sexual exploitation. I felt there were no longer any rules; on what grounds did one decide to say no? If the rule was casual sex and if you engaged in it on what grounds did you say no? . . . without protection of some sort, the sexual liberation meant that women were free to be exploited more by men . . . the laws of *taharat ha'mishpakhah* make so much sense. . . . The separation restores our passion and places control of it in my hands.[19]

Disillusionment with what one observer called the "sexual wilderness" created by rampant individualism and the feminist version of that individualism is shared by some Jewish and non-Jewish women alike.[20] Thus, even postfeminist retreat from sexual liberation into religious structure may have a component of coalescence. Creating a fictionalized dialogue between a liberated, intellectual, antireligious mother and her newly Orthodox daughter, novelist Anne Roiphe chronicles the wild experimentation which, in the case of some *ba'alei teshuvah*, leads unexpectedly into the most traditional of all lifestyles. For the mother, religious laws are "the invention of the human mind, petty, bizarre, and self-righteous"; in contrast, for those in the Yeshiva Rachel community, religious laws are God-given and nurture wholesome natural functions:

> "I was always waiting for some definitive, end-of-the-line call. We've found your daughter in a ravine outside of Las Vegas with her throat cut, we've found your daughter dead of an overdose in a pickup truck with a Hell's Angel, we've found your daughter naked hallucinating on the L.A. freeway. I had anticipated a lot of phone calls. I had not thought of the Yeshiva Rachel."
>
> ... "My body has stopped being simply a means to a quick fix. My body is also intended to serve Gd. Mr. Cohen says I no longer look like a chicken bone. My periods are coming regularly and they never did that before. Mrs. Cohen says that the periods are set in tune with our prayers and move in cycles toward fulfillment of womanhood. I know you won't like this but I believe that my body is like the earth, rhythmic and fertile. At least I hope I'm fertile. I told Mrs. Cohen about the abortions. ... She puts extra spoonfuls of honey on my bread. I know you didn't believe that we should mix up food with love, but it seems to me you separated the things that belong together and mingled the things that should be separated, like dairy and meat. The world without covenant confused you."[21]

Cultural Artifacts Illustrate Coalescence among
Young Orthodox Jews

Although they might vigorously deny it, coalescence suffuses the covenantal world of traditional young American Jews, both *ba'alei teshuvah*, colloquially known as B.T.s, and the far more numerous Orthodox young adults who have been raised in Orthodox homes, colloquially known as F.F.B.s—*Frum* (pious) From Birth. This coalescence is particularly evident in their material culture, where their distinctive consumer needs have spawned new species of product advertisements. A clothing catalogue from California, distributed in Fall, 1996 by direct mail, for example, is called: *Any Wear You're Frum: Fashionable Modest Attire.* The models, young women and children from the Calabasas, California synagogue community, wear youthful hats and casual footwear—running shoes, basketball sneakers, flats—with trendy, long skirts, denim, broomstick skirts, natural fabrics, Indian prints. While their blouses modestly cover the upper arm and their hats cover all but the tiniest portion of hair at the forehead or ear, their overall appearance is breezy Americana.

The advertising text quotes from the praise of the Woman of Valor in Proverbs or from "Fiddler on the Roof," and describes the fabrics and styles in terms of the young matron's busy life: "Always comfortable and stylish because it's knit dressing. Dresses that move when you do./ She is robed in strength and dignity and she smiles at the future." "This pale check in shades of yellows and sage will keep you looking cool through the long, hot summer./ May you be like Ruth and like Esther. . . . You asked for it so here it is . . . Mommy and Me!" Most pages refer to traditional, domestic women's roles: carpooling, picnicking with the children, conversations with female friends, running errands. However, one page refers to the professional lives of many Orthodox young mothers by offering: "A little something more. These pretty two piece sets will take you from a business meeting to Shabbos!"

A long letter from the designer fills the first page of the catalogue. Its language flows unselfconsciously from world to world, describing how she and her husband decided to become Orthodox—"I want to give thanks to the Rosh Yeshiva of Aish Ha Torah, Rabbi Noah Weinberg. . . . It is directly because of his efforts my husband and I chose to return to our heritage"—and how she went into business "with little more than this concept and a lot of *emuna*. . . ." She offers the reader "*tsniess* (modest), durable fashion" by phone, fax, or mail.

A different blend of contemporary American culture and trendy traditionalism is found in another new publication, a magazine called *Natural Jewish Parenting*. This publication is geared to young parents who are concerned about ecological and religious criteria for pregnancy, childbirth, and childrearing—a kind of eco-Orthodox *Parent's Magazine*. The cover of the premier issue—"B"H. Fall 1996/5757. No. 1"—features an appealing picture of the editor's toddler and a sampling of article subjects: "A Natural Foods Shabbat," "Disability's Hidden Gifts," "Fathers and Childbirth," "Spirituality and Nursing." In an opening "Editor's Note" entitled, "Transcending Ourselves," the editor shares her goals with readers:

> My hope is that *Natural Jewish Parenting* will help to increase awareness and appreciation of a holistic approach to living that is fully integrated with Jewish values. . . . I hope that *Natural Jewish Parenting* will, in some small way, help to strengthen Jewish families and inspire us to raise our children with a commitment to their total health and well-being—physical, emotional, and spiritual. And may they grow up in a world where Jews of all types transcend their perceived limitations and their individual differences, and join together with a commitment to the ultimate goal: their perfection of ourselves and our world, with the coming of Moshaich.

In the pages of the magazine, women are urged to nurse their babies well into toddlerhood, and men are urged to participate with their wives in natural childbirth and unmedicated deliveries. In the exploration of each section, both halakhic and psycho-social issues are considered. Looking at "Husbands in the Delivery Room?" author Yehudah Hoffman, a married "technical writer" with two children, suggests:

> If a couple plans to have the father present in the delivery room, they should first familiarize themselves with the *halachos* (laws) of *Niddah* as they pertain to

childbirth. Consult a *Rav* (qualified religious authority) to help you determine how much physical support the husband may provide during the early and later stages of labor and delivery. You should be aware that some authorities hold that a husband should not be in the room during delivery. In general, once a woman is past the early stages of labor, a *mechitza* (divider) should be used if the husband is present, but individual circumstances vary. YR

Much of the focus in *Natural Jewish Parenting* is on the intricacies of "The Kosher/Organic Lifestyle." On the closing page, the conflicts between the standards of health and kashruth are explored, and readers are urged to consistently evaluate food choices on the bases of ecological responsibility and Jewish tradition.

Outmarriage and the American Dream

American-Jewish lifestyles have clearly undergone dramatically overt and subtle changes over the past several decades. No change has excited more commentary from scholars, Jewish professionals, lay leaders, and mainstream American Jews than the seemingly inexorable rise of rates of outmarriage. The percentage of Jewish households including one Jewish and one non-Jewish spouse has escalated from about 7 percent in the 1950s to about half of first marriages conducted in the 1980s. While scholars working with data from the 1990 National Jewish Population Survey have argued as to whether the percentage of recent first marriages that are outmarriages is closer to 40 percent or 50 percent, the trends are clear. Rates of outmarriage for second marriages are considerably higher, and with increasing rates of divorce among Jews these mixed marriages increase outmarriage figures. The results of the 1990 NJPS startled the American-Jewish community into a reassessment of itself, as it revealed that well over one-third of Jews who married during the years 1985–1990 had married a non-Jew, and over one-half of children of at least one Jewish parent were not being raised as Jews.

However, contemporary patterns of outmarriage are instructive, since outmarriage no longer functions as a ticket to socio-economic advancement and upward status movement as it did decades ago. It may seem ironic that under these conditions the rates of outmarriage are far higher than they were when marrying a non-Jew positively benefited one's chances in life. Outmarriage among Jews must be put in the context of outmarriage among the general American population. Compared to other white ethnic Americans and compared to Americans of Asian heritage, Jews have a comparatively lower outmarriage rate.

High rates of outmarriage themselves are testimony to the Americanization of the Jewish population: in a culture that emphasizes the autonomy of the individual, the epitome of individualism is romantic choice. From childhood onward, American children are indoctrinated with motifs of romantic individualism. Even Disney creations such as "The Little Mermaid," promulgate romantic attraction rather than loyalty to family and community; Ariel, the sea king's daughter, gives up not only the glorious diversity of her father's kingdom "under the sea" and even her own beauti-

Not to be a yenta, but aren't these conversational!

(Center) Loved this dress – had to put it in the book! This is an all year round item, appropriate for almost any event. 100% Cotton. Machine washable. Color as shown. Sizes S, M, L: Item No. D171 $98. 1X, 2X, 3X: Item No. D172 $110.

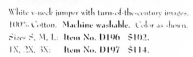

White v-neck jumper with turn-of-the-century images. 100% Cotton. Machine washable. Color as shown. Sizes S, M, L: Item No. D196 $102. 1X, 2X, 3X: Item No. D197 $114.

Mock neck poorboy sold separately (see page 23).

CONVERSATIONAL

From Biel Bonne, a retro look in rich tones. But it gets better, it's machine washable! 100% cotton & 100% linen pieced. Shown in Cocoa, also available in Taupe, or Ecru. Sizes 4-12. Item No. D125 $152.

Figure 6.1 **CULTURAL ARTIFACTS ILLUSTRATE COALESCENCE AMONG YOUNG ORTHODOX JEWS.** *ANY WEAR YOU'RE FRUM: FASHIONABLE MODEST ATTIRE* (DIRECT MAIL, OCTOBER 1996).

She plants a vineyard with the fruit of her labors.

Telephone Print

(left) As easy as a stroll through the park, Autumn Moon's drop waist **washable rayon dress**. Shown in Black & Ivory Piano print. One size fits most.
Item No. D191   **$140.**

(right) Fun for under denim, a striped tee... one of three separates we've put together to create a contemporary look. A Lycra blend you won't want to take off once you slip it on. Dry clean only. Shown in Black & White, also available in Taupe/White and Red/White.   *See page 23.* Sizes S,M,L.
Item No. T153   **$56.**

A crinkle Rayon button front straight yet generous skirt. 100% Rayon. **Machine washable**, gentle cycle, twist dry. Shown in Black and White Floral, also available in a charming telephone print. Sizes S,M,L.
Item No. K171   **$66.**

Matching tichel for skirt, 40" x 9". Available in both prints.
Item No. G150   **$18.**

Adorable denim vest to pull it all together (can be worn with almost any skirt we have. **Machine washable**. Sizes S,M,L.
Item No. G110   **$22.**

A little comfort while we work, Barbara Lesser's **100% Cotton fleece** top with **100% Rayon** crinkle bottom. Machine washable. Shown in Birch *(left)* and Black *(above)*. Sizes S,M,L.
Item No. D131   **$140.**

discussion with your OB/GYN and the head obstetrical nurse of your hospital (if you should choose to give birth in a hospital).

We went over every point of our plan with our doctor. The opening paragraph expressed our faith in him and that his judgment would be followed in case of an emergency if there is no time for discussion. (There usually *is* time for brief discussion when complications arise, but the mother is often too exhausted to represent herself. She needs an advocate!) Our birth plan then went through all the routine things we wished to avoid, among them: intravenous fluids (the IV inhibits mother from walking around and thereby slows down labor); episiotomy (research does not support its routine use in first time mothers); pitocin (it causes unnaturally strong and painful contractions); epidural (dangerous to the mother and slows labor). Epidurals and pitocin tend to go together; the former slows the labor so the latter has to be used to get it going again. Why not skip the whole routine? (See Dr. Sears' book and many others for balanced, factual presentations of all of these procedures. Each has its place when necessary; none is valuable on a *routine* basis or for the convenience of the doctor or hospital.)

The head nurse also went over our birth plan in full detail. She appreciated our interest in doing the best for mother and baby. She explained that it was a challenge to balance the wishes of each individual patient with the need to service the large number of patients passing through her department. While she could offer only minimal verbal support, our visit with her may have been the key to the level of cooperation we received when the time came. (When I stopped by the maternity wing a week before the due date, one of the nurses

pointed to our birth plan hanging conspicuously at the nurses' station. It stayed there until our daughter was at least three months old!)

When we arrived at the hospital we immediately faced our first hostile native, a scratchy old nurse fully prepared to push me out of the way and start poking my wife with hospital routine while babbling about her liability: "If anything were to happen..." I wanted to throw her into a labor pool, but none was to be found in our high-volume, Brooklyn hospital. Fortunately, before I had a chance to take any action, our well-prepared head nurse looked in and said, "Would you like me to replace your nurse?" I nodded and that was the last we saw of her. She was soon replaced by a very helpful nurse wearing a bright red shaitel and a much better attitude. Kind as she was in keeping the bed clean and mopping Helaine's brow, the nurse understood that the birth was Helaine's task and she served her well by staying out of the way.

We had known for weeks that the baby was in the posterior position—head down, but facing mother's belly instead of her back. Our preparation, therefore, included some research on how best to deal with this. Our doctor was conscientious in performing his duties, but over the years the medical profession in general has moved

away from its proper role as health *educators* and it is now incumbent on the parents—both of them—to learn all they can and ask questions of whomever has the knowledge and experience to answer them. We had learned that a posterior birth is no different or more threatening than any other. It just takes longer in the pushing stage.

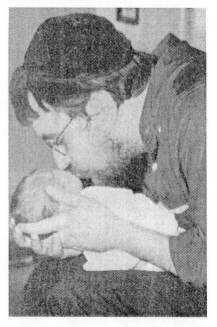

(That's easy for me to say. Giving birth to our daughter took four hours of my powerful wife's pushing, an Olympic performance that no man could have come close to achieving.)

Helaine had several things going for her. First, she had prepared her body by exercising, using a wonderfully designed (if inanely titled) videotape, *Buns of Steel 8: Pregnancy Workout*, by Madeleine Lewis. These exercises took away the back pain she had started to

Figure 6.2 NATURAL JEWISH PARENTING, PREMIERE ISSUE. B"H. FALL 1996/5757, NO. 1

experience in the second trimester. Posterior birth typically leads to back labor, which Helaine completely avoided by preparing herself with these exercises daily.

Second, she had learned the best positions in which to push. Initially, she was lying on her back as the doctor and nurse pressed against her feet. When the doctor went out to catch up on TV with the other miracle workers in the physicians' lounge, she switched to squatting without any assistance from anyone. Big improvement.

Third, she had me to fend off the offers for a variety of medical diagnostic tools and interventions. After three hours of pushing, contractions became less effective; i.e., they came one on top of another, not allowing her any rest, but each one was small and ineffective. Our one mistake may have been not continuing to drink juice throughout this period. I gave in to the doctor's second request to insert an IV when he promised that it was only for glucose water, which, as he suggested, did give her a little more energy to finish the job. A glass of mango juice would probably have been even more effective, and less invasive.

Following a final effort of pushing assisted by the doctor's applying fundal pressure (a low-tech measure, most likely invented by

the Flintstones, in which the doctor presses with all his might on the mother's belly as she pushes), our daughter, Shoshana, was born. This was the moment when a mother's love, having been put to the test during childbirth, is fulfilled with the joy of her life.

About ten minutes before the birth, the attending pediatrician had tripped over the external monitor cord, sending the monitor hurtling across the delivery room. The anesthesiologist blurted out, "Doctor, if you would have done an episiotomy, the baby would have been out long ago." I doubt it. Helaine is also a lot happier to have one unnoticeable stitch instead of a cut that may have hurt for considerably longer.

My wife had succeeded by her own wisdom and effort. She had learned to go beyond the pain instead of enduring it like a righteous victim. Shoshana was born fresh and natural, without the influence of powerful drugs—a good first step in learning to take command of her life with faith in her own strength and Hashem's guidance. And I, the father, who could have been in my own busy world for nine months, would have missed the opportunity to be an advocate, a defender of my family, and a participant in Hashem's miracle of creation. ✍

Yehudah Hoffman is a technical writer, Windows Help file author, and web site designer. He lives in New York with his wife and daughter.

KOSHER & HEALTHY

In a perfect world, all kosher food would be healthy, and all healthy food would be kosher! But in the real world, we all know that this just isn't so. We have all had the experience of walking down the aisle of a natural foods store and seeing a product that we know "*should* be kosher!" Likewise, we are often stuck compromising our health standards when the only kosher option available contains ingredients or additives we wish weren't there. ✍ What can we do? Well, let's find out. In each issue of *Natural Jewish Parenting* we will present three products or product categories: the first of which is kosher, but in some way lacking in the good-for-you department; the second of which is healthy and potentially a great asset to the kosher consumer's kitchen—except that it is not certified kosher; and the third, a kosher and healthy product we are pleased to recommend. ✍ We will provide the companies' addresses, and, when possible, customer service numbers, and we encourage you to make your opinions known by writing a letter (preferably) and/or calling the company. We'd love to hear about any replies you receive, and we'll publish the news of any positive developments. ✍ Which products do you think should be listed here? Send your suggestions to "Kosher and Healthy," *Natural Jewish Parenting*, 173 Speedwell Ave., Suite 127, Morristown, New Jersey 07960 (or e-mail to NJPmail@aol.com). ✍

KOSHER, BUT...

It would be nice to be able to recommend **Rokeach**'s line of 100% vegetarian, ready-to-serve soups as an easy and tasty way to grab a nutritious meal. They do taste good, but with their added sugar, artificial flavor and color, MSG, and extremely high salt content, these aren't soups we can afford to stock up on. Someone needs to let them know what vegetarians (and other health-conscious people) want— and don't want—in their soup.
Rokeach Foods
Newark, NJ 07105

HEALTHY, BUT...

Since they have a monopoly (for the moment) on the organic baby food market, it seems almost shameful that **Earth's Best Baby Food** isn't kosher. Maybe all they need is to know we kosher/organic parents are out here! Drop them a line and tell them we exist.
Earth's Best, Inc.
Boulder, CO 80301
(800) 442-4221

KOSHER & HEALTHY!

Lightlife's meatless Lightburgers, SmartDeli slices (try bologna), and SmartDogs are more-than-reasonable facsimiles of the "real thing." (Of these, Lightburgers stand up best on their own; the others are awfully convincing when dressed up with condiments in a sandwich.) If you haven't already, try them and then let Lightlife know what you think!
Lightlife Foods, Inc.
Greenfield, MA 01302
(800) 274-6001

Figure 6.3 **NATURAL JEWISH PARENTING, PREMIER ISSUE, B"H. FALL 1996/5757, NO. 1**

ful voice to be "part of his world," part of the human world of her conventionally handsome prince charming. From Bambi and Thumper and the forest creatures on upward, the American birthright is the right to make erotic life choices individualistically and freely. The person who would interfere with that right is viewed as the "Grinch Who Stole Christmas."

In a cultural environment that views interethnic relationships positively, the likelihood of outmarriage is deeply affected by familial attitudes. For some American Jews, assimilation is the family tradition, sanctified by generations. It is their American-Jewish heritage to live in an area where there are some Jews (but not too many), to affiliate with organizations that are Jewish (but not too Jewish), and to have friends of many types, although perhaps very secretly preferring the company of Jews. As one Florida grandmother lamented the fate of her children:

> My sons both married non-Jewish women, and their children are being brought up in homes with no Jewishness. My daughter, on the other hand, married a Jew, and they have now left the Reform temple and have joined a Conservative temple so her children can go to the Conservative school. I am very upset about my daughter. She came to me two weeks ago and said, "Mom, we're going kosher." Can you imagine? When I think of my mother and her sisters—their hair, and their clothing—all they wanted was to look American and to be American. If she knew that her granddaughter was going to make her home kosher, she'd be so upset.

In the area of romantic and marital choices, as in other aspects of American-Jewish lifestyles among younger American Jews, Jewish education is a key factor. Formal Jewish education such as supplementary afternoon school or day school which extends over the elementary and high school years has a positive link with the propensity to marry a Jewish mate, to establish a Jewish household, and to raise Jewish children. Among Jewish adults ages 25 to 44, only one-third of those who received no Jewish education married Jews; among those who received six or more years of supplementary school education, over half married Jews; among those who received six years of day school, 80 percent, and those who received nine or more years 91, percent married Jews. The apparent impact of Jewish education persisted even when denomination of parental home was factored out.[22]

Households that choose to affiliate with synagogues of any type are much less likely to involve an outmarriage than non-affiliated households within the same denomination. Thus, among NJPS respondents identifying as Orthodox, 3 percent of those currently synagogue members were outmarried, compared to 17 percent of nonmembers; among Conservative respondents, outmarriage rates were 6 percent members compared to 36 percent nonmembers; among Reform respondents, outmarriage rates were 17 percent members compared to 49 percent nonmembers.[23] The causes of this disparity between members and nonmembers probably run both ways: more synagogue-oriented individuals are less likely to date and marry non-Jews, but synagogues may also be perceived as inhospitable to outmarried households.

As Peter Medding has pointed out, children who grow up in mixed married households are likely to grow up with a unique form of compartmentalization: a seg-mented religious identity.[24] That is, they believe their religious identity to include Ju-daism and something else, such as partly Jewish and partly Italian Catholic. The fact that the religious component of their ethnicity is divided into two or more parts cre-ates a qualitative difference, especially for marginally active groups within the popu-lation for whom Jewish religious identity often meant something along the lines of, "I am Jewish because I am not a Christian." Moreover, in a country that celebrates ethnic options, a person with segmented identity possesses the ultimate in American ethnic options.

For American Jews, who face a potentially shrinking Jewish population due to the complementary forces of assimilation into an open society, a low birthrate, and in-termarriage, concerns about the religious identity of children raised in Jewish homes are significant. Intermarriage between Jews and non-Jews, once rare, is now common-place, as the above figures indicate. This change in the underlying social and religious structure of the American-Jewish community has important implications for the pres-ent and future state of that community. The presence of numerous non-Jews in Jew-ish households is in one way a kind of victory, indicating as it does the successful in-tegration of Jews into American society, and their achievement of a high level of social acceptance. However, the presence of not only Jewish and non-Jewish persons, but of Jewish and non-Jewish religions and cultures within the home base worries many in the Jewish community. Their concern is not about biological "mixtures," but about the dual identity of Jewish children and the dissolution of cultural distinctiveness.[25]

Adding to these concerns are the facts that among younger American Jews rates of outmarriage rise and rates of conversion fall. Within those households in which Jews live, a growing proportion of non-Jews reside in the under age 45 adult popula-tion. Almost one-third of Jews who married out in the 1970s have spouses who con-verted into Judaism at some point in their relationship, a level that falls dramatically among persons who married in the 1980s. Whatever the causative factors, the "bot-tom line" is that Jewish households today are more likely to include non-Jews as fam-ily members than at any time in recent Jewish history. Robert Bellah and other social scientists have suggested that such a family constellation, in which the emotional and cultural boundaries between Jew and non-Jew have lost their power, is far more likely to produce children who have an ambiguous identity.[26]

In many ways, the factors surrounding the phenomenon of non-Jews living in Jewish households have changed from decade to decade. The educational, occupa-tional, and income levels of the Jewish partner are salient today in the opposite way from the way they were salient earlier. In the 1950s and 1960s, when Jews married out, they were likely to be the most highly educated, highly placed professionally, and affluent individuals. Marrying out was one way up the ladder of social mobility. To-day, the opposite is true. Jews are currently among the most highly educated, affluent, professional Americans. Jews who marry non-Jews are likely to be less educated, less professional, and less affluent as a group than Jews who marry other Jews. However, romantic choice still carries the enormous emotional valence of control over one's own individual destiny. In the climate of American values, insisting on the social ramifications of personal choices is difficult at best.

The high rates of intermarriage but low rates of conversion are of concern to many American Jews because within outmarried households connections to Jews and Judaism are much weaker than they are in inmarried households. Children growing up in outmarried households are less than half as likely as children in inmarried households to receive formal Jewish education. Rates of home-based rituals, organizational affilation, and Israel trips are all strikingly lower in outmarried households. In conversionary households, in contrast, most aspects of Jewish identification are very similar to those in inmarried households. Thus, the difference between households at present seems to lie not in whether both spouses were born Jewish, but in whether they currently identify themselves as Jews.

Individualism, Jewish Households, and "Jewish Family Values"

Many contemporary American-Jewish parents express their Jewish commitments primarily by channeling them into providing their children with "Jewish values." National Commission focus-group participants seemed to have incorporated some of the energy, activism, and self-confidence of their work lives into their Jewish parenting roles as well, seeing transmission of Jewish values as their "job." Jewish mothers frequently described themselves as being transmitters and interpreters of Judaism to their children, and it is to this role as cultural interpreters and transmitters that they feel the most passionate attachment. These commitments to Jewish parenting can be viewed as a very positive indicator of continuity. However, the opposite interpretation is possible as well: if American Judaism is primarily a pediatric phenomenon, what happens to parents Jewishly when their children leave home, and what happens to the growing population of Jewish nonparents?

For many adults, Judaism does not become a significant aspect of their lives until their children are born. As one mother talked about this life cycle impact, "After I had children, I had a different sense of responsibility about my Judaism. It was very important that they had a strong sense about being Jewish." Another woman, a mother of young children stated, "I try to teach them values and ethics. They know how important it is to us. They are picking up on that between tradition and teaching. They are getting it, and there is a sense of love that I see growing in them." Many focus-group participants agreed with the woman who consciously teaches her children both formally and by example:

> It really revolves around holidays and tradition. We are not a particularly observant family, but by the same token everyone is observant in terms of holidays and traditions and things that everyone did when they were growing up ... every time we get to another major holiday we explain what it is about and what is going on and why we do certain things. I think to my oldest at this point it is more storytelling than anything else. I don't think he knows yet what religion is.

Another woman, who said that she keeps a kosher home "so my grandmother can eat at my house and feel comfortable" and lights candles on Friday night "before we go out," explained that, for her, family, morality, and charitable giving are the cornerstones of her Jewish identity: "Your giving, charity, just the moral issues that go along with it are more what I identify with than the religious aspect. I am not very religious. I can't quite believe that there is really someone up there that's making decisions as to whether you are here next year or not."

Mothers described themselves as being concerned that their children should experience a very positive version of Judaism, and should not be alienated by a version of Judaism that appears too rigid or demanding. Many spoke about a process of editing Judaism which they engage in so that their children are "exposed" only to those aspects of Judaism that their mothers deem attractive and appealing. One mother said,

> I only do the positive things that are fun and relate to kids and sort of build memories. The Hanukkah candles are important, Purim is important, just the things that you touch, that you do. The blessings. My kids started at a very early age and I hope that it will stay with them. It is all the positive stuff. The fun stuff. My Judaism relates to children. My focus is always children.

For most, the American values of emotional health and self-esteem, blended with ethnic pride, have completely replaced more traditional Jewish values of knowledge, piety, or deep belief. As one woman said,

> I feel very positively about being Jewish and that is something that I would like my children to feel. But in terms of Hebrew school, my main goal is for my children to view themselves as Jewish, not necessarily to learn that much about Judaism per se or religion per se. It really wouldn't bother me if they become nonbelievers in God, if they feel good about themselves as Jewish people.

When American Jews make the decisions that shape their lives and the lives of others, few of them presumably focus consciously and directly on the balancing act presented by the secular and Jewish pieces of their lives. And yet it is in the realm of personal choices and changing patterns of family formation that the coalescence of Jewish and secularized American Protestant values have had the most sweeping impact on the lives of American-Jewish men and women.

Table 6.1 Raised and Current Denominations of American Jews

Denomination	Current	Raised
Orthodox	6	27
Conservative	35	34
Reform	38	26
Reconstructionist	1	—
Just Jewish	10	7

Source: 1990 NJPS data. Adapted from Sidney Goldstein, *Profile of American Jewry*, pp. 170–171. Percentages have been rounded.

Table 6.2 Current Denominations of Born Jews
Percentages by Denomination Raised

Raised	Current Denomination				
	Orthodox	Conservative	Reform	Recon.	Just Jewish
Orthodox	89	32	12	17	16
Conservative	5	60	26	44	18
Reform	—	4	59	14	15
Reconstructionist	—	—	17	—	—
Just Jewish	5	2	2	6	47
Non-Jewish	1	2	1	2	5
Total Percent	100	100	100	100	100

Source: 1990 NJPS data. Adapted from Goldstein, pp. 170–71. Percentages have been rounded.

Table 6.3 Ritual Practices of American Jews
Percentages Answering Always, Usually, or Yes

Practice	Percent of Jews Consistently Performing Practice
Attend Passover Seder	62
Light Hanukah Candles	60
Fast on Yom Kippur	49
Light Sabbath Candles	17
Home Kosher / 2 Sets of Dishes	13

Source: 1990 NJPS data. Percentages have been rounded.

Table 6.4 Current Religious Identification of Born Jews
Percentages by Age

Ages of Individuals	Currently Jewish	Currently Something Else
0–5	97	3
6–9	98	2
10–13	100	0
14–17	95	5
18–24	94	6
25–34	91	9
35–44	89	11
45–54	92	8
55–64	91	9
65+	94	6

Source: 1990 NJPS Data. Percentages have been rounded.

Table 6.5 **Current Religious Identification of Persons Who Were Born Non-Jews Living in Survey Households Percentages by Age**

Ages of Individuals	Currently Jewish	Currently Something Else
0–5	1	99
6–9	2	98
10–13	3	97
14–17	3	97
18–24	3	97
25–34	7	93
35–44	12	87
45–54	14	86
55–64	11	89
65+	7	93

Source: 1990 NJPS Data. Percentages have been rounded.

Table 6.6 **Sabbath Observances in 1990 NJPS Households Percentages Lighting Candles, Not Handling Money by Age and Denomination**

Respondent Age	Denomination			
	Orthodox	Conservative	Reform	Reconstructionist*
30–49				
Lights Sabbath Candles	66	21	8	15
Doesn't Handle Money	70	13	6	9
50–64				
Lights Sabbath Candles	58	27	4	54
Doesn't Handle Money	55	9	5	0
65–74				
Lights Sabbath Candles	37	25	17	—
Doesn't Handle Money	49	9	3	—

Source: 1990 NJPS data, all respondents reporting denomination. Percentages have been rounded.

*Small cells throughout.

SEVEN

PROFILING JEWISH ORGANIZATIONAL CONNECTIONS

Communalism as Covenant

Institutional vitality is a burning practical issue in contemporary American-Jewish life. Numerous organizations are engaged in self-evaluation and redefinition, as they attempt to meet new challenges, such as attracting and retaining members, volunteers, and philanthropists in order to maintain established infrastructures and programs. In addition to internal institutional anxiety, Jewish organizational participation is currently a crucial concern not only for the institutions involved, but for the entire Jewish community, for several reasons.

First, American-Jewish institutions and organizations provide the contexts for personal, familial, and communal Jewish activities that facilitate Jewish connectedness among individuals and social groups. In the American environment, religious and secular Jewish communal institutions are for many individuals and families the primary context in which Jewish identification is tangibly expressed. Second, Jewish secular institutions provide an arena for Jews who describe themselves as nonreligious to express their Jewish connections. Not least, members of and volunteers for Jewish organizations have higher levels of Jewish activism and involvement in other areas of Jewish life as well, and a process of mutual reinforcement may be at work.

American Jews behave very similarly to other Americans vis-à-vis their voluntaristic behavior, according to data from the 1990 National Jewish Population Survey. About half of both Jewish men (48 percent) and women (51 percent) and non-Jewish American men (50 percent) and women (53 percent) volunteer some time for good works. As seen in Table 7.1, Jewish men and women are each twice as likely to volunteer time for non-Jewish causes (40 percent and 39 percent, respectively) as for Jewish causes (17 percent and 23 percent, respectively). Moreover, Jews volunteer less time per week (about three hours on average) than non-Jews (more than four hours).[1] Slightly over one-third of American Jews are currently paying dues to a synagogue (although most Jews will or did belong at some point in their lives), only about one-fifth are actively involved in Jewish organizations, and, contrary to popular impressions, about one in ten belong to a Jewish Community Center, far fewer than to synagogues.

The current paucity of Jewish institutional involvement among American Jews is most striking when compared with the mutual interdependence of Jews and their communal representatives and institutions in historical Jewish communities, and even when compared with American-Jewish life earlier in the twentieth century, when Jew-

ish organizations became very central to personal Jewish identification and group social cohesion.

Traditional Jewish Communal Patterns

In traditional Jewish communities, communal concerns were historically intertwined
with the daily activities of Jewish individuals, families, and societies. Communal responsibility was sacralized through a dense network of laws. From biblical law onward, Jewish codes aimed to provide safety nets for the most vulnerable members of
society, dictating, for example, that the corners of grain fields be left for widows, or-
phans, and impoverished persons, and that a coat taken as collateral for a loan be returned to its debtor-owner with the onset of cold weather. Some biblical laws dealt
with public safety: the owner of a building with a flat, walk-on roof was required to
fence it so that no one would tumble off and injure themselves. In addition, rabbinic
law, the *halakhah*, mandated that Jews take responsibility for creating and maintaining such communal institutions as cemeteries, ritual baths, synagogues, and study
houses. Each religious holiday provided specialized occasions for *tzeddakah*, fund-raising for the poor, so that indigent members of the community could purchase the appropriate foods and accoutrements. Life cycle events also evoked religious laws which
made members of the community responsible for facilitating and enhancing individual and familial moments of joy and grief: divine approval was thought to rest on those
who attended the *brit milah* (circumcision ceremonies), collected dowries to enable
the marriages of poor, young women and danced entertainingly before the bride
(*hakhnasat kallah*), washed and prepared deceased Jews for burial (*khevrah kaddishah*),
and comforted the bereaved during their mourning period (*menakhem avel*).

In the immediate post-Exilic period, the centrality of the synagogue and the importance of Jewish communal autonomy emerged as durable organizational factors in
Jewish life. The synagogue and study hall were the hallmark, male-oriented communal institutions of most traditional Jewish societies. Within Jewish societies' clear gender-role definitions, men were strongly encouraged to participate in group prayer and
devote as much time to study of sacred texts as possible on a regular basis. In contrast,
women's spiritual expressions were primarily home based, and their roles in public
religious arenas were usually marginal or enabling—creating or purchasing decorative
coverings for tables, lecterns, and Torah scrolls, participating in adjunct women's
prayer groups, and in some oriental communities (*aidot hamizrach*) cleaning the area
around the ark. The impetus for group worship was reinforced by the fact that rabbinic law forbade the recitation of many central parts of the worship service unless the
requisite quorum of ten men (*minyan*) was present. In many communities, women
were also expected to attend worship services on Sabbaths and holidays, especially to
hear the public readings of particular sacred texts which had been identified as incumbent upon all members of the community.[2]

Communal activities and influence were reinforced by the geographic proximity and population density that were typical of Jewish societies. Partially because all
transportation but walking was prohibited on Sabbaths and many holidays that stud-

ded the Jewish year—and even walking was not to exceed a specific distance on some holy days—Jews tended to live close to each other and their communal institutions. In addition to this voluntary physical togetherness, boundaries imposed externally by antisemitic edicts often reinforced physical togetherness, and thus gave local Jewish societies additional formal and informal control over the lives of individuals.

Over centuries of Diaspora existence, diverse Jewish communal leadership roles were institutionalized.[3] In small communities a single person might manage many tasks, but in larger communities roles were divided, often with an elaborate pecking order of clearly defined and named functions. Some leadership tasks were primarily nonreligious, such as tax collection, and some were invested with religious authority. Among the most critical personages in larger towns was the *shtadlan*, a regional representative or negotiator upon whom the welfare of the Jewish community depended; the *shtadlan*'s success—and the fate of his Jewish community—were directly linked to his sophistication, resourcefulness, and skills at pleading/negotiating with the princes and potentates who comprised the non-Jewish governments in the areas where Jews were (more or less) tolerated, usually without any intrinsic rights. The authority of communal (but often impoverished) rabbis grew slowly during the middle ages, and some rabbinic leaders began to specialize in particular activities, such as Jewish civil law, ritual law, or homiletics. The Jewish communal court composed of rabbis (*beit din*) adjudicated religious, familial, and communal issues; however, in many communities Jews turned to non-Jewish courts as a last resort. Records of Jewish presence in non-Jewish courtrooms provide rich historical materials for contemporary scholars.

In some locations and historical periods, Jewish communal organizations were government controlled and centralized, with one organization for each Jewish settlement; many communities had a community board, or *kahal*. In other areas authority structures tended to be congregational, rather than citywide. Relationships between communal leaders and the populations they represented and controlled varied widely and shifted over time. Many communities functioned through socio-economic stratification, in which only established personages took part in the process of choosing or advising leaders. Local Jewish communal leaders were charged with collecting taxes and fees, and, in some pre-emancipation locales, with providing Jewish youths for military conscription. The power (and sometimes abuse of power) wielded by some Jewish leaders as they engaged in these tasks exacerbated lower-class Jewish perceptions of internal inequities.[4]

The official and unofficial authority and power of Jewish communal institutions were gradually and unevenly eroded during the eighteenth and nineteenth centuries through intersecting forces of modern social change. Jewish populations tended to shift from the social and religious authority of tightly knit villages to larger and more anonymous urban areas. The religious iconoclasm of *haskalah* (Jewish Enlightenment) thinkers fanned the flames of resentment of Jewish lower classes against the perceived imperiousness and unfairness of Jewish oligarchies. In some countries, political emancipation seemed to promise that diminished Jewish distinctiveness would lead to complete Jewish enfranchisement. The hegemony of Jewish educational institutions gave way as Jews started being admitted into non-Jewish schools and universities. Not least, the influence of communal religious authorities declined as individualism and secularist movements, such as socialism, nationalism, and Zionism gained a hold in the minds of many young Jews.

Whatever hold traditional Jewish communal institutions retained over individual Jewish lives was physically terminated for many immigrants in the passage to America. On American shores, Jewish communal institutions and the relationship of individuals and families to communal authority were reinvented in ways that echoed Jewish traditional patterns in some ways and diverged from them in others. Perhaps most significant, as American Jews acculturated and were accepted into the socio-economic structure of mainstream American communities, it became clear that Jewish communal associations would be purely voluntary. Jewish communal institutions and authorities would have few means of imposing their will—or even communal participation—upon Jews in the United States.[5] American-Jewish organizations, like American Jews, adapted to the voluntaristic nature of American religious life.

American Jewish Men and Women and Their Organizations

In twentieth-century America, the sacramental nature of Jewish communal affiliations was transformed. In the minds of many American Jews, communal activities became the primary expression of covenantal identification. For some men, the synagogue continued to be a compelling communal structure; regular synagogue worship provided spiritual and social outlets, and gave participants a feeling of solidarity with the Jewish people and its destiny. For others, putatively nonreligious Jewish organizations were more appealing. Jonathan Woocher elegantly describes the secularized notion of *Sacred Survival,* which flourished for decades among Jewish communal activists who believed that "problems of theology are somewhat irrelevant," and that the group identification and cohesiveness of the Jewish people would be maintained "through voluntary community, through loyalty to Israel, through the recognition that Jewish unity transcends nationality and opinion."[6] As Woocher articulates the official core belief that animated many American-Jewish institutions:

> Jewish unity, expressed in the commitment to Jewish continuity, is a signal to the world that Jews will not abandon their self-definition as a distinctive people. It is a basis of strength in the struggle for self-perpetuation. . . . Jewish community is the vehicle through which the abstract principle of Jewish unity and the values which that unity enshrines are made manifest in contemporary Jewish life. . . . The polity has to accept responsibility for the spiritual, as well as the physical, well-being of Jews throughout the world."[7]

For Jewish women, organizational activism provided arenas both for accomplishing Americanization and expressing their Jewishness. American Christian middle-class society had characteristically approved of women who devoted themselves to domestic tasks and communal good works, including church-related communal activities. American-Jewish women for many decades viewed Jewish voluntarism as "their" Jewish activity, analogous in some ways to the public religious roles of groups of Jewish men in the synagogue and parallel to the activism in prestigious church-related activities.

Throughout the first half of the twentieth century, distinctively American communal organizations were formed that reflected the needs of both volunteers\philanthropists and client populations. While a complete listing of such organizations is outside the focus of this discussion, a brief summary of the types of Jewish organizations that developed indicates the impressive scope and range of American-Jewish interests that have been expressed through organizational life. Daniel Elazar categorizes the Jewish organizational world within several overarching mandates, although there is overlap between groups and many organizations fit into more than one category: *Communal welfare* is funded and overseen by Jewish federations and by their national leadership group, the United Jewish Communities (UJC), formerly the Council of Jewish Federations (CJF), and provided by constituent local and national social service agencies (Jewish Family and Children's Services, Jewish Vocational Services, Jewish Hospitals, etc.), as well as by the Jewish Community Centers Association (JCCA), B'nai B'rith lodges and projects, and United Hebrew Immigrant Aid Society (HIAS), among others. The *community relations* category includes both umbrella organizations such as the Jewish Council for Public Affairs (JCPA) and Jewish Community Relations Councils or Committees (JCRC), and more targeted organizations such as the Anti-Defamation League (ADL), American Jewish Committee, American Jewish Congress, the National Council of Jewish Women (NCJW), the Simon Wiesenthal Center, the Holocaust Museum in Washington, D.C., and the World Jewish Congress, among others. Support for *Israel and Jews overseas* is the goal of Zionist organizations such as the new UJC, which incorporates the former United Jewish Appeal (UJA). Zionist organizations include the Israel Bonds Association, Jewish National Fund (JNF), Hadassah, Pioneer Women/Na'amat, Organization for Rehabilitation and Training (ORT), the American Israel Public Affairs Committee (AIPAC), the Joint Distribution Committee (JDC), and many others. While many educational activities take place under the rubric of congregational, denominational synagogue life, other *educational and cultural activities* do not have a specifically denominational orientation, and are promoted by organizations such as Jewish colleges, university-level Judaic studies programs and departments, cultural institutions and organizations, and foundations, and scholarly, artistic, and educational associations.[8]

Religious education on the transdenominational level is supported locally by Bureaus of Jewish Education (BJE) and nationally by the Jewish Educational Service of North America (JESNA), the National Center for Jewish Learning and Leadership (CLAL), the Coalition for the Advancement of Jewish Education (CAJE), and foundations that have created programs devoted to educational leadership. Many all-day Jewish schools are organized denominationally and receive guidance from Orthodox, Conservative, or Reform national educational institutions; others are conceived of as transdenominational community schools, and receive primarily local guidance. The *religious/congregational* world is also devoted to Jewish educational goals, in addition to meeting the Jewish spiritual worship and life cycle celebratory needs of its constituents, but is frankly denominational in its organization.

As the decades passed and Americanization proceeded, local and national Jewish organizational activity became the signposts of Jewish commitment and prestige. Given the almost exclusively materialist focus of American Jewish men's daily lives, philanthropy and organizational activities were a good fit for their expressions of religious solidarity. Philanthropy and organizational activism were also the ideal arenas for successful Jewish male entrepreneurs to establish their status in the Jewish worlds in which most of them functioned socially.[9]

Some observers have suggested that Jewish men who sought out leadership positions in the Jewish community may have been influenced by practical necessity as much as by loyalty to the Jewish community. Rather than becoming inconsequential "little fish" in big, cold gentile philanthropic lakes, many materially successful American-Jewish men chose to become "big fish" in the more navigable ponds of Jewish organizational life. Thus, while some successful professionals or business Jewish men in the pre– and post–World War II years might have preferred to use their money and communal activism to position themselves in prestigious non-Jewish philanthropic and communal voluntaristic spheres, overt or subtle antisemitism often excluded Jews from nonsectarian volunteer leadership positions. Herbert J. Gans notes that many such leaders were "lone wolves" in terms of personality and expressed needs.[10] Power and status—rather than social support and conviviality—were the rewards they sought for the gifts of their time and money.

For the rank and file of organizational membership—and for most women, including those who have sought out leadership roles, according to anecdotal reports—voluntarism for Jewish organizations has always served a social function, in addition to whatever religious and communal ideals it represented. As Gans and other observers of middle-class Jews during the middle decades of the twentieth century have noted, Jews found a comfort level with coreligionists which they often did not find with non-Jewish colleagues. Organizations and friendship groups with non-Jews made them feel self-consciously that their words and actions would be perceived as representative of the Jews; as one of Gans's respondents observed (1958), "You can't give vent to your feelings. If you talk to a Christian . . . you feel you are doing it as a Jew. With Jewish friends you can tell 'em point blank what you feel."[11] With non-Jews, they often felt they had to be on their best behavior, so as not to cause antisemitism or to fit into negative antisemitic stereotypes, while with Jews they could relax and be themselves.

American-Jewish organizational life was greatly enhanced by untold millions of hours of free labor and organizational ability, especially that donated by American-Jewish women. Women's Jewish organizations often developed a cultural ambience that was different from that of male-dominated philanthropies. Within women's organizations, hard work and organizational ability were as important as the ability to donate money if women aspired to leadership positions. This culture of earned progression up a leadership ladder was reportedly very fulfilling for many talented, energetic women. From the 1920s through the 1950s, many Jewish women were relatively highly educated; they had fewer children than their gentile cohort; and the majority avoided labor force participation after marriage. They devoted themselves to Jewish organizations with professionalism and passion. Any one Jewish woman often worked for several Jewish organizations or causes. Jewish organizations, for their part, gave women a religiously and culturally approved, non-threatening outlet for their intellectual, organizational, and social energies.

In addition, anecdotal evidence reveals that for many women, meetings and other activities held on behalf of synagogues, Jewish schools, and other Jewish organizations provided a chance to get out of the house and to socialize with like-minded women, as well as to engage in good works. The important role that Jewish organizations played in the social, cultural, and religious lives of women is amply attested to by veteran volunteers, who describe not only hours of hard work but hours of friendship as well, plans mapped out and goals attained, and warm feelings of accomplishment. Even rote tasks such as preparing mailings and labor-intensive tasks such as organizing bake sales and rummage sales could be experienced as enjoyable and worthwhile in such a context.

In addition to differences in organizational culture between men's and women's organizations, Jewish organizational activities have often been perceived by participants as being divided between the "religious" realm of educational and synagogue-related activities, and the non-religious "alphabet soup" world of Jewish organizations. For decades, this perception had some basis in reality. Jews who chose to become active in so-called secular Jewish organizations often had little interest in synagogue life or religious expressions of Jewishness. They found in the secular Jewish organizational world diverse and manifold opportunities for connecting and contributing to American-Jewish life and Jewish communities around the world.

Before the late 1960s, Jewish communal activists often saw in their organizational activities an alternative to religious and synagogal modes of Jewishness. This sacralization of nonreligious organizational activity has sometimes permeated even the synagogue world. Among organizational activists, Jewish men and women who join, work for, and contribute money to congregational Sisterhoods and Brotherhoods and to other Jewish organizations have been perceived as "good" Jews, while those who did not are viewed as apathetic, unaffiliated, or marginal—even though they might be more ritually observant or culturally literate. Especially for those older generations of American Jews who had taken organizational life as their primary form of religious expression, the importance of institutional participation suffused even nominally Orthodox environments.

Current Organizational Involvements

The landscape of contemporary Jewish organizations has been changing in response to internal and external transformations in the lives of American Jews. American Jews today, across age, gender, and socio-economic divisions, are much more likely to donate time and money to non-Jewish causes than to Jewish causes. 1990 NJPS data reveal that Jewish men as a group are more than two and a half times more likely, and Jewish women almost twice as likely to work for non-Jewish causes as for Jewish causes, as seen in Table 7.1. In terms of gender, contemporary American-Jewish men and women volunteer for Jewish causes at very similar rates overall, although women are slightly more likely to volunteer and to volunteer more hours. Jews with higher levels of secular education are slightly more likely to work for Jewish causes and dramatically more likely to work for non-Jewish causes than are those with lower levels of secular education, as Table 7.2 demonstrates. Older Jews are somewhat less likely than younger Jews to volunteer for non-Jewish causes, but they are not much more likely to volunteer for Jewish causes. In terms of hours spent volunteering, more hours are devoted to non-Jewish causes than to Jewish causes.

The current greater likelihood of Jews working for and giving to non-Jewish causes is linked to the fact that external boundaries, which excluded Jews from becoming leaders in high status non-sectarian social, communal, and cultural activities, have virtually disappeared. As a result, individuals who seek voluntaristic and philanthropic activism are not forced to find an outlet in the Jewish communal world. Additionally, today the internal discomfort level, which many American Jews felt when interacting with non-Jews earlier in the twentieth century, has diminished impact on behavior. American-Jewish secular education and occupational status facilitates interactions with the non-Jewish world, and professional life leads today's Jews into involvements with non-Jewish communal good works.

Persons with higher levels of Jewish education are the most likely to volunteer time for Jewish causes. As Table 7.3 shows, men and women who receive the most lengthy and intensive Jewish education which is perceived as the norm within their denomination are much more likely to volunteer for Jewish causes. For Jews who have been raised in Orthodox homes and have received six or more years of day school education, percentages volunteering for Jewish organizations are 54 percent for women and 68 percent for men, compared with only 17 and 16 percent, respectively, for those receiving six or more years of supplementary school education. For Jews raised in Conservative homes, in comparison, those receiving six or more years of supplementary school are the most likely to volunteer, with 54 percent of women and 59 percent of men who had received this level of education volunteering. For Jews raised in Reform families, the "center of gravity" shifts upward still further, with those receiving six or more years of Sunday school education (27 percent and 37 percent, respectively), when added to those receiving three or more years of supplementary school (43 percent and 37 percent respectively) yielding voluntarism rates of 70 percent for women and 74 percent for men. Rates for those receiving minimal amounts of Jewish education were mostly dismal: For those receiving anything less than six years of Sunday school, voluntarism rates were 21 percent and 8 percent for Orthodox women and men, 18 percent and 15 percent for Conservative women and men, and 31 percent and 16 percent for Reform women and men.

Philanthropic Activities and Jewish Profiles

While older activists may still view their activities as secular, younger activists tend to perceive organizational activism as one aspect of religious Jewish connectedness, even spirituality. For example, in the late 1980s at a Federation Women's Division Caucus in the New Jersey suburbs of New York, a young woman stood to declare her yearly pledge with the words:

> My daughter came home from school having learned for the first time about the Holocaust. She asked me, "Mommy, how could it have happened? Where was *Hashem* (lit. "the name," polite euphemism for God in Hebrew) when the Holocaust happened?" I didn't know what to answer my daughter—I don't know where *Hashem* was then, but one thing I do know. When I look around this room at all of you who are working so hard for Jews in America and in Israel, I know that *Hashem* is right here in this room today.

This young woman's religious or spiritual motivation for giving is a very significant clue as to why and which American Jews give money today. The giving patterns of American Jews defy common perceptions of Jews as a people more generous than most; clearly, Jewish philanthropic patterns are undergoing change. Among younger Jews, percentages donating money are lower than those of other Americans, according to Gabriel Berger's study based on the 1990 National Jewish Population Survey.[12] In addition younger American Jews are more likely to give money to general, non-Jewish causes than to Jewish causes, with a steady decline in Jewish giving by age. Among Jews ages 25 to 34, only 44 percent give to Jewish causes, 63 percent give to general causes, and 70 percent give to Jewish and general causes; this compares to 71 percent of Americans donating money.

Younger Jews also give a smaller percentage of their household income to charity than do other Americans. American Jews ages 25 to 34 give one third of one percent of their income to charity—compared to 1.6 percent given by Americans of the same age. Jews ages 35 to 54 give slightly over one-half of one percent, compared to over two percent of income given by all Americans. Giving to Jewish organizations increases more than four times between the age 25 to 34 group and the group ages 75 and over, while giving for non-Jewish organizations increases more than 1.5 times.[13]

Jewish patterns of Jewish philanthropy differ from those of general philanthropy: The relationship between voluntarism and philanthropy is strong when Jews give money to non-Jewish causes, but not when they give money to Jewish causes: a Jew who works for a nonsectarian cause tends to give money to it as well. Second, the relationship between income and philanthropy is direct when Jews give money to non-Jewish causes but not when they give to Jewish causes: a Jew who has more money is incrementally more likely to give more money to non-Jewish causes than one who has less money. In other words, Jewish giving to non-Jewish causes seems to follow intuitive rules of common sense much more directly than Jewish giving to Jewish causes. Jewish giving to Jewish causes seems to be more complicated and harder to predict.[14]

Understanding the link between religious feelings and Jewish philanthropy is helpful in understanding those younger Jews who do decide to give money to Jewish causes. Despite the widespread idea that higher education and careerism have a negative impact on Jewish commitments and communal activities, the 1990 National Jewish Population Study data demonstrate that failure to give money to Jewish philanthropies is not linked to high levels of secular education. As Tables 7.4 and 7.5

demonstrate, individuals with higher levels of secular educational achievement are more, not less, likely to donate money to Jewish causes, and higher levels of Jewish education has a strong positive relationship with likelihood of donating money to Jewish causes.

Table 7.4, which divides respondents by age, secular education, and the simple fact of having or not having formal Jewish education, shows that the Jewish classroom makes a positive difference in almost every category. However, the truly dramatic differences are found once we divide respondents by duration of Jewish education and by age, as seen in Table 7.5. For college graduates, for example, substantial Jewish education made respondents twice as likely as minimal Jewish education to give to Jewish causes: among respondents ages 30 to 49, 33 percent of those with one to three years of Jewish education donated money to Jewish causes, compared to 61 percent of those receiving seven to nine years of Jewish education. Among Jews ages 30 to 49 with graduate or professional degrees, 58 percent who had received one to three years of Jewish education gave money, compared to 77 percent of those who had received seven to nine years of Jewish education.

Jews who give money or volunteer time for Jewish causes today do so by choice, not automatically or by necessity. Rather than two separate worlds, the religious-congregational world overlaps with the educational-cultural, community relations, communal welfare, and Israel-overseas worlds. Especially for those under age 50, when American Jews become involved with Jewish organizations as lay leaders, organizational members, or as Jewish professionals, they are likely to perceive their activities as complementary to religious modes of expression and synagogue involvement. Younger Jews drawn into Jewish "religious" activism and into Jewish "secular" activism are no longer two distinct populations. Instead, a common population of individuals seeking out Jewish behaviors and associations are found in synagogue and organizational spheres.

The sacralization of organizational involvements differs from the twentieth-century American past, with its "sacred survival" psychology, because younger American Jews who get involved with secular-Jewish organizational activities are most likely to be drawn from the ranks of those who also have relatively higher levels of Jewish education. Persons who remain committed to Jewish organizational life today tend to be those who have the strongest Jewish backgrounds and/or the strongest Jewish activist profiles in other ways. 1990 NJPS data corroborates the fact that younger Jews who are involved with Jewish organizations tend to be those who define themselves as Jewish by religion, belong to synagogues, have a higher than average level of ritual observance and a stronger than average profile of Israel connections.[15]

While giving to general causes is clearly affected by income level, giving to Jewish causes does not show a clear pattern, especially at income levels below $80,000 a year. Jewish Americans making $50,000 to $59,000 per year are 10 percent less likely to give to Jewish causes (49 percent) than are Jews making $40,000 to $49,000 per year (59 percent). When looking at giving to general causes, however, Jews, like all Americans, are quite affected by income, with general giving reported by over half of Jews making less than $20,000 and $20,000 to $30,000 per year, two-thirds of Jews making $30,000 to $49,000 per year, three-quarters of Jews making $50,000 to

$79,000 per year, and 87 percent of Jews making over $80,000 per year. For all Americans, percentages of giving show a similar income-related rise from lower to higher incomes.[16] It should be noted that survey participants are more reticent about revealing their incomes levels than about almost any other subject, so reliability in this regard is somewhat more questionable than in other areas.

Berger notes that "the relationship between giving time and money is different in the Jewish and non-Jewish domains." He speculates, "In the non-Jewish realm, to contribute money would lead people to give time, while in the Jewish sphere, the path may follow the opposite direction: volunteering leads people to making contributions to Jewish causes."[17]

The lack of an unambiguous relationship between income and Jewish giving is very important. Giving charity for Jewish causes seems to be more tied to attitudes and habits than directly tied to income. Like voluntarism, philanthropic profiles are closely related to levels of Jewish connectedness. Jewish giving is most related to contemporary factors such as synagogue attendance, having mostly Jewish friendship circles, being married to a Jewish spouse, and volunteering time for Jewish organizations, and by the background factor of having received a substantial Jewish education.

In the case of women's giving, levels of philanthropy may also be affected by the fact that women have historically seen their contributions as "extra" donations over and above family or household gifts. Since they are perceived as supplementary, rather than basic money gifts, they have often been modest; while Jewish women have been quite forthcoming with volunteer time, they have often been more conservative than their family finances might have dictated when it comes to giving money.

Today's Jewish women are getting more secular education and they are working for many more years in much more lucrative jobs than Jewish women did in the past. However, it is not at all clear that contemporary Jewishly committed women working outside the home for pay are equally likely to write out checks of an appropriate size to Jewish causes. This gender gap in philanthropy exists in non-Jewish as well as Jewish organizations. In a *Radcliffe Quarterly* article, Keller Freeman notes that there are critical differences in the ways in which men and women solicit and give money. Among men, says Freeman, "there was a recognition that who made the solicitation call was a matter of paramount importance."

> Something like the dominance hierarchy in a band of mountain gorillas was established so that calls were made peer to peer, or superior to subordinate. . . . This fund raising campaign had a public face. It was robust, confident, assertive. It assumed that individuals and corporations would want to stand up and be counted, counted in bills of large denomination.

Women, on the other hand, were much more likely to "give generously of their time and energy to causes and institutions beyond the circle of the family." However, says Freeman, "they rarely take responsibility for a comparable fiscal generosity," and she wonders how we can "decide to shape a future in which women and men aspire to philanthropic equality. In the present, we might at least continue the questioning begun by Carol Gilligan: Do women have not only a different voice, but also a different philanthropic hand? Some of our gender differences are, of course, essential to the continuation of the human species. Some are desirable contributions to a rich, multivalent society. But some are evidence of women's failure to claim equal philanthropic responsibility." She advises feminists: "It is time for us to come of age; time to exercise our powers of philanthropy; time for us to learn to give at the highest level of our capacity."[18] To the extent that such considerations still hold sway, Jewish communal organizations face the challenge of educating women to be as independent in their gift giving as they are in other aspects of their personal and professional lives.

A Culture of "Machers" Alienates Some Potential Activists

As the National Commission for Jewish Women focus-group research clearly revealed, younger American Jews who choose Jewish communal involvements often assert that they seek out Jewish organizational activities with goals such as building community, finding a sense of social destiny, and participating in a spiritual mission. Some focus-group participants argued that although the demographic realities of potential volunteer and philanthropic populations have changed, many Jewish organizations are still preoccupied with wealthy, older, often Jewishly ignorant *machers* (big shots, powerful persons). These organizations, according to their young adult detractors, are still geared toward the leadership motivations of the "lone wolf" types discussed by Gans, providing the greatest rewards for the biggest givers and putting enormous stress on monetary concerns. Such emphases are not a good match with the motivations and contemporary personal goals of younger Jews who are attracted to volunteer leadership.

Among single urban professionals in Manhattan, for example, many voiced great hostility toward the current Jewish organizational establishment. One woman talked about Jewish organizations repeatedly sending her mail addressed to Mr., rather than Miss or Ms. She felt that not even knowing which gender she belonged to was the ultimate in impersonal fund-raising. Many in the group expressed bitterness toward what they perceived as an incessant preoccupation with fund-raising, a disinterest in individuals, and a kind of institutional hypocrisy that consisted of organizations "asking for time when what they really want is our money."

In contrast to an impersonal "unrelenting focus on money" which they thought was typical of many established Jewish organizations, focus-group participants talked about the kinds of activities they find satisfying. Several Manhattan women mentioned the emergence of new, more personalized types of Jewish organizations, such as the US/Israel Women's Network: "We raise money to support shelters for abused women, and our whole focus is on the needs of women. That happens to be one of the projects, which is fund-raising, but we also bring groups of Israeli women to the United States and show them around, and raise American Jewish consciousness about the situation of women in Israeli society."

Another woman talked about her "pet charity," which supports Ethiopian Jews: "It is all right to do the fund raising, but when I go to Israel I try to work with the Ethiopians because that's the overall goal. It is hard to organize. Anyone who works with Israeli-related charities has had that difficulty. There is also lobbying for them." An insistence that organizational activity should be focused on discernible and meas-.urable achievement of goals, and a desire to become involved in a hands-on way with real people was common to many participants.

In response to the disaffectedness that many American Jews report about some established, "standard" Jewish organizations, a plethora of new Jewish organizations have sprung up over the past few decades, which purport to more closely match the organizational goals of many American Jews. For example, the New Israel Fund is an umbrella organization that collects funds and distributes them among diverse projects and programs in Israel, especially those believed to advance civil rights, democracy, religious freedom, and improved Jewish-Arab relations. The Jewish Fund for Social Justice tries to address social ills in the United States.

Other new Jewish organizations are geared toward more specialized constituencies. Among many examples, P'tach works to provide Jewish educational opportunities for children with developmental challenges; Pareve is an organization for the children of interfaith marriages; ICAR (International Coalition for Agunah Rights) and GET (Getting Equitable Treatment) deal with the issue of women who have difficulties obtaining a religious divorce. Jews with hearing disabilities have their own rabbinical seminary. Health issues have spawned numerous Jewish responses, with organizations focusing on Jewish genetic disposition toward certain congenital diseases, Jewish women's propensity to breast cancer, and the location of organ and bone marrow matches for Jewish victims of debilitating conditions.

These new Jewish organizations, specifically created to match the belief system of contributors, are an excellent example of coalescence. Whereas Jews in the past often said that they joined, volunteered time for, and donated money to Jewish organizations out of a sense of duty—"Just like paying taxes," as one older activist put it—many younger American Jews feel they should have direct representational impact on the giving patterns of the organizations they give to. They are implying that Jewish organizations should be more democratic in their giving decisions. They are also implying that human rights issues, which their coalesced belief systems tell them are the essence of Jewish "tradition," ought to be reflected in Jewish organizational life.

Positive new trends in established Jewish organizations were also spoken of by focus-group participants. Among working Jewish mothers in Long Island, for example, several spoke of community building activities that they had recently enjoyed in Jewish organizations. One woman talked about a blend of professional and Jewish communal identities that were met in a satisfying way at one of Hadassah's nurse's groups:

> I don't like Manhattan at all, but on a Thursday night in Manhattan 135 Jewish nurses showed up and we all looked at each other and had the same reaction: Did you know that there were that many Jewish nurses? When I went to school, there were only two other Jewish nursing students. It was a wonderful experience, very enlightening and positive. And just think that I have become a more well-rounded person as a result of that experience. There is a lot

to be said for having both professional identity and the commonality of a communal relationship.

Another professional Long Island working mother said she would find great personal and religious fulfillment in a synagogue-sponsored family retreat: "What happens when you have a family? You have only weekends. You would love to do something with your family and you would love to be with other Jewish families. I saw this and said this would be a great idea for a family outing in the Jewish sense."

A concern with Jewish knowledge and spiritual experiences surfaced again and again among focus-group participants. Among Reform women in Atlanta, Georgia, for example, one woman spoke about the fact that she and her husband had both served for years in leadership positions on synagogue boards, but were now much more involved in inculcating Jewish cultural and ritual literacy in their children:

> I put in too much time too fast over a six-year period and totally burnt myself out and said I need a break. Now I have a twelve year old and a fourteen year old and my focus is totally on their youth group, identification both here at the synagogue and through Jewish camps that they have attended in the summer. I want to provide for my kids not just the Jewish identification that I grew up with which was very strong, but I want them to have more than that. I want them to understand rituals, I want them to understand the history, and I want their identification to be as Jewish people.

Perhaps not surprisingly, this woman remarked that her daughter "is going into the ninth grade and is already a vice president of the junior youth group. She is the youngest kid to sit on the board." Within her own family unit, the relationship between knowledge, ritual, and organizational activism is clearly illustrated.

For some American Jews, ancient rituals can attain personal immediacy, and many focus-group participants said they want their Jewish organizations and synagogues to respond to their sense of spiritual urgency. As one Atlanta Reform focus-group participant reflected:

> After moving from New York to the South, I became much more hungry for a stronger Jewish identification and knowledge base. So I started doing that through involvement in our synagogue, but just as much from finding sources that I liked and just reading and then going back to a rabbi and asking him to talk to me about this. What I am doing right now that I am really excited about is writing a Haggadah play for the Passover seder, that is meant to be read around the dinner table. It is looking at the concepts surrounding Passover from women's standpoints.

Focusing on Women's Voluntarism

The focus-group data quoted above provides an important window into the kinds of emotional investment that women have often brought to their Jewish volunteer work, and the kinds of satisfactions they may seek through it. Voluntarism by both men and women has had important impact on the Jewish communal world. However, voluntarism by women historically is particularly significant. American-Jewish women today have participated in sweeping demographic changes, and many of these changes have aroused the anxiety of Jewish communal leaders, who wonder if the very success of American Jewish women in education and labor force participation will undermine the passionate involvement of Jewish women in Jewish organizational life. However, as Tables 7.1 through 7.5 illustrate, 1990 National Jewish Population survey data indicate that Jewish connectedness, not new educational and career patterns, pose the greatest challenge to voluntarism.

It is quite possible that, unlike volunteers of the past, who were more content to rise slowly up the ranks through a progression of tasks, gradually acquiring more responsibility and power, today's highly educated volunteers, most of whom have been labor force participants, are more likely to volunteer and to keep on volunteering if they have access to volunteer roles that are commensurate with their roles in the outside world. Given the high proportion of such women who do volunteer time for non-Jewish organizations, it is well to keep in mind that such a woman has other options for her limited volunteer time. It is important for opportunities in Jewish volunteering to be as attractive as possible. For today's Jewish woman, attractive voluntarism opportunities often imply access to decision making, public prominence, and power.

The married mother of two children ages nine and thirteen, working part-time outside the home doing legal research, for example, is not likely to be attracted to a morning demonstration of kosher gourmet cooking or an evening session stuffing envelopes for an upcoming meeting, no matter how worthy the cause; however, if she is asked to do legal research determining the feasibility of a public rally in support of overseas Jewry, she may very well agree. The currently unemployed mother of two children under age six, formerly an advertising executive, may be totally uninterested in a rummage sale for the synagogue; however, the same woman may enthusiastically plan and supervise a telethon for her synagogue afternoon Hebrew school. A gastroenterologist whose last child has entered college may be quite willing to deliver a fascinating series of lectures as fund-raisers for the Jewish hospital on diseases that are prevalent in the Jewish community.

NJPS data show that Jewish milieu, both in the form of Jewish husbands and Jewish friendship circles, is an important predictor of whether or not women volunteer time for Jewish causes. Jewish women who are married to non-Jewish men have drastically lower rates of voluntarism for Jewish causes than other married Jewish women, as seen in Table 7.6. Among married Jewish women ages 18 to 44, only 6 percent of born Jewish women married to non-Jewish men volunteer any time for Jewish causes—compared to 42 percent of Jewish women married to Jewish men (either born Jews or converts) and over half of women who are themselves Jews by choice. This fits in with the general picture of outmarried households as environments that are less likely to include Jewish activities. These data suggest that the prevalence of mixed marriage, rather than rising rates of careerism, provides the greatest single challenge to levels of Jewish voluntarism.

Similarly, Jewish women who do not have predominantly Jewish friendship circles are far less likely to volunteer than those who do. Jewish women who say that none of their best friends are Jewish almost never volunteer for Jewish causes, although 40 percent of them volunteer for non-Jewish causes only. Thirteen percent of Jewish women who have some Jewish friends volunteer for Jewish causes, and 40 percent volunteer for non-Jewish causes only. Among Jewish women who have mostly Jewish friends, however, 35 percent volunteer for Jewish causes and 19 percent volunteer for only non-Jewish causes. (These friendship circles do not seem to be employment related: within each of these groups, between half and two-thirds of the women are employed for pay outside the home.)

Synagogue membership and attendance among Jewish women is also strongly associated with volunteering behavior. Half of Jewish women who attend synagogue services frequently also volunteer time for Jewish causes or a combination of Jewish and non-Jewish causes. The picture of Jewish women who rarely attend synagogue services is almost the reverse of this pattern: among such women, about one-fifth volunteer time for either Jewish only or a combination of Jewish and non-Jewish causes. Among Jewish women who never attend synagogue services, the picture is even more dramatic: fewer than five percent volunteer any time for Jewish causes.

As one example of the close relationship between Jewish activism in "secular" Jewish organizations and the Jewishness of women's lives, a 1987 study, done by the Cohen Center for Modern Jewish Studies at Brandeis University, of the women who were involved on leadership levels in the Women's Division of Federations of Jewish Philanthropies around the country[19] revealed that seder attendance, Hanukkah candle lighting, and High Holiday observance were almost universal, and 70 percent said they always or usually light Shabbat candles. Well over half—57 percent—said they attended synagogue at least once a month. While the general population has shown a strong drift toward Reform Judaism over the past two decades, the proportion of Conservative Jews among the Women's Division leaders rose steadily from the older to the younger age groups: 44 percent of women ages 55 to 64, 48 percent of women ages 45 to 54, and 57 percent of women ages 35 to 44 defined themselves as Conservative Jews.

In other ways, these Women's Division leaders fit into current demographic trends, as discussed in chapters 2 and 5. Although they had more children than other American-Jewish women, an average of three per household, they had very high levels of secular education and labor force participation. Only 16 percent of Women's Division leaders ages 35 to 44 identified themselves as homemakers. Like most American-Jewish women, these Jewish leaders were more likely than not to work outside the home for pay, even when they had children between the ages of 6 and 13 at home.

Leadership seems to be a habit, so that women who are leaders in general organizations are more likely to be leaders in Jewish organizations as well. NJPS data reveal that 30 percent of women who lead non-Jewish organizations also lead Jewish organizations, compared to 22 percent of women who do not lead non-Jewish organizations. Leadership may thus be a mutually reinforcing activity (as voluntarism itself is). Jewish organizations do not need to make leadership of non-Jewish organizations unattractive, but to make Jewish leadership more attractive, in order to take advantage of the leadership abilities of today's Jewish women.

American Jewish Leaders Receive High Secular and Jewish Education

Decades ago the persons who filled secular Jewish positions had often grown up within intensely ethnic Jewish environments, but few had substantive formal Jewish educations. Many of them subscribed to the "sacred survival, civil religion"[20] mode of Jewish identification. They cared passionately about Jews in America, Israel, and around the world, but knew little about classic Jewish history, texts, and culture, and did not think such knowledge especially salient to their tasks. Some had absorbed the ideals of secular Jewish labor and/or Zionist movements; some were proudly against "organized religion"; some saw synagogues and synagogue-goers as rivals in Jewish life. One finds representatives of this older mode of Jewish activist identification primarily among the over-60 generation in Jewish organizational life. At the 1996 B'nai B'rith International Meeting, for example, one older leader blended old traditional and liberal vernaculars as he articulated his bafflement at what he saw as a confusion in his coreligionist's Jewish values: "I am so frustrated at people in my temple. I keep trying to get them to join B'nai B'rith. They think that going to the temple to daven every morning is more important than joining an organization like B'nai B'rith, which is so much more important for world Jewry. These people don't know what is important in Jewish life."[21]

In contrast, the contemporary generation of younger Jewish thinkers and lay and professional leaders include those who are searching for spiritual substance, or have already learned how to merge deep Jewish commitments with American liberal values. Many of them are personally rather observant of Jewish home-based and synagogue rituals, but also prize American pluralist freedoms and see secular education and personal autonomy as their birthrights. Utilizing the four-group typology of American secular and Jewish education introduced in chapter 4, the group that has received high levels of both secular and Jewish education are now prominent among the younger activist segment of Jewish life.

Among contemporary examples of the high secular/high Jewish educational mode, today's younger American-Jewish leaders, such as research heads of major (secular) national Jewish organizations, editors of widely-circulated Jewish newspapers and periodicals, executives in large-city federations, writers and scholars of Judaic studies include a disproportionate number of Jewishly and secularly well-educated men and women. Younger American Jews who are attracted to Jewish organizations today are a special breed, and have often been influenced by Jewish educational experiences.

Jewish Professionals and Lifestyles of Service

Most of this chapter has focused on American Jews who volunteer time and give money to Jewish organizations. Some of them are members, who simply pay dues and may give occasional small extra donations; some are activists, who work many hours and take on leadership roles; some are philanthropists, who make substantial donations.

However, Jewish organizations are dependent not only on their members and lay leaders, but also on their Jewish professionals—rabbis, Jewish educators, and Jewish communal workers. Our discussion of trends in American-Jewish organizations as part of the context of Jewish lives would not be complete without exploring the unique role played by these professional leaders.

Jewish communal professionals comprise an elite cadre in terms of their knowledge of and their commitment to the Jewish people, the Jewish cultural and religious heritage, and the Jewish future. But despite their leadership status, the powers of Jewish communal leaders are limited. American Jews are a hybrid group whose concepts of Jewish values are shaped more by the general values and behaviors of American society than they are by distinctive Jewish traditions. Jewish professionals serve as leaders of individuals in an open society, individuals who can only be called a community to the extent that they choose to be part of that community. When Jews have been relatively isolated from the cultures surrounding them, either voluntarily or because of antisemitism, individuals have formed a structurally more cohesive group. In such situations, the leadership cadre has often had significant power over societal norms and over the daily lives of individuals.

However, in the United States today, far from being isolated as a group, American Jews can choose whether or not to affiliate with a broad spectrum of groups. Thus, unlike the *rav* and the *shtadlan* and other communal leaders who dealt with physically and/or spiritually dependent historical Jewish communities, contemporary American professional Jewish leaders have limited authority or influence within their voluntaristic communities. The partial power that enables Jewish communal professionals to lead and serve their constituencies derives both from institutional structures and from the constituencies themselves.

Data gathered for this author's 1994 Wexner Foundation Research Project on Contemporary Jewish Professional Leadership, entitled "Training for a Life of Jewish Service—Working in the Real World" reveal basic demographic information and insights into the sources of satisfaction and dissatisfaction in the current professional lives of persons who have trained to be rabbis, Jewish communal workers, and Jewish educators.[22] The 280 respondents in this study included sixty-one men and seventy-one women who had completed their professional training about ten years before the study, and fifty-six men and ninety women who had completed their professional training about four years before the study.[23]

The Wexner respondent data revealed that Jewish communal professionals are a unique group of individuals, in many ways shaped by the fact that they have chosen to devote their time and energies to the task of guiding and facilitating contemporary Jewish life. Men and women who choose to train for the rabbinate, Jewish communal service, and Jewish education in the contemporary American environment are by definition a self-selected group of people. Within an open American society that now tolerates Jews in virtually every strata of educational, occupational, and social arenas, Jewish professionals have nonetheless chosen to focus their energies on Jewish concerns. They are very often persons with a strong sense of vocation, sometimes referred to as a "calling." Data gathered in this survey underscore the fact that for this particular group of people, job satisfaction cannot be measured only—or even primarily—by financial or status rewards.

Persons who choose to devote their professional lives to the Jewish community tend to have one of two basic formative experiences: either one is "groomed" for Jewish leadership by many and varied early experiences in the Jewish world, or one is "hooked" in young adulthood by some transforming experience. Jewish communal professional aspirations seem primarily to begin during the college years. For respondents in this survey, the college and graduate school years seemed to be the most critical time for deciding on a career in Jewish communal leadership.

The Jewish professionals studied had often entered their fields in order to combat assimilation and to revitalize American-Jewish life. They reported that they often find themselves coping with a working environment that is very different from the one for which they had hoped and trained. Many encounter challenges for which they feel underprepared. Ironically, it is often manifestations of assimilation itself that eat away at their own personal and professional vitality. When the individuals and the communities they serve seem apathetic or lacking in communal Jewish will, the professionals said they often feel as though they are struggling against discouraging odds.

For many Jewish communal professionals, these larger, ideological issues, are intertwined with feelings of personal professional frustration. They sometimes feel that because Jewish culture is not very important to their clients/congregants/students, they are not treated as well as they should be on many fronts. Jewish professional standards, job status, salary, and work expectations often seem to be negatively affected by the status of Judaism itself within the lives of individual American Jews.

At the same time, many American-Jewish professionals find their professional lives gratifying. They find satisfaction in enhancing the personal and Jewish lives of their clients, congregants, and students. They enjoy serving as role models, and often feel that their own spiritual lives are made more meaningful by the work that they do.

For those Jewish professionals who are essentially satisfied with their professional lives, a sense of calling both shapes and nourishes their daily activities. For those who find their professional lives to be essentially unsatisfying or frustrating, a failed sense of calling often colors and embitters their perceptions.

The survey explored sources of job satisfaction in two ways: respondents were asked to react to a series of statements about job satisfaction, specifying whether a given statement was true, somewhat true, mostly not true, or does not apply. They were also asked two open-ended questions, "Now tell me, in your own words, what has most contributed to your feelings of satisfaction and success?" and "In your own words, what would you identify as your most important professional achievement?"

Information from the closed-ended sequence of questions show that Jewish professionals most universally articulate their greatest sources of satisfaction on the job in ways that are connected to their calling. They emphasize their ability to (1) make a difference in people's lives, (2) have warm interpersonal relationships, and (3) enhance Jewish continuity in the United States. In the open-ended questions, these altruistic, calling-related sources of satisfaction are fleshed out: making a difference in people's lives and enhancing Jewish continuity in the United States can mean, for a fund-raiser, "making donors feel good about their giving." For a rabbi, it can mean providing people with counseling that saves a marriage, or serving as a Jewish role model who "turns on" a teenager to more intensive Jewish life.

Conversely, in the close-ended sequence of questions about job frustrations, respondents report that the greatest source of dissatisfaction is assimilation in the American-Jewish community. This sense that their very calling is irrelevant to the people they serve exacerbates the frustrations they feel in the professional aspects of what they do.

Overwhelmingly, respondents pointed to altruistic aspects of fulfillment and human connections as yielding their greatest sources of satisfaction. Well over three-quarters (78 percent) of respondents said that "I feel I am making a difference in people's lives" is a "true" statement about their work, and another 20 percent said it is "somewhat true." Similarly, 77 percent said the statement that "I have warm interpersonal relationships with students, clients, congregants, or lay leaders," is a "true" statement and another 17 percent said it is "somewhat true." Sixty-five percent of respondents said that "I feel I am enhancing Jewish continuity in the U.S." is a "true" statement, and another 22 percent said it is "somewhat true." Almost two-thirds of respondents said it is "true" that "I have a strong sense of personal fulfillment," and another 30 percent said that statement was "somewhat true."

No other sources of satisfaction came close to this kind of unanimity. Responses to open-ended questions about job satisfaction and achievement yielded a wide variety of responses. Indeed, it is striking that questions about satisfaction and achievement evoked a far greater variety of response than questions about frustration and job burnout. In direct contradiction to Tolstoy's observation that happy families are all the same, while unhappy families are each miserable in their own unique way, among Jewish communal professionals happiness seemed to stem from many sources, while unhappiness wells from a few, bitter streams.

Most of the answers reveal how profoundly Jewish communal professionals perceive themselves as persons who are in the process of improving people's lives and revitalizing American-Jewish life. Statements about personal ambition, money, and power are few, and limited to respondents who talked about creating a "good reputation" for their own work or for their institution, or about the high quality of their scholarly output.

Responses to the open-ended question, "What contributes most to your feelings of job frustration or burn-out?" indicated that much is troubling today's Jewish communal professionals. Often they are expected to be fund-raisers as well as educators, spiritual leaders, or administrators. Many described situations in which they struggle with overwhelming amounts of work, in which there are few recognized personal boundaries, in which they feel called upon to meet the needs of many and at all times—and in which they simultaneously feel isolated and lacking in appreciation and support.

In addition, in every field except for the rabbinate, standards of professionalism either have not been clearly established or are not universally honored by institutions, and persons who have not received professional training sometimes receive desirable jobs and promotions. Salaries sometimes seem inappropriately low, and professionals must struggle to put together several jobs to make a living.

When, as a backdrop for these struggles, the community at large seems indifferent to the professional's goals for Jewish continuity, when money and communal support are inadequate to accomplish what should be mutual goals, the sources of discouragement frequently seem greater than the sum of their parts. Professionals complained that the conditions under which they worked were inappropriate, and also that the community did not share and support their goals. These two types of complaints are often deeply linked in their own minds.

Consumers and Covenant Keepers

The attitudes voiced by Jewish communal professionals in the Wexner study, and their perceptions of the dramatically diverging goals of their client populations, underscore the differences in attitudes toward communal affairs historically and today. American Jews tend to be consumers in their relationship to Jewish institutions. They belong to synagogues and Jewish community centers when they need services that those institutions provide. They are less likely to belong during the years before they marry and have school-age children, and less likely to continue membership after their children have left home. Moving to retirement communities often spells the end of organizational affiliations.

Many also approach the Jewish organizational world with a consumer rights attitude. They often have a specific sense of what they are "looking for," and are likely to join and maintain memberships in those organizations that fulfill their practical, social, or spiritual needs. If they identify as Jews primarily through awareness of anti semitism and memories of the Holocaust, the Anti-Defamation League, the Simon Wiesenthal Center, or the Holocaust Museum may claim their loyalty. If they have a classic Reform prophetic vision of the Jewish ethical mission to the world, local synagogues that focus on community aid to the homeless or AIDs victims, or organizations such as the Jewish Fund for Social Justice may resonate. Family members of women who have suffered inequitable divorce situations are galvanized by organizations that work to provide women with religious divorces despite recalcitrant husbands. Family members of children or adults with developmental challenges often work for Jewish organizations that aim to alleviate special problems. Attachment to organizations supporting Israel may fluctuate according to the political correctness of Israeli governments—although crisis situations tend to temporarily erase feelings of alienation. Nevertheless, the older idea that one joins umbrella Jewish organizations because one has an obligation to support them seems less salient to the majority of contemporary younger American Jews. Alienation or apathy are found among Jews who have generally weak ties to diverse areas of Jewish social, cultural, and religious life.

It becomes more and more apparent that individuals who choose lay or professional leadership roles in Jewish organizations have been educated for Jewish leadership at the same time that they are being educated for Jewish living. In the past, this education for Jewish leadership and Jewish life was accomplished in a "by the way" fashion, and was often perceived as a secular value, separate from Jewish religious concerns. The current sweep of demographic trends and the words of younger American Jews illuminate the correlation between Jewish leadership and Jewish education, Jewish marriage, Jewish friendship circles, and Jewish lifestyles. If the American community aims to reproduce its Jewishly oriented leadership, membership, and philanthropic cadres—rather than to increasingly supply leadership for general civic and secular causes—an infusion of traditional Jewish religious, spiritual, and communal values must complement the coalesced values of general voluntarism and communal activism.

Table 7.1 **Jewish and American Volunteers**
Percentages of 1990 NJPS Respondents by Sex,
Compared to All Americans

Gender	Jewish Organizations	General Organizations	Either or Both	All U.S.
Men	17	40	48	50
Women	23	39	51	53

Source: 1990 NJPS data, adapted from Gabriel Berger, *Current Philanthropic Patterns of American Jews* (Waltham, Mass.: Cohen Center for Modern Jewish Studies Research Report 7, 1992). Percentages have been rounded.

Table 7.2 **Volunteers for Jewish and Non-Jewish Causes**
Percentages by Education and Sex

Education Level Attained	Jewish Causes		Non-Jewish Causes	
	Women	Men	Women	Men
High School or Under	15	11	23	20
Attended College	22	14	39	43
Bachelor's Degree	23	13	47	49
Master's Degree*	27	18	57	48
Ph.D., M.D., DDS., J.D.	27	19	44	47

Source: 1990 NJPS data. Percentages have been rounded.
*Includes nursing degree.

Table 7.3 Current Volunteers for Jewish Organizations Percentages by Jewish Education, Denomination Raised, and Sex

	Orthodox		Conservative		Reform	
	Women	*Men*	*Women*	*Men*	*Women*	*Men*
None	17	4	7	5	15	5
1–2 years Supplementary or Sunday School	—	—	4	5	4	11
3–5 years Sunday School	4	4	7	5	12	—
6+ years Sunday School	4	—	2	2	27	37
3–5 years Supplementary School	4	4	16	16	12	5
6+ years Supplementary School	17	16	54	59	31	32
1–5 years Day School	—	4	4	2	—	5
6+ years Day School	54	68	7	7	—	55
TOTAL	100	100	101	101	101	100

Source: 1990 NJPS data. Percentages have been rounded.

Table 7.4 Jews Giving Money to Jewish Charities Percentages by Age, Secular Degrees and Did or Did Not Receive Jewish Education

Highest Secular Degree	*Age*	*Received Jewish Education*	*Did Not Receive Jewish Education*
High School or less	30–49	34	14
	50–64	61	49
	65–74	73	57
Some College	30–49	37	15
	50–64	70	0
	65–74	100	57
Bachelor's Degree	30–49	48	40
	50–64	67	77
	65–74	74	80
Master's or Nursing Degree	30–49	56	37
	50–64	69	16
	65–74	75	100
Other Graduate and Professional Degrees	30–49	60	61
	50–64	68	21
	65–74	100	27
Totals	30–49	48	30
	50–64	66	49
	65–74	76	58

Source: 1990 NJPS data, respondents born or raised Jewish. Percentages have been rounded.

Table 7.5 Jews Giving Money to Jewish Charities Percentages by Age, Secular Degrees, and Years of Jewish Education

Highest Secular Degree	Age	Years of Jewish Education Received			
		1–3	*4–6*	*7–9*	*10 or more*
High School or less	30–49	31	29	20	55
	50–64	70	61	56	44
	65–74	65	91	100	69
Some College	30–49	4	45	33	55
	50–64	100	64	100	21
	65–74	100	100	100	100
Bachelors Degree	30–49	33	45	61	57
	50–64	92	66	54	68
	65–74	59	59	100	94
Masters or Nursing Degree	30–49	49	57	48	71
	50–64	46	66	100	65
	65–74	70	60	100	100
Other Graduate and Professional Degrees	30–49	58	40	77	67
	50–64	75	74	59	59
	65–74	100	100	100	100
Totals	30–49	37	45	51	61
	50–64	73	65	64	66
	65–74	66	81	100	80

Source: 1990 NJPS data, respondents born or raised Jewish. Percentages have been rounded.

Table 7.6 Jewish Women Volunteering for Jewish Causes Percentages by Marriage Type

	All	*Ages 25–44*	*Ages 45+*
Jewish Women Married to Born Jewish Men	33	42	29
Jewish Women Married to Converted Jewish Men	31	39	18*
Jewish Women Married to Non-Jewish Men	6	6	5
Converted Jewish Women Married to Born Jewish Men	52	53	48*

Source: 1990 NJPS data. Percentages have been rounded.
*Fewer than 10 cases.

Table 7.7 **Women's Voluntarism for Jewish and Non-Jewish Causes Percentages by Age, Marital Status, Family Formation, and Labor Force Participation**

Category	Jewish Causes	Non-Jewish Causes
Married	23	41
Under Age 45	23	46
Over Age 45	24	36
Never Married	16	47
Divorced	16	37
Widowed	23	24
No Children Born	14	44
Children 6 & Under	22	48
Children 18 & Under	24	46
Children 19 & Over	27	33
Homemakers	21	41
Under Age 45	29	49
Over Age 45	13	32
Students	13	54
Work Part-time	32	39
Under Age 45	24	43
Over Age 45	45	32
Work Full-time	18	43
Under Age 45	18	45
Over Age 45	18	39
Unemployed	27	30

Source: 1990 NJPS data. Percentages have been rounded.

EIGHT

NEGOTIATING BOTH SIDES
OF THE HYPHEN

Coalescence, Judaism, and Historic Syncretism

Coalescence is an American phenomenon, and it has arisen as a response to the unprecedented conditions of Jewish life in America. It is not just that for most contemporary American Jews the authority of historical Judaism has been diminished, not just that the past has a vote but not a veto. Taken together the quantitative and qualitative data demonstrate that for most American Jews today distinctions between Jewish tradition and American context are seldom recognized; the two value systems can thus hardly be compartmentalized. External boundaries have become increasingly indistinct; internal aspects of Americaness and Jewishness—the contents of liberal American and Jewish cultures—appear to many American Jews as almost identical.

Jews often experience and believe what other Americans do—but to a perhaps surprising extent, many American Jews tend to reinterpret these belief systems as deriving from their Jewish identity. This tendency to see Americanisms as Jewishness is reinforced by the continuing Judaization of American culture. Jews are perceived as being distinctive, but the sources of their distinctiveness reflect coalesced perceptions of Jewish tradition. As we have seen, coalescence manifests itself in almost every sphere of American-Jewish life. Even everyday phrases reflect coalesced pictures of Jews:

"Jews are the people of the book": When American Jews acquire extraordinary levels of secular education, they and others believe that a "traditional" Jewish emphasis on education is part of their motivation. Few Jews or non-Jews remember the central traditional role of sacred learning, or the very different role played by secular education in weaning Jews away from their parental faith and its strictures.

"A nice Jewish doctor," or "Get me a smart Jewish lawyer": When Jews aspire to professional excellence, they are perceived by themselves and others as part of the "traditional" Jewish gravitation to such professions. Almost forgotten are the American quotas that once kept Jews out of professional schools; one imagines instead Jewish professionals going back to Moses.

When Jewish parents "edit" Judaism and transmit only the "fun parts" to their children, omitting ideas or activities they believe might be onerous or intimidating, they picture themselves as exercising "free choice," which they believe to be an essential part of "traditional" Judaism. Similarly, when Jewish women plan their families carefully, they are following in the footsteps of their mothers, and often their grandmothers. This "tradition" of contraceptive punctiliousness has surely played a role in the readiness of Jewish organizations to lobby on behalf of reproductive "choice."

When American Jews say they look to Jewish organizations and institutions to meet their needs, whether these are needs for Jewish life cycle ceremonies, or for a sense of community, or for memorable spiritual experiences—rather than saying they affiliate out of a sense of duty—they often think they are behaving according to Jewish "tradition." Ironically, Jewish professionals who come to their calling with a similar coalesced desire for "fulfillment" are the group most likely to leave the field when they discover the consumer mentality of their client population.

An awareness of societies in which Jews were distinguished by their clothing and food has largely been subsumed by observations about contemporary American-Jewish preferences in clothing and food. When American-Jewish teenagers are asked if there is such a thing as "Jewish clothing," the responses center around expensiveness, high style, and jewelry; except for those youths who live near Hasidic populations or have recently seen a film featuring black-garbed Jews, the whole concept of modest or distinctive clothing is alien. It may even be appropriate to consider such sources as jokes about Jews and food, such as, "What do Jewish women make for dinner? Reservations!" The subtext of the joke, once one has gotten past the offensive attitude toward Jewish women, is about Jewish affluence and affection for Chinese or trendy restaurants. Again, traditional Jewish culinary concerns around kashruth are usually far from the general consciousness.

At the same time, the America that Jews experience at the turn of a new century is one in which the senior foreign policy leadership, for example, the Secretary of State and the United Nations Ambassador, the senior economic leadership, for example, the Chairman of the Federal Reserve and the Under-Secretary of the Treasury, and the Secretary of Defense are all of Jewish descent. This is an America where Jews see themselves in government offices and college presidencies, as well as in books, television, and film. Jews are white, mainstream Americans; their Jewish ethnicity and religion is seldom a serious impediment to success, and may even be perceived as an advantage. Jewish names and Jewish noses are more likely now than ever before to remain in place, because American Jews have negotiated both sides of the American-Jewish hyphen. When they look into the mirror of America, they see themselves.

In differentiating the current American situation, one faces the difficult task of distinguishing between the varieties of contemporary American Judaism, on one hand, and historic evidence of earlier syncretism, on the other hand. Looking back at the Judaisms of the past two thousand years is much like peeling layer after layer of an onion: which layer is the real thing? In this book, authentically Jewish values and behaviors have been defined as those that can be located within Ashkenazi, Sephardi, or Oriental Jewish societies where traditional religious imperatives (*halakhah*) and social attitudes and norms (*hashkafah*) held sway.

The merging of foreign ideas, attitudes, and values with whatever comprised the Judaisms of the time has repeatedly and substantively taken place in most earlier eras of Jewish history. Cultural merging has taken place on an elite stratum, in the intellectual realm, and in the mundane lives of the masses of Jewish individuals, affecting lifestyle factors such as cuisine, music, and dress. In both elite and folk realms, what Ann Swidler calls the "cultural toolkit"[1] of Jewish communities has been profoundly influenced by external societies.

One could cite the examples of Philo's superimposing Greek thought onto Judaic texts, and of Maimonides' Aristotelianism. Rabbinic textual emphasis on notions of heaven and hell, reward and punishment, arguably were encouraged by interactions with Christian thought and culture. Incrementally restricted roles of Jewish women and growing preoccupations with menstrual taboos and misogynist mythology tended to occur within Jewish societies located in countries with relatively repressive treatment of women. Jewish cuisine and cultural artifacts have been widely syncretic: adapted to the strictures of the dietary laws and the requirements of Sabbath and holiday celebrations, the Jewish foods of Russia, Budapest, Yemen, and Morocco each reflect their country of origin. Jewish music echoes the motifs of Ukraine, Turkey, Rumania, and Syria. Many a cherished Sabbath melody has the lilt of a Viennese waltz or a German drinking ditty.

Some crosscultural developments have been revitalizing to Jewish life. Language is one powerful example: two or more languages were combined to produce linguistic instruments of extraordinary flexibility and range in the traditional Jewish communities that spoke and wrote in Yiddish, Ladino, or Judeo-Arabic. Michael Brenner argues that third generation assimilated Jews in the Weimar period in Germany (1918–1933), stimulated by an intimidating culture, produced a rich and moving array of transformed Judaica, using "distinct forms of Jewish traditions, marking them as authentic," and presenting them "according to the demands of contemporary taste and modern cultural forms of expression. What might have appeared as authenticity was in fact a modern innovation." The Weimar Jewish cultural output included multivolume encyclopedias, music, texts, and museums. The search for a Jewish authenticity that was acceptable to secularized moderns led in Berlin and elsewhere to the promotion and support of the study of Hebrew culture.[2] Some German-Jewish writers in the 1920s actually tried to turn the largely negative German notion of Asiatic or orientalized Jewish culture into a positive quality, arguing that Jewish orientalism gave Jews access to the wisdom of ancient Asiatic civilizations.[3] Similarly, analyzing *A Great Awakening: The Transformation That Shaped Twentieth Century American Judaism*, Jonathan Sarna demonstrates that some of the "most successful and creative innovations" of late nineteenth-century American Jewry "turned past wisdom on its head. New historical conditions created new movements, new emphases, and new paradigms—the very opposite of the tried and true."[4] In such cases, the challenges of change produced a new fascination with Jewish tradition—and a transformation of that tradition.

Jewish historians and their historiographies illustrate this critical tension between participation in the external contemporary cultural context, on the one hand, and a grounding in distinctively Jewish internal history and tradition, on the other hand. David Myers describes the overtly diverging historiographical biases of the nineteenth-century German-Jewish *Wissenschaft des Judentums* and those of the twentieth-century Hebrew University-based Jerusalem School of scholars, both of whom shared a nationalistic desire to shape and invent an appropriate history. David Biale sees Myers as the epitome of "a new tendency in Jewish studies: to see beyond the belief in Jewish uniqueness toward an understanding of Jewish culture as one moment in human culture and to situate the Jews in their larger cultural heritage as children of their age."[5]

Thus, the evolution of the Judaisms of the past seems to support Frederik Barth's foundational assertion that ethnic history is not a series of events happening to a social group with one defined and unchanging culture, but instead ethnicity functions as a kind of boundaried vessel, within which the enclosed culture is continually adjusted, with some elements being emphasized and others deemphasized according to a shifting spectrum of influencing factors.[6]

Nevertheless, despite many impressive examples of syncretism in Jewish history, I have argued that compared both to eras when Jewish societies were relatively untouched by outside cultures and to those that were deeply transformed by interactions, the coalescence of American values and behaviors into American Judaism in late twentieth-century America truly represents a distinct phenomenon, albeit one that has been foreshadowed by certain crosscultural developments of the past in both pre-emancipation and modern societies. Jews in pre-emancipation Jewish societies usually functioned in a densely constructed Jewish environment. They shared a complex cultural milieu composed of distinctive languages; highly prescriptive religious law; communal Sabbath, holiday and life cycle celebrations; communal models of male study and worship, in which the female auxiliary role was societally reinforced; restrictive dietary laws; and, to a greater or lesser extent, communal governing bodies.

After emancipation and the various secularized social movements of modernity transformed such tightly knit Jewish environments, the lines between Jews and non-Jews remained clear from the outside, even when they were less obvious from the inside. Firm boundaries, including the discriminatory boundaries of antisemitism, separated Jews from their host cultures. Although Jews imported foreign customs, cultural artifacts, and intellectual trends into their lives, thoughts, and texts, the structural boundaries of their ethnicity remained in place. Indeed, nineteenth-century intellectual trends often displayed a stunning tendency toward antisemitism which made secularized Jewish thinkers painfully aware of their own difference.[7] The shared declaration of Herzl and Nordau in 1895—"Only antisemitism has made Jews of us"—accurately reflected certain European realities.[8] The persistence of boundary lines between Jews and non-Jews was powerfully reinforced by the fact that Jews lived in countries in which one ethnic group defined the main culture. Jews were always the other—perceived as a foreign body among the Germans in Germany, English in England, French in France, Poles in Poland, and Russians in "mother" Russia amongst whom they lived.

The United States that American Jews inhabit today presents an environment which differs profoundly from such historical situations in its current lack of a single, overriding mainstream culture and in the extraordinary permeability of its internal ethnic and cultural boundaries. Philip Roth's protagonists may have lumped non-Jews into one mainstream sweep of turned-up noses and yellow hair, but to themselves they were ethnic Irish and Germans and Poles and Italians in a country composed of immigrants. Sporadic discrimination against Jews was played out against similar injustices against other white European ethnic groups, and far more systemic discrimination against persons of color.[9]

In the years since World War II, overall discrimination in the United States has eased dramatically.[10] American culture seems to be telling ethnic Americans that to be ethnic is to be more, not less American. Jewish creative artists no longer have to tell the story of Jewish experience by putting on blackface, encoding Jewish life in some other ethnic or racial story, as Edna Ferber, George Gershwin, Aaron Copland, and even Leonard Bernstein had done at first. In recent decades Jewish films, fiction, plays, and music have proliferated; National Public Television features Israeli violinist Yitzhak Perlman playing Klezmer music on the streets of Warsaw, and American Jews who decades ago would have cringed in shame at being associated with such "old world" music thrill with pleasure at having their culture thus validated and send large donations to their local station. Indeed, even stories about assimilation seem dated, as Jewish creative artists reach further and further into the esoteric reaches of the "authentic" Jewish experience represented by earlier periods of Jewish history or by Israel, the Holocaust, or Orthodox societies.

Ethnic boundaries, as quantitative and qualitative data and cultural artifacts demonstrate, are blurred not only externally but internally as well. Unlike Jews in earlier eras of American history, who were all too aware of what it meant to be a ghettoized Jew, for the vast majority of American Jews, as for the majority of ethnic white Americans, ethnicity is not a limiting factor of life. Jewishness and Judaism, for most, is not a daily, pervasive, defining condition of existence. As a result, when American Jews import Jewishly unprecedented ideas, attitudes, and behaviors from external cultures into their concept of Judaism, these elements are not being merged into an otherwise clearly defined Jewish culture, but instead into a culture that is already overwhelmingly Americanized.

Of the various coping mechanisms employed by American Jews, coalescence is both the least self-conscious and the one perceived to be the most organic and American. In contrast, American Jews who are conscious of the fact that they are using compartmentalization do not find it a culturally approved or permanent technique, as psychic divisions have a way of threatening to break down. Resealing the boundaries is often viewed by both practitioners and opponents to be the least "American," functioning as a kind of cultural resistance. None of these coping mechanisms truly eliminates the tension between secular and Jewish components of American-Jewish life, although probably coalescence comes closest. In these negotiations from both sides of the American-Jewish hyphen, American Jews are supremely American. They, like other white American minority ethnic and religious groups, are now negotiating opportunities and challenges that may be unprecedented in the history of the world.

Recent writing by and about other hyphenated American ethnic groups is useful in illuminating the American-Jewish experience. As Esmeralda Santiago in a *New York Times* "Hers" column describes the "Puerto Rican Stew" which became her life when she emigrated to the United States at age thirteen, she—like Jewish immigrants a century ago—quickly took up the challenge "to learn English, to graduate from high school . . . to assimilate into American society." Having accomplished these goals splendidly, she reads in her mother's face that she is on one level a failure, because she has become too "Americanized," and hovers at the edge of "becoming something other than the person" she was intended to be:

> In the United States, her children would challenge her authority based on different rules of conduct. . . . I never considered myself any less Puerto Rican. I was born there and spoke its language, identified with its culture. But to Puerto Ricans on the island during my summer there, I was a different creature altogether. Employers complained that I was too assertive, men said I was too feminist, my cousin suggested I had no manners, and everyone accused me of being too independent. Those, I was made to understand, were Americanisms.

Santiago insists that she can construct her own variety of Puerto Rican-American identity, "one not bound by geographical, linguistic, or behavioral boundaries, but rather by a deep identification with a place, and people and a culture which, in spite of appearances, define my behavior and determine the rhythms of my days."[11] However, she does not reflect on what the Puerto Rican identity of her children—who will not necessarily hear the rhythm of Spanish in their ears as they speak English or be brought back to associations with an island homeland when they smell *arroz con pollo*—might be. In her reliance on intense memories for her own ethnic identification, Santiago is reminiscent of Jewish immigrants who imagined that their own memories might somehow be transferred to their children—and were shocked to discover that their "Jewish hearts" were not replicated in their successfully Americanized offspring.

Chinese-American Tony-award winning playwright David Henry Hwang dramatizes the predicament of such "hyphenates" in his play "Golden Child." Hwang characterizes himself and other "third wave" ethnic Americans as a group "no longer willing to pit race-based separatism against assimilation." Instead of what he sees as pressure toward "fundamentalist" separatism, Hwang advocates "dynamic assimilation that is the American experience," and explains, "as I am changed, so is the society changed by me."[12] Similar issues are explored by hyphenated authors such as Gish Jen, Amy Tan, Cynthia Kadohata, David Ware, and others, each of whom describes transformations in the values and behaviors of second and third generation American descendants of rich and ancient cultures.

For the children and grandchildren of Jewish immigrants, the issue of transference is even more complicated, because few immigrants wanted their children to share their associations with an Old World Jewish culture planted in muddy villages or antisemitic cities. For Jews, their birthplaces were usually not synonymous with the emerging nationalist homeland of their heart, which came to be called Israel. Israel was a place beloved by many, sometimes idealized and idolized, but usually from a distance. As Philip Roth cleverly captures the three-way split of Jewish identity for many American Jews, "Grandpa didn't come from Haifa. Grandpa came from Minsk."[13]

When American Jews send children to Israel to be enculturated to an often vague notion of Jewish commitment, they are not sending them "back" to a familiar culture that produced their own parents or grandparents, but "over" to a different language, Jewish culture and identity. Above all, few American Jews have wanted their children to leave America and to live in their new Israeli homeland. For most American Jews, Zionism does not obviate a passion for the adopted homeland, America. Nevertheless, Israel continues to play an extremely important role in the education of American Jews, and in the broader issue of American-Jewish identity.

Jewish Culture of Disbelief

One of the ways in which Jews participate in American liberal middle-class culture is their anxiety about not being too pious. Today's Americans often suffer from the fear of being "too Jewish." In the current multicultural environment, Jewish distinctiveness has few realistic negative repercussions, and yet many American Jews are apprehensive about religiosity. As a result, despite the overwhelming data showing Jewish education to be the most powerful positive tool in combating cultural impoverishment, many individuals express an anxiety that religious educational settings may succeed too well.

Jews are not alone in this anxiety. Piety often has been derided in liberal American culture, and the vast majority of American Jews, according to comparative studies of non-Jewish and Jewish attitudes and voting patterns, believe their interests to be most accurately represented by the liberal camp. Working hard to maintain such principles as the separation of church and state, Jews have been deeply affected by what Stephen L. Carter calls *The Culture of Disbelief;* Carter argues that a passionate devotion to the First Amendment encourages a kind of reflexive suspicion of religious devotion, leading to the idea that piety of any kind is irrational and irrelevant.[14] Harvard political scientist Samuel Huntington, describing *The Clash of Civilizations and the Remaking of World Order,* suggests that Jews are intrinsically Western, and as Westerners are locked in a fight to the death with religiously fundamentalist and aggressive cultures such as Islam.

Reacting to the antireligious bias of American liberalism, a recent article in *Commentary* magazine urges American Jews to rethink their attachment to liberal attitudes and behaviors. Some historians, rabbis, and sociologists assert that conservative politics may be more consistent with and friendly to Jewish tradition.[15] However, it is closer to the truth that American-Jewish hostile attitudes toward religious ritual observance and dissonance with American social norms transcend political orientation because they derive from historical Westernization. In the minds of many Americans, secularism has become confused with modernity, and religiosity has become confused with backwardness. Meaningful Jewish continuity is entangled with destructive confusion between Jewish traditions and fundamentalism. This very genuine fear that increased knowledge levels can lead to increased Jewish practice and from thence to a fundamentalist mindset has sometimes worked against the clear data-based policy mandate to increase the scope of Jewish education.

The general fear of increased Jewish distinctiveness is often exacerbated by turf wars between lay and professional leaders in the different streams of American Judaism. Religious leaders have sometimes indulged in rhetoric that delegitimates the Judaism of persons who affiliate with other Jewish denominations. In particular, some ultra-Orthodox leaders have tried to divest more liberal forms of Judaism of legiti-macy, urging the Israeli government to revoke the right of return for Jews who have been converted by non-Orthodox clergy, and the children of such converts. Some ul-tra-Orthodox groups have violently opposed tolerance and respect for non-Orthodox Jews worshipping in public, especially at the Western Wall in the Old City in Jerusalem. These attempts have often drawn sweeping critiques from Conservative, Reform, and Reconstructionist leaders, who are understandably agitated that their un-derstanding of Judaism has been labeled "not Judaism." The resulting public and pub-lished accusations and counter-accusations have undermined connections to Israel and have deflected communal will from working cooperatively toward the increased accessibility of more extensive and intensive forms of Jewish education.

Making Coalescence Work for Jewish Life

This book has argued throughout that the unprecedented freedom that American Jews enjoy has been a source of extraordinary advantages, accompanied by a tendency to-ward the erosion of the rich cultural legacy of Jewish history. We have suggested three reactions to coalescence. The most extreme model, utilized by right-wing Orthodox groups comprising perhaps 3 percent of the American-Jewish population, is that of resisting coalescence by resealing permeable boundaries, so that fewer elements of Americanization can enter their societies and the lives of their individual members. Living in close-knit communities where societal pressure can be a real force for be-havior modification, making high levels of Jewish education a social imperative and discouraging college education except as a kind of vocational training, maintaining as norms early marriages and large families, the boundary resealers regard American cul-ture as a pollutant, rather than as a potential source of enrichment. Even they, who see any amount of cultural diffusion or coalescence as a national and religious tragedy, have been affected by American values and behaviors, but levels of Americanization are limited.

The second model, employed to a large extent passively or unwittingly by more than two-thirds of American Jews, is that of minimal resistance to coalescence. The majority of younger American Jews have grown up in homes with little Jewish cul-tural ambience, receiving low levels of Jewish education. High levels of secular edu-cation and high levels of geographical mobility and independence have characteristi-cally been facilitated by American-Jewish parents; there is little indication that they also emphasized the importance of the Jewish environment of the universities at-tended. For this large proportion of the American-Jewish population, a dearth of cul-tural literacy becomes a kind of self-fulfilling prophecy. When formal Jewish educa-tion is minimal, it may well provide only a very narrow level of acquaintance with the Jewish cultural heritage, articulated by a woman in her sixties who had attended Sun-day school: "My formal religious education taught me that bribes work, women were always wrong, and Jews had an obligation to survive. Not to learn, believe, or under-stand, just to survive. There were no answers so there was no point in asking ques-tions." In addition, marriages are often late, and single-person households are unlikely to affiliate and bring Jewish organizational activities into the mix. Outmarriage by about one-third of the younger population brings even more Americanized elements into these Jewish homes.

However, a third model of reacting to coalescence, by reinforcing the intensity of Jewish life without resealing the boundaries, is employed by around one-quarter of American Jews. They enhance Jewish connections through cognitive and affective experience, and yet are open to the inward and outward flow of Americanisms. For those Jews who are concerned about maintaining Jewish cultural literacy and strong connections with Jews and Jewishness, but do not uniformly reject the American version of Western culture, the infusion of Jewish distinctiveness presents a far more attractive option for meaningful Jewish survival than does isolation.

By observing these high Jewish education-high secular education American Jews, we see that learning experiences work because they enable Jewish individuals to engage in a dialogue with historical Judaism. Effective learning experiences change the way an individual views and interacts with the world; Jewish learning can enable the individual to respond to his or her American environment with a Jewish consciousness. When Jewish learning is both broad and deep, when it engages the individual in the intellectual, emotional, artistic, and social realms, it becomes a natural element in a complex Jewish consciousness of the full spectrum of life's joys and challenges.

Jewish formal and informal educational experiences provide the twin initial and lifelong bases for the infusion of Jewish cognitive and affective materials into American lives. Cognitively, individuals have a more genuinely Jewish consciousness when they have acquired intellectual tools that include familiarity with the Jewish religious belief system; Jewish texts and literatures; Jewish laws, codes, and rituals; Jewish languages; Jewish prescriptions for familial behaviors; Jewish ideas of communalism; Jewish preferences for gender role construction; and the diversity of Jewish cultural expressions.

Affectively, individuals are more likely to be actively connected to other Jewish individuals and Jewish religious and communal structures when their experiential lives have included cultural reinforcements, such as those provided by Jewish families, youth groups, camps, and friends, along with Israel trips. Respondents in focus groups, individual interviews, and other settings repeatedly spoke about the powerful role of family and home-based rituals both in educating them as children and in reinforcing their Jewish connections as the years pass.

This model for harnessing coalescence to make it the vehicle for dynamic Jewish life is not limited to any one wing of Judaism. A powerful example of how it works was articulated by a middle-aged Reform man, who remarked that Judaism "provides me with some spiritual and ethical guidelines by which I can seek to live a meaningful life," and "provides me with an overwhelming sense of Jewish continuity," but most importantly,

> gives me the most marvelous and enjoyable social and cultural framework I have ever encountered. Its holidays and rituals bring the family and community together in an atmosphere of meaningful learning and fun. When we annually retell the story of the Exodus from Egypt, we concurrently remind ourselves of

the importance of freedom, of family and community, and manage to do so with food and song, a sense of togetherness and a healthy dose of good humor. In virtually every Jewish home will be found certain constants: an emphasis on learning and education, a sense of responsibility to the family as well as to the community, and an awareness that forces of movements which threaten others may someday threaten ourselves and must therefore be resisted. These are the essential components of my Jewish identity.

Within this rose-colored depiction of the American-Jewish family Seder table, American values (fun, good humor, secular education) have been creatively coalesced into solidly Jewish values and behaviors. Others spoke passionately about the positive effects of Jewish camping experiences and Israel trips. In the context of contemporary permeable boundaries, both quantitative and qualitative data support the hypothesis that formal and informal Jewish educational experiences yield complementary types of Jewish enculturation. Substantive formal education that extends over the teen years has the most reliable predictive association with adult Jewish connections; informal Jewish education, almost always experienced today by persons who are also in the highest categories of formal educational cohorts, is closely correlated with adult connections. Together, they provide the best chance to ensure that what Hwang calls "dynamic assimilation" does not lead to the extreme type of coalescence that is tantamount to cultural impoverishment.

Religion and the Future of American Jewish Distinctiveness

An exclusive focus on the construction of ethnic identity, while a useful tool for understanding the behavior of ethnic groups, leaves critical religious concerns insufficiently explored. Joanne Nagel, after effectively discussing current applications of constructionist theory, poses some critical unanswered questions: "What is driving groups to construct and reconstruct ethnic identity and culture? What is it about ethnicity that appeals to individuals on so fundamental a level?"[16] Phillip Hammond and Kee Warner have suggested that for some Christian denominations "decline of ethnic identity appears to precede decline of ethnic religious loyalty," although they warn that "just because religion is a matter of choice, its importance declines; it may actually take on greater psychological significance even as its social and ethnic importance diminishes."[17] Queries about the persistent salience of membership in the Jewish entity may require more direct focus on the sociology of religion. To understand the current Jewish communal obsession with "continuity," for example, we can learn much by turning to Peter Berger's theory that religious group identification serves as a spiritual antidote to randomness and mortality:

> This does not mean that nothing terrible could happen to the individual or that he is guaranteed perennial happiness. It does mean that whatever else happens, however terrible, makes sense to him by being related to his ultimate meaning of things. Only if this point is grasped can one understand the per-

sistent attractiveness of the various versions of this world view to the Israelites, even long after their own religious development had decisively broken with it.[18]

Berger argues that to the extent that individuals can locate themselves within an ancient and continuing spiritual community, they can perceive themselves as part of an immortal chain, even in a radically secularized universe. The chain of Jewish history has had powerful appeal in Jewish traditional life, partially because the communal imagination, shaped among the masses as well as the elites by daily Jewish liturgy and holiday celebrations, has, until quite recently, brought the patriarchs and Jewish heroes of the past into the imagined community of Jews in every century and in every place. This imagined community was particularly important because of the pan-ethnicity of Jewish communities spread out across the globe.

Hyphenated Jews, both scholars and lay people, have continued to re-invent their Jewish past in ways that resonate in their own cultural context. From the most liberal to the Orthodox worlds, across the denominational spectrum, serious contemporary Jews look to the past for precedents and anchors. For example, much of the focus of Jewish feminist effort in the United States has been to insure that the imagined community of past Jews is not composed exclusively of men but also includes female matriarchs and heroines. Jewish women are urged to include biblical females in their list of invited guests to the *Succah,* the matriarchs, Deborah, Esther, and Yael along with the traditional *Ushpizin* of patriarchs and beloved male biblical heroes.

Similarly, when Orthodox women in feminist groups and as individuals justify their participation in separate *tefillah* worship communities, they often turn to the existence of women's prayer groups in Eastern Europe, as though there were a direct line between the excluded East European Jewish women and their *firzogerin* prayer leaders and the feminists who are their great-great-granddaughters. In truth, although their activities are strikingly similar, the prayer activities of contemporary Orthodox women began in the early 1970s in a very contemporary feminist response to perceived inequities. It was only later that female and male scholars looked back to traditional Jewish societies and found "precedents" for the women's *tefillah* groups. In choosing to link their own activities, so influenced by contemporary attitudes and mores, to those of Jewish women in the past, American Jewish feminists are inventing a history of their own, composed of factual evidence, but with a fresh new emphasis.

This ability to link traditional behaviors with Jewish feminist liturgical interventions is very significant to many women. For example, one Orthodox attorney celebrating her son's Bar Mitzvah in 1997 stated in an address to the congregation that she looked to her own pious East European grandmothers for an example of a prayer that a traditional woman could utter on such an occasion. Addressing both men and women from the *bimah* of her modern Orthodox congregation on Saturday morning, she spoke about the fact that in some communities no women, even mothers, were present at the occasion of their sons' Bar Mitzvah, "it was an exclusively male activity." She talked about the prevalence of European women praying together "in what amounted to parallel prayer in a virtually separate room." Ultimately, like some feminist scholars, the attorney turned to retrieving the homely Yiddish prayers, *tekhinnes,* which devout Jewish women recited as they went about their daily tasks and confronted life cycle events. She concluded her talk by reciting the translation of one such traditional Yiddish prayer which had been composed for the purpose of a son's Bar Mitzvah. Thus, she recited the same words on the same occasion as her grandmothers might have, but in a radically different context.

Coalescence has changed the terms of the interplay between American and Jewish values in contemporary American Jewish societies, and it has, in certain ways, supplanted assimilation as a primary vehicle for the Americanization of Jews in the United States. However, the impact of coalescence is not necessarily destructive to Jewish connections. Unlike assimilation, coalescence allows highly educated, highly achieving Jews to feel that their achievements bond them to, rather than separate them from, their Jewish ethnicity. Because of internal ethnic identity reconstruction and external boundary permeability, contemporary Americans need not reject—or even "tune out"—their Jewish identity. How far that connection goes and how deep it reaches depends on factors such as the extent of formal and informal Jewish educational experiences and the consistency of Jewish commitments in the parental home.

The depth of Jewish identification will increasingly be related to religious aspects of ethnicity. Benedict Anderson may be correct that for many emerging nations modern communications and technology have been critical to creating an imagined community which includes characters from the past as well as living citizens of their contemporary world.[19] For Jews, however, the religious consciousness of daily life and liturgy ensured that an imagined community of belief and common destiny was repeatedly transmitted long before the age of the global village. In its own way, Jewish history was a global village.

Today, as each Jewish generation moves further and further away from immigrant origins, ethnic memories fade. Spiritual questions, in contrast, feel fresh to each new generation of individuals facing life's existential and sequential mysteries, including mortality. The prominence of religious, rather than ethnic, components of Jewish identity, may be increased by the entry into Jewish communities of converts who come from other ethnic groups, for whom the only feasible type of Jewish identity is arrived at via a spiritual journey. During the coming years, there will be no easy answers via default bagels-lox-and-guilt models of Jewish distinctiveness, because those thin, stylistic aspects of Jewishness have already been diffused into general American culture. Instead, aspects of American Jewish identity that relate to spiritual community will occupy more prominent places in the psychic maps of meaning of identified American Jews.

APPENDIX

The Methodology of the National Jewish Population Survey

Joseph Waksberg

Large-scale sample surveys are frequently carried out in a number of discrete steps and the National Jewish Population Survey (NJPS) followed such a pattern. The steps consisted of: determination of the subjects to be included in the survey; development of specific question wording; testing questions and procedures, decisions on survey procedures; preparation for data collection, including recruitment and training of staff; sample selection; data collection; weighting and other aspects of data processing; internal analysis of potential sources of errors; tabulations; analyses and preparation of reports. This methodological report concentrates on the technical aspects relating to sampling, survey procedures and data collection, weighting, and issues relating to accuracy of the data. There is a brief description of the questionnaire development. Data analysis and preparation of publications, both of the monographs and of less detailed reports, are not part of the survey methodology and are not discussed here.

1. GENERAL SURVEY PROCEDURES

United Jewish Communities, formerly known as The Council of Jewish Federations (CJF), established and supports a National Technical Advisory Committee on Jewish Population Studies (NTAC). At the time the NJPS was planned, the NTAC consisted of researchers who worked for the CJF or local Jewish federations and outside demographers and statisticians interested in Jewish issues. The NTAC endorsed an initial recommendation of the October 1987 World Conference on Jewish Demography in Jerusalem to conduct a U.S. National Jewish Population Survey (NJPS) in the spring and summer of 1990. The CJF concurred in this recommendation and agreed to support such a survey.

The choice of 1990 was a deliberate one since it placed the survey at about the same time as the 1990 U.S. Census, thereby insuring maximum comparability between the Jewish survey data and census statistics. Further, the time period chosen for the conduct of the detailed interviews—late spring and early summer—both corresponded to the timing of the Census and is a time when most college students can be reached in their families' residences or other dwelling places that are more permanent than dormitories or other college housing. The interviewing period is also the time that most Sunbelt residents are in their more permanent homes.

The NTAC had independently come up with 1990 as the logical period for the survey as part of more general considerations of appropriate survey methodology. In a series of meetings in the decade leading up to 1990, the NTAC had discussed the many aspects of planning and implementing a Jewish Population Study and had submitted the following recommendations to the CJF:

- *That a large scale survey of the Jewish population be conducted in 1990.*
- *Data collection should be by telephone.* Over the past twenty to thirty years, survey researchers had demonstrated that the quality of responses to inquiries over the telephone were, for almost all subjects, about the same as for face-to-face interviews. Response rates to telephone surveys are generally lower than in face-to-face interviews, but the cost of telephone surveys is so much lower that the NTAC felt that the substantial cost advantage of a telephone survey more than compensated for the adverse effect on quality of a lower response rate.
- *A sample of 2,000 to 2,500 Jewish households should be selected by random digit dialing (RDD), without any use of Federation or other lists of Jewish households.* RDD gives all households with telephones in the United States (both Jewish and non-Jewish) a known chance of selection into the sample so that lists are not necessary. Furthermore, it was the NTAC's judgment that the effort involved in trying to construct a national list, and the likely small percentage of U.S. Jews that would be on the list, would make the construction of the list counterproductive. It should be noted that households without telephones were not intended to be covered in the survey. In 1990, about 7 percent of U.S. households did not have telephones. However, the percentage is undoubtedly much lower for Jewish households, and the NTAC did not believe their omission would have any detectable effect on the quality of the survey results. The survey also was to omit the nonhousehold population, principally persons in nursing homes, long-term hospital units, religious institutions, military barracks, and prisons. College students in dormitories (as well as those in private residences) were to be covered in the survey, usually as members of their parents' households.
- *Data should be collected only for the civilian population living in the households,* omitting the institutional and other nonhousehold population. The survey thus would exclude those in prisons, hospitals, nursing homes, hotels, religious institutions, and in military barracks. Estimates of the relatively small number of Jews in such places were added to the survey results for the estimate of the total number of Jews in the United States. However, their characteristics would not be reflected in the breakdowns of the totals by age, sex, etc.
- *A screening questionnaire that defines and identifies Jewish households should be administered to the sample of telephone households.* Since random digit dialing

produces a sample of all U.S. telephone households, non-Jewish households would then be dropped and Jewish households retained for the survey.

- *That the survey include a wide variety of topics.* The NTAC developed a broad set of questions designed to shed light on the demographic, social, and economic characteristics of the Jewish population, and to provide information on items of specific Jewish concern, such as intermarriage, Jewish education, philanthropy, observances of Jewish rituals and practices, synagogue membership, utilization of social services, volunteerism, attitudes to certain issues of Jewish concern, etc. The questions were divided into two groups: (a) ones for which reasonably accurate information for all household members could be provided by any adult in the household (e.g., age, education, observance, etc.) and (b) questions for which the accuracy of proxy responses would be in doubt (e.g., attitudes). For the first set of questions, data would be obtained for all members of the sample households. For the second group, the NTAC recommended that one adult be selected at random in each sample household and that the sample for these items should be considered as consisting of only the selected persons.
- A second, and independent, partition of the questions was also made. In order to reduce the considerable interview length, the questionnaire was divided into a "core" component, to be asked in all sample households, and "modules" to be asked in subsamples of households. More specifically, respondents were randomly allocated to three equal subsamples, and each subsample was assigned one of the three following areas of inquiries:

  1. Jewish identity
  2. Social services
  3. Philanthropy

- *After the survey information was collected, weights should be inserted into the data file.* The weights should be constructed so that when they are used in tabulations of the survey data, they provide approximately unbiased estimates of the U.S. Jewish population in each category shown in the tabulations.
- *The individual responses to the survey questionnaire as well as the appropriate weights should be entered onto a computer tape.* Copies of the tape would be available for researchers interested in making detailed studies of particular aspects of Jewish life.
- *A high priority was put on speed of data processing, tabulations of the data, and publication of the major results,* first in a summary report highlighting the major findings in the survey, and then in a series of analytic studies focusing on particular topics.
- *That the survey be conducted outside of CJF or its member organizations.* More specifically, that a contract be let by competitive bidding to a company experienced in the conduct of such statistical studies.

The CJF approved the NTAC recommendations, provided a budget for the survey, and asked the NTAC to make the necessary arrangements. A Request for Proposals (RFP) that described the work to be done, the procedures outlined above, and the scope of work was prepared and distributed to interested statistical and market research companies. A subcommittee of the NTAC received the proposals submitted by organizations that were interested in carrying out the survey, and selected the ones that were judged best. These organizations were invited to make personal presentations of their plans and their experience in such activities before the subcommittee. A contract was then awarded to a team consisting of ICR Survey Research Group and Marketing Systems Group (also known as Genesys Sampling Systems). The Marketing Systems Group was responsible for the sample selection and all weighting and estimation phases of the project. ICR was responsible for all other aspects of the survey, from questionnaire pretesting through data collection, coding, and data tape preparation.

The choice of ICR and Marketing Systems Group was based on a number of factors: understanding of the requirements of the study, the reputation of the team in doing high-quality work, experience with large-scale telephone sample surveys, an existing staff of experienced telephone interviewers and a system for training and supervising them, a capable statistician to oversee the sampling and related activities, and cost. A main, and overriding advantage of the team, was the fact that they carried out, for other sponsors, a weekly RDD national household sample survey of 2,000 households. They agreed to add the screening questions that identified Jewish households to the questionnaire then in use. It was estimated that the approximately 100,000 households screened over the course of a year would supply the 2,500 responding Jewish households desired in the final sample. (The screening actually covered more than a year, and consisted of over 125,000 households which yielded over 5,000 households that indicated the presence of a Jewish member.) By attaching the screener questions to an existing national sample survey, the NJPS was able to avoid the expense of selecting and interviewing the very large sample needed to locate 2,500 Jewish households. Instead, the survey incurred only a fairly modest marginal cost of the added time to administer the screening questions. If the NJPS had to pay the entire cost of selecting and screening more than 100,000 households, the additional cost probably would have been well over $1,000,000.

An additional advantage of using the ICR's ongoing weekly survey was that it provided flexibility in achieving the desired sample size. The amount of screening necessary to achieve a sample of 2,500 Jewish households could only be approximately estimated in advance. With the weekly samples screened by ICR, a cumulative tally of Jewish households could be kept, and the weekly samples terminated before the end of the year if fewer than 100,000 households provided the required sample size, or it could be continued for longer than a year if that was necessary.

2. SAMPLE SELECTION

The telephone numbers selected for the NJPS were based on random digit dialing (RDD), and are a probability sample of all possible telephone numbers in the United

States. The sampling procedure utilized a single-stage sample of telephone numbers within known residential working banks (the first two digits of the four-digit suffix, e.g., 212-555-XXxx). Telephone exchanges were strictly ordered by census geographic variables (i.e., Division, Metro/Non-Metro, Central City/Suburban, etc.) creating a sample frame with fine implicit geographic stratification. This procedure provides samples that are unbiased and in which all telephones have the same chance of selection. Since the random digit aspect allows for the inclusion of unlisted and unpublished numbers, it protects the samples from "listing bias"—the unrepresentativeness of telephone samples that can occur if the distinctive households whose telephone numbers are unlisted and unpublished are excluded from the sample. The RDD sample is referred to as the "screening sample." It consisted of 125,813 households that were asked whether any household members was Jewish. (See Section 4 for specific questions.) All qualified Jewish households were followed up with requests for the detailed interviews.

The household sample selection was accompanied by an automated scheme for scheduling callbacks for telephone numbers at which there was no response to the initial call. A three-callback rule was followed—the timing of the callbacks was scheduled by the computer to cover various times of the day, but within a narrow time frame. This narrow time frame was required by the short field period for each weekly survey. There were actually two weekly sample surveys, with 1,000 households in each survey. One weekly survey ran from Wednesday evening through Sunday evening; the second from Friday evening through Tuesday evening. The initial call and callback schedule ensured a minimum of two week-end attempts (if necessary) on each sample number.

The tight time schedule for the screening interviews undoubtedly reduced the response rate, as compared to a survey with more time for callbacks. (For example, persons on a vacation during the survey week were never given an opportunity to respond.) However, the NTAC believed that the advantages of using an ongoing survey for screening outweighed the disadvantages.

3. PRESURVEY OPERATIONS

Two major sets of activities preceded the data collection. They consisted of the development and testing of the survey questions, and the interviewer training and briefing.

3.1. Development and Testing of Survey Instruments

Three stages of data collection were planned: screening, recontact and in-depth interviewing. The questionnaires for all three phases were initially developed by the NTAC. These documents were then edited, reformatted, and programmed for CATI interviewing by ICR staff. The development phase included several questionnaire drafts and a series of "live" pretests.

CATI stands for Computer Assisted Telephone Interviewing. It is a system in which the questionnaire has been entered into a computer, each interviewer is provided with a computer screen and keyboard, and the questions to be asked appear on the screen instead of having to be read from a paper questionnaire. The responses are entered directly into the computer. In addition to speeding up the data processing, CATI has the capability of carrying out editing for consistency and completeness of data and flexibility of operations. Almost all large-scale telephone surveys are now done by means of CATI.

All interviewing in both the Screening, Recontact/Validation, and the Main Study Phases were conducted by professional interviewers by means of computer-assisted telephone interviewing. From an interviewing standpoint, the CATI system removes the potential for interviewer error relative to skip patterns and possible response options. Moreover, the CATI system provides inherent response editing capabilities relative to both range edits and conditional requirements based upon prior responses. Computerized questionnaire control allows interviewers to better establish rapport with respondents and concentrate on responses rather than attempting to contend with the extreme complexity of the Recontact and Main Study questionnaires.

Finally, CATI capabilities allowed for access to up-to-the-minute interviewing production measures including production rates, refusal and refusal conversion rates, and results of dialing attempts.

In each pretest, personnel from NTAC and ICR monitored interviewers as they were being conducted. Any unforeseen deficiencies in question content, sequencing, and nomenclature were corrected during this stage. In most cases, indicated changes were incorporated immediately, providing pre-test capabilities during the same pretest session.

The final CATI questionnaires were reviewed and tested extensively by both NTAC and ICR personnel prior to "live" interviewing. In addition, the pretest data served as a "live" test of output, data format, edit checks, etc.

3.2. Interviewer Training and Briefing

All interviewers selected to work on the 1990 NJPS were personally briefed, trained, and supervised during all hours of interviewing. In addition to participating in the standard ICR ten-hour interviewer training session, all interviewers who worked on the survey participated in a detailed briefing session developed specifically for this study.

This special briefing included an item-by-item discussion of each question and module contained in the interview; a discussion of special respondent "handling" for specific interview situations, including providing the CJF's telephone number to respondents who questioned the authenticity of the survey and suggesting that the CJF be called; and a review of areas and issues relating to Jewish heritage including customs, holidays, and proper pronunciation of Hebrew words and phrases that interviewers would be likely to encounter during the course of the study. In addition to the briefing, written interviewer aids were provided and made available during all hours of interviewing.

4. ORGANIZATION OF DATA COLLECTION ACTIVITIES

For approximately one year preceding the survey, beginning in April 1989, ICR conducted Stage I of the National Jewish Population Survey. This entailed incorporating a series of four screening questions into its twice weekly general market telephone surveys. The screening questions determined Jewish qualification and thus were the basis for the recruitment of households. The four screening questions in Stage I were asked in the following order:

1. What is your religion?
   If not Jewish, then . . .
2. Do you or anyone else in the household consider themselves Jewish?
   If no, then . .·.
3. Were you or anyone else in the household raised Jewish?
   If no, then . . .
4. Do you or anyone else in the household have a Jewish parent?

This screening stage of the survey obtained information on the religious preference of 125,813 randomly selected adult Americans and the Jewish qualification of their respective households. It was determined initially that 5,146 households contained at least one person who qualified as "Jewish" or Jewishly affiliated as determined by the screening questions. Stage II, the inventory stage, consisted of attempts to recontact Jewish households to requalify potential respondents and solicit participation in the 1990 NJPS. The households classified as Jewish in the last three months of screening were omitted from Stage II because the Stage III interviewing was to follow so closely. Stage II included 4,208 households. During Stage II, a number of households that were initially classified as Jewish dropped out of the survey sample due to changes in household composition or to disqualification based upon further review.

Stage III, the final interviewing stage of the survey, yielded a total of 2,441 completed interviews with qualified respondents. The statistics reported here are drawn from these households. Through a process of scientific weighting procedures utilizing all 125,813 Stage I interviews, the sample of Jewish households represents about 3.2 million American households nationally.

The survey interviews collected information about every member of the household. Thus, the study was able to ascertain important personal information about 6,514 persons in the surveyed households. Appropriate weighting procedures indicate that the number of persons in the surveyed households represents about 8.1 million individual Americans, a number of whom are not themselves Jewish, reflecting the mixed composition of the households in the Jewish sample.

5. DATA COLLECTION: FIRST TWO HASES—SCREENING AND RECONTACT AND VALIDATION

5.1. Phase I: Screening

The entire screening phase was conducted as part of the ICR Survey Research Group's twice weekly telephone omnibus survey. The use of a telephone omnibus vehicle as opposed to a custom survey has obvious cost advantages; on the other side, there may be trade-offs relative to response rates, length of field period, placement of the screening questions on Jewish identity with the ever changing instrument, etc. However, these were thought to be small.

As mentioned earlier, 125,813 screeners were completed for this project. Although no formal disposition of call results is available, it is known that the proportion refusing to participate in any given weekly survey averages about 45 percent. In order to assess the potential bias resulting from this response rate, two separate analyses were conducted. They are described in Section 9.

5.2. Phase II: Recontact and Validation

The second phase of the study was conducted with respondents from Jewish households identified during the initial Screening Phase. This phase was designed to validate the initial screening process; to initiate contacts with qualified households to explain the purpose of the study and gain cooperation; and to provide a means of keeping in touch with the qualified respondents given the extended time period between the initial screening and final interview.

The primary informational objectives of the Recontact/Validation Phase were as follows:

1. Validate that the respondent/household was, in fact, Jewish;
2. Explain the purpose of the call and encourage respondents to participate in the in-depth Study during the summer of 1990;
3. Collect detailed household data relating to age, sex, and relationship of each household member, and type of residence and location; and
4. Request and secure a third party reference to assist in the future recontact for the in-depth Study.

Recontact Phase interviewing was conducted over a 52-week period, from 7 April 1989 through 2 April 1990. The process was continuous, with most recontacts occurring within two weeks of the initial qualification in the Screening Phase.

Upon successful recontact, the household member who participated in the Screening Phase was asked to reverify the Jewish character of himself/herself and other household members relative to:

- Being Jewish;
- Considering himself/herself Jewish;
- Being raised Jewish; and
- Having a Jewish parent.

Respondents were asked to participate in an in-depth Main Study Phase interview to be conducted at a later date. This recruitment included an explanation of the study, the size of the study, an explanation of how and why they were selected to participate, and the naming of CJF as the study sponsor.

Substantial efforts were made to "convert" respondents who refused to participate. Respondents who refused to participate at the introduction or during the interview itself were recontacted by specially trained interviewers. These interviewers used specially developed and proven techniques to convert refusals into participants. In some cases, alternative respondents within a given household were recruited to participate. In addition to specially trained interviewers, letters of explanation were mailed to refusals in an effort to establish credibility for the study and, in turn, to increase likely participation.

A household inventory of requalified Jewish households was created; this roster of household members included age and sex, along with each member's relationship to the primary contact person. Specifically, four questions were asked about each household member:

1. Name;
2. Age and sex;
3. Relationship to the respondent; and
4. Religious qualification.

Additional information relating to household characteristics was also requested; specifically, the type of household unit (e.g., multiple family, single unit, apartment, etc.) and whether this particular unit was the primary residence or a seasonal or similar recreational dwelling.

Finally, information about third-party references (i.e., a relative or close friend) was requested for use in the event that respondents could not be reached at their original location. This third-party information was utilized to "track" the original respondents during the final phase of interviewing.

Not every Jewish household identified in the Screening Phase was included in the Recontact Phase. Specifically, households identified during the final three months of Screening were excluded because of the rather short time until onset of the full National Survey; it was thought that the risk associated with alienating respondents by attempting multiple contacts over a very short period of time outweighed the few households likely to be lost due to relocation.

In total, 4,208 Jewish households identified in the Screening Phase were included in the Recontact Phase. The results of attempted recontact are shown in table A.1. It should be noted that there was no strict callback rule, but rather "nonrespondent households" were continually recycled, with many receiving 20 attempts or more.

Over 81 percent of the screened and qualified households were successfully contacted and reinterviewed; of these, 15.5 percent did not requalify and 6.3 percent disavowed knowledge of the previous interview. Just over 9 percent refused the Recontact interview.

None of the original respondent households were excluded from the 1990 Survey based on results of the Recontact Phase; the purpose here was to facilitate tracking of respondents and increase ultimate cooperation, not to requalify, validate, and

Table A.1 Results of the Recontact Validation Phase

	Number	*Percent*
Requalified and willing to participate	2,124	52.1
Requalified and not willing	316.	7.5
Not requalified	652	15.5
No such respondent	266	6.3
Refused at start	315	7.5
Refused during interview	75	1.8
Language barrier	27	0.6
Nonworking	135	3.2
Nonhouseholds	20	0.5
No Contact	278	6.6
Total	4,208	100.0

reject sample households. Although the Recontact data were retained, all sample households (including those that failed to qualify in Phase II) regardless of the outcome were again attempted during the Final Phase of interviewing.

6. PHASE III: MAIN STUDY—DATA COLLECTION

In the spring and summer of 1990, the third and final phase of data collection was undertaken. The survey instrument itself was initially developed by the NTAC, jointly pretested with ICR, and prepared for CATI interviewing by the ICR.

In the Main Study Phase, households that were identified as being Jewish in the screening phase were recontacted between May 8, 1990, and August 12, 1990, in an effort to complete the in-depth, detailed information requested on the Jewish character of the household, its members and related issues. Due to the considerable interview length (approximately 30 minutes), the questionnaire was divided into two parts: the "core" questionnaire and three shorter questionnaire "modules."

The core questionnaire was asked of all respondents. In addition to this core, respondents were randomly assigned to one of three groups and asked a series of more detailed questions relating to one of the following areas of inquiry (referred to as modules):

1. Jewish identity
2. Social services
3. Philanthropy

The Screening Phase had identified a total of 5,146 Jewish households over more than fifteen months of interviewing, and surveying a total of over 125,000 households. As table A.2 shows, 49 percent of these resulted in completed Phase III interviews; just over 15 percent refused to participate; and in only 13 percent of the cases was it impossible to contact any household members.

Table A.2 Results of the Main Study Phase

	Number	*Percent*
Nonworking	366	7.1
Nonhousehold	63	1.2
No Answer/Busy	191	3.7
Respondent no longer there	23	0.4
Answering machines	101	2.0
Refused at start	670	13.0
Refused during interview	126	2.4
Language barrier	21	0.4
Ineligible	146	2.8
Not requalified	908	17.6
Deleted/Not used interviews	25	0.5
Completed Interview	2,506	48.7
Total	5,146	100.0

The most difficult and puzzling result however, was the roughly 18 percent of respondents and/or households which failed to requalify; all of these respondents were recontacted a second time during Phase III, and all failed to validate their replies in the Screening Phase. Sections 7 and 9 contain a discussion of this group of respondents and describe how they were used in estimating the size of the Jewish population.

It was also a standard practice to attempt conversion of all refusals, so that all of this group represents "double refusals." All telephone numbers reported as "nonworking" were verified and attempts to secure new numbers were made, although this was not very successful. There was no limit on number of followup attempts, which explains the relatively low proportion of "no answer" and "busy" sample dispositions (<4%).

7. WEIGHTING PROCEDURES

7.1. Overview of Weighting Procedures

After the survey information was collected and processed, each respondent was assigned a weight. When the weights are used in tabulations of the survey data, the results automatically provide estimates of the U.S. Jewish population in each category shown in the tabulations.

The weighting method first insured that key demographic characteristics of the adult population of the total weighted sample of the 125,813 screened responding households matched the most current estimates of these demographic characteristics produced by the Census Bureau. The weighting procedure automatically adjusted for noncooperating households, as well as for those who were not at home when the interviewer telephoned and for households that did not have telephones or had multiple lines.

A second step in the weighting was carried out on the questionnaires completed in the recontact and validation phase and the main study phase of the study. This step made the weighted totals of completed questionnaires in each phase of the survey conform to the geographic and demographic profile of Jewish households at the earlier phases.

In addition, a separate weighting routine was established for each of the modules that was based on a subsample of the full set of Jewish households, so that the weighted total of each module corresponded to the full sample.

7.2. Detailed Description of Weighting

There were four stages in the preparation of the screening sample weights. First, households with more than one residential telephone number were assigned weights designed to compensate for their higher probabilities of selection—one-half for households with two telephone numbers, and one-third for households with three or more numbers. Secondly, cooperating households were poststratified, using 18 geographic strata—9 Census Divisions, and 2 categories for in or out of metropolitan areas. In the third stage, a weight was derived by poststratifying the weighted counts of the population in the sample households, using geographic-demographic strata, to the best current estimates of those strata. The strata comprised Census Region (4), age by sex (12), education of respondent (3), and race, i.e., white or other (2). The fourth stage was geographic poststratification at a state, metropolitan statistical area (MSA), or county level, depending on the size of the area. Individual counties with 75,000 or more households became individual strata. The remaining counties were grouped by individual MSAs or when necessary linked to a larger county (over 75,000 households) within the same MSA. Counties outside MSAs were grouped at the state level.

Following the weighting processes described above, the completed screener interviews were classified by their initial level of Jewish qualification and the results of the subsequent data collection efforts. During the various interviewing phases, a significant number of Jewish households that were initially considered qualified, subsequently became classified as non-Jewish. The largest proportion of these households were originally qualified because the respondents or others in the households "considered" themselves to be Jewish. Table A.3 details weighted respondents by the basis for qualification and response category in the Phase II follow-up interview.

The critical issue was how to treat the "not qualified" in estimating the total number of Jewish households. The extreme alternatives were to ignore the requalification information altogether, essentially treating the "not qualified" as refusals; or to take the additional information at "face value" and reduce the estimates of Jewish households by 789,000, to just under 3 million.

Of course, there were a wide range of options in between. To aid in the evaluation of this situation, a DJN (Distinctive Jewish Name) analysis was conducted on the respondents qualified through the screening process. The first step in this process was obtaining a reverse match for these telephone numbers; for each telephone number corresponding to a household that was listed in the white pages of any U.S. tele-

Table A.3 Qualified Jewish Households in Screener by Reporting Status in Validation Interview

Reporting status of later interviews	Total	Basis of qualification in screener			
		Religion	*Consider*	*Raised*	*Parents*
Known Jewish households	1,896,000	1,167,000	460,000	80,000	189,000
	100.0%	61.6	24.2	4.2	9.9
Refused Phase III	506,000	242,000	176,000	29,000	59,000
	100.0%	47.9	34.8	5.8	11.6
Other nonresponse	563,000	200,000	246,000	29,000	88,000
	100.0%	35.4	43.8	5.1	15.7
Non qualified	789,000	128,000	466,000	57,000	138,000
	100.0%	16.2	59.0	7.2	17.5
Total	3,753,000	1,737,000	1,347,000	195,000	474,000
	100.0	46.3	35.9	5.2	12.6

phone directory, the name and address of the subscriber was obtained. The surnames were then matched against a data file of distinctive Jewish surnames provided by the NTAC. The results are shown in table A.4.

As is evident from table A.4, the Not Qualified segment exhibits strikingly different proportions of DJN's from the other groups. Based on this and related information, the determination was made that all respondents originally qualified on the basis of Religion were most likely Refusals, and should remains as qualified Jewish households; conversely, among the other groups, the unweighted ratios of DJN's indicated a likely true qualification rate of 17.5 percent.

Based on these assessments, the estimated Jewish households were adjusted to those shown in table A.5. The impact of these adjustments were to reduce the estimates of Jewish households from 3.753 million to 3.208 million, a reduction of about 14.5 percent.

Table A.4 Percentage of Sample with Distinctive Jewish Surnames (Base = Qualifiers with a Located Surname)

Reporting status in later interviews	Total	Basis of qualification in screener			
		Religion	*Consider*	*Raised*	*Parents*
Known Jewish household	16.7	23.3	5.6	10.5	4.8
Refused Phase III	13.8	20.0	8.0	9.5	7.8
Other nonresponse	10.9	21.21	4.9	6.7	3.8
Not qualified	2.6	8.6	1.5	0.0	1.6

Table A.5 Final Estimates of Jewish Households Reflecting Adjustments to "Not Qualified"
Call Results

Reporting status in later interviews	Total	Basis of qualification in Screen			
		Religion	Consider	Raised	Parents
Known Jewish HH	1,896,000	1,167,000	460,000	80,000	189,000
	100.0%	61.6	24.2	4.2	9.9
Refused Phase III	506,000	242,000	176,000	29,000	59,000
	100.0%	47.9	34.8	5.8	11.6
Other Nonresponse	563,000	200,000	246,000	29,000	88,000
	100.0%	35.4	43.8	5.1	15.7
Not Qualified	244,000	128,000	82,000	10,000	24,000
	100.0%	52.4	33.6	4.1	9.9
Total	3,208,000	1,737,000	963,000	148,000	360,000
	100.0%	54.1	30.0	4.6	11.2

The adjustments to the weighted estimates of Jewish households in table A.5 required a two-phase adjustment to the weighted dataset:

1. The indicated proportions of Not Qualified respondents needed to be weighted downward to the indicated totals, while non-Jewish households required a compensatory weight to maintain Total Household in the entire Screening Sample.
2. The completed Phase III interviews were then weighted to the estimates of Total Jewish Households, for analyses based on Jewish households only.

The first step was accomplished by stratifying based on Census Division, and within Division, by (1) non-Jewish Qualifiers; (2) Households qualified in the screener as Jewish based on other than Religion, who became "not Qualified in Phase III; and, (3) all other Jewish households. The second group represents those respondents whose estimate of Jewish affiliation was to be adjusted in this process. The revised weights were substituted in the individual data records, completing reconciliation of the full Screener Data set.

The procedure described above was carried out for the full sample and is therefore applicable to the core questionnaire that was administered to all sample households. However, each sample data record also includes a module weight in addition to the household and population weights for the core questions. The weighting procedure for the modules duplicated that of the previous section: a poststratification scheme incorporating census region and level of Jewish qualification. A simple expansion factor, to weight each module's sample total in each cell was computed, multiplied by the household weight, and incorporated into the sample record.

Separate population weights were also developed for the statistics obtained from the randomly selected adult in each household. Essentially, these weights incorporated the household weights multiplied by the number of adults in the sample households.

8. APPLICATION OF WEIGHTS

Given the character and complexity of the survey instrument itself, a determination as to which of the weights described above to utilize for a particular statistic is not always apparent. The following explanation and examples should help in eliminating uncertainties.

Household weights should be used for developing estimates in the following types of situations:

1. Where the analysis, table, or distribution being produced is clearly based on household demographics. Examples include:

    • The number of households by level of Jewish qualification;
    • Distributions of households by number of children, number of adults, number of Jewish adults, age of oldest member, or household income distributions.
    • Household distributions based on qualification of one or more members; such as "are you or any member of your household currently a member of a synagogue or temple?"

2. Where the analysis or distribution utilizes variables constructed from the roster of household members. Examples include:

    • Age or educational attainment of all household members or subsets of all members.
    • Country of origin, or employment status, of all household members or adult household members.

The populations weights are applicable only in those situations where the respondent answers to a specific question about himself or herself, and are to be utilized to represent all adult members in Jewish households. For example:

• Opinions about various public issues.
• Distributions of Jewish religious denomination, or Jewish ethnicity.
• Personal attendance at Jewish religious services.

In certain rare situations users may need to devise their own weighting schemes to establish a fully weighted sample base. This is most likely to occur when the adult members of a sample household exceed the number for which data was requested. For example, detailed information as to marital status was requested for only four members 18 years of age and older. If a particular sample household had five members, there are a number of options depending upon one's objectives and the characteristics of the household:

• A balance line of "not-reported" could be incorporated into the tables being produced.

- The simplest weighting method would be to weight each of the four responses by 1.25 in addition to application of the household weight. Depending, however, upon the characteristics of the member for whom no data is available, alternative approaches might prove more desirable.
- If the missing number's data represented one of three adult children, a better approach might be to weight the data for the two children for which data is present by 1.5, while keeping the parent's weight at 1.0.
- Alternatively, one could compensate for the missing member information on an overall basis. For example, one could categorize all qualified members by age, sex, region, etc., using the household weights; categorize those for which data was reported in a similar matrix using the household weight; and finally computing a weight for each cell which would increase the base of those responding to the weighted total in the first matrix.

In most cases, the bias created by simply ignoring the small discrepancies will be minimal. However, the user needs to make these decisions on a case-by-case basis, possibly trying alternative methods and comparing the results.

Finally, the module weights should obviously be used for tabulations of items in any of the modules regardless of whether simple totals of module items are tabulated or there are cross-classifications with other nonmodule items.

9. ACCURACY OF DATA

9.1. Nonsampling Errors

All population surveys are subject to the possibility of errors arising from sampling, nonresponse, and respondents providing the wrong information, and the NJPS is no exception. The response rate to identify potential Jewish households was approximately 50 percent. This Is lower than most surveys that make efforts to insure high quality strive to achieve. (The low response rate was partially caused by the contractor's need for each set of sample cases assigned for interview to be completed in a few days. This made intensive followup in the screener impractical.) The concern over the effect of nonresponse on the statistics is not so much on the size of the nonresponse since this is adjusted for in the weighting, but on the likelihood that nonrespondents are somewhat different from respondents. Although variations in response rates by geography, age, sex, race, and educational attainment were adjusted for in the weighting, there was still the possibility that Jews and non-Jews responded at different rates.

To test whether this occurred at an important level, the telephone numbers of approximately 10,000 completed interviews and for about 10,000 nonrespondents were matched against telephone listings to obtain the household names, and the percentage of each group having distinctive Jewish names was calculated. The percentage for the completed cases was 1.38 percent and for the nonrespondents was 1.29. The difference between the two is well within the bounds of sampling error. Although distinctive Jewish names account for a minority of all Jews, this test does provide support for the view that nonresponse did not have an important impact on the reliability of the count of the Jewish population.

In regard to errors in reporting whether a person is Jewish, previous studies indicate that the errors are in the direction of understating the count of the Jewish population, although the size of the understatement does not seem to be very large. A particular concern in the NJPS was the fairly large number of cases where respondents in households reporting the presence of one or more Jews in the screening operation, reversed themselves in the detailed interview. Of all households reported as having Jews in the screener, 18 percent were reported as nonqualified in the detailed interview. There was a possibility that this was a hidden form of refusal, rather than errors in the original classification of the households or changes in household membership.

A test similar to the one on refusals was carried out for the nonqualified households. The telephone numbers for the 5,146 households were reported as Jewish in the screening interview were matched against telephone listings, and those with distinctive Jewish names (DJN) were identified. The detailed results of the match are reported in Section 7. They can be summarized as follows: In households that reported themselves as Jewish in the detailed interviews, 16.8 percent had DJN's. The rates were slightly smaller for refusals (13.9 percent) and for those who could not be contacted (10.9 percent). However, the percentage was only 2.9 percent for households who were reported as not Jewish in the detailed interview. It is, of course, possible that DJN households are less reticent than others in acknowledging to a telephone interviewer the fact that all or some of the household members are Jewish, but the evidence is that underreporting did occur, but not to a very serious extent. An adjustment in the weights of about 8 percent was made to account for the unreported Jews in the estimates of the total number of Jews. Since questionnaire information was not obtained for them, the statistics on characteristics of Jews may be subject to small biases if the Jewish nonqualifiers are very different from those who responded.

As mentioned earlier, other studies have reported that there is some understatement of reporting of Jewish heritage in interviews surveys. No adjustments were made for such possible understatement since firm data on its size does not exist. As a result, the estimate of the size of the Jewish population is probably somewhat on the low side.

It is not possible to quantify the effects of the relatively high nonresponse rates, the possibility that some respondents might have deliberately misreported their religious affiliations, errors arising from misunderstanding of the questions, or other problems in the data. As indicated above, the test done with the presence of Distinctive Jewish Names did not detect any important problems. Furthermore, comparisons of the estimates of total Jewish population with the results of local area surveys carried out in or near 1990, did not show any important discrepancies. The screener questionnaire that inquired about Jewish affiliations also identified other major U.S. religious groupings, and estimates of their membership corresponded reasonably well with independent estimates of the membership.

Consequently, all of the tests we were able to carry out failed to turn up any major problems in the data. However, it seems reasonable to assume that persons who did not respond are somewhat different from respondents, and the other potential sources of error must also have had some impact. When comparisons are made, either over time, or among subgroups of Jewish persons (e.g., between those with a relatively high level of Jewish education and others, persons with synagogue affiliation and unaffiliated, etc.), it would be prudent to avoid analyses or explanations of small differences, even if they are statistically significant. However, the evidence is that large and important differences do reflect real phenomena, and can be relied on.

9.2. Sampling Variability

Sample surveys are subject to sampling error arising from the fact that the results may differ from what would have been obtained if the whole population had been interviewed. The size of the sampling error of an estimate depends on the number of interviews and the sample design. For estimates of the number of Jewish households, the sample size is 125,813 screened households. The screened sample was virtually a simple random sample. As a result, it is very likely (the chances are about 95 percent) that the number of Jewish households is within a range plus or minus 3 percent around the estimate shown in this report. For estimates of the Jewish population, the range is slightly higher since sampling variability, will affect both the estimate of the number of Jewish households and of the average number of Jews in those households. The 95 percent range is plus or minus 3.5 percent. These ranges are the limits within which the results of repeated sampling in the same time period could be expected to vary 95 percent of the time, assuming the same sampling procedure, the same interviewers, and the same questionnaire.

Unfortunately, due to the complex nature of the sample design and weighting method used in estimating the characteristics of the Jewish population, it is not possible to give a simple formula that will provide estimates of the standard errors for all types of estimates. To begin with, there are three basic samples embedded in the survey:

1. The household sample can be considered as the equivalent of a simple random sample of 2,441 households.
2. For population statistics based on data reported for all household members, the sample size is 6,514. However, for most estimates of this type, the standard errors will be greater than what would be achieved with a simple random sample of 6,514 because of the presence of intra-class correlation, that is the tendency of household members to be more alike than would be the case of persons chosen at random. The intra-class correlation introduces a design effect that should be superimposed on the simple formula for the standard error.
3. Population statistics based on data reported for only one household member, selected at random, are also based on a sample size of 2,441. However, since the chance of selection of any person depends on the number of adults in the household the sample is not equivalent to a simple random sample of 2,441. The varying probabilities of selection also create a design effect.

The standard error of an estimate of a percentage can be approximated by:

$$\sqrt{D.p.(1-p)/Rn}$$

where p is the estimated percentage, D is the design effect, R is the proportion of Jews in the segment for which percentages are computed, and n is the sample size, that is 2,441 or 6,514. When percentages are computed of all Jewish households or persons, R is equal to 1; when the base of the percentage is a subgroup of all households or persons (e.g., households observing certain rituals, all females, persons in a particular group), the value of R is the fraction of all households or persons in that subgroup.

The value of *D* is 1 for household statistics. For population statistics, the value will depend on the item being estimated. Although it is possible to calculate an estimate of the value of *D* for each item (or alternatively, a relatively unbiased estimate of the standard error), we assume most analysts will not want to make the fairly extensive effort needed for such calculations. Guidelines for approximating *D* follow.

- As stated earlier, *D* can be considered equal to one for household statistics.
- For items based on data reported for all household members, *D* will be in the range 1 to 2.7. It will be close to 1 for percentages based on a subset of the Jewish population (e.g., adult males, currently widowed persons, persons born abroad, disabled, etc.) At the other extreme, the value will be close to 2.7 on items for which household members are likely to have similar characteristics (e.g., the percentage of Jews who belong to conservative congregations). The 2.7 is the average size of Jewish households, and when *D* has this value, the effect on the standard error is to treat the statistic as a household item with a sample size of 2,441 rather than a population item. For other types of percentages, the value of *D* will be somewhere in the 1 to 2.7 range; the more alike members of a household are likely to be, the greater should be the value of *D* used in the calculations.
- The value of *D* is about 1.2 for items based on data reported for only one adult in the household. This design effect reflects the effect on sampling errors of having varying probabilities of selection, depending on the household size. For example, adults living in one-adult households will have twice the chance of selection as those in two-adult households, three times the chance as those in households containing three adults, etc.

It should also be noted that the value of n is lower for items in the modules asked for a subsample of respondents than for other items. Since the modules are based on a one-third subsample, the sample size of 2,441 and 6,514 are reduced to 814 and 2,171. When the sample sizes used in the base of percentages are obtained by simply counting the number of records used in the calculations, the count automatically provides the value of *R*, and it is unnecessary to calculate R, or to be concerned over whether or not the item is one of the modules.

NOTES

Introduction

1. For a discussion of this technique, see Sylvia Barack Fishman, "Triple Play: Deconstructing Jewish Lives, " *Contemporary Jewry* 14 (1993): 23–47.

2. The 1990 National Jewish Population Survey, the first national survey of American Jews in two decades, randomly screened over 125,000 households and located 2441 Jewish households, comprising some 6500 individuals, upon whom the sampling was based. A summary of findings can be found in Barry A. Kosmin et. al., *Highlights of the Council of Jewish Federations National Jewish Population Survey* (New York: CJF, 1991).

3. Sylvia Barack Fishman, "Training for Jewish Leadership and Service—Working in the Real World," in Charles Liebman, ed., *Expectations, Education and Experience of Jewish Professional Leaders: Report of the Wexner Foundation Research Project on Contemporary Jewish Professional Leadership,* Research Report 12 (Waltham, Mass.: Brandeis University Cohen Center for Modern Jewish Studies and Bar Ilan University Argov Center for the Study of Israel and the Jewish People, 1995), 61–126.

4. Sylvia Barack Fishman, "In Many Voices: Diversity and Commonality among American Jewish Women," *Report of the National Commission on Jewish Women* (Waltham, Mass. and New York: Cohen Center for Modern Jewish Studies and Hadassah, 1995).

5. Some aspects of these interview data are included in Sylvia Barack Fishman, *A Breath of Life: Feminism in the American Jewish Community* (New York: Free Press, 1993).

6. Eight focus groups were planned and implemented by the Morning Star Commission, a project of Hadassah Southern California, in the Los Angeles area. My analysis of these data can be found in Sylvia Barack Fishman, *I of the Beholder: Jews and Gender in Film and Popular Culture* (Waltham, Mass: International Research Institute on Jewish Women Working Paper Series, No. 1, 1988).

7. Catherine H. Zuckert, "Why Political Scientists Study Fiction," *The Chronicle of Higher Education,* March 8, 1996, A48.

8. Yosef Haim Yerushalmi, *Zakhor: Jewish History and Jewish Memory* (New York: Schocken Books, 1989), 100.

9. Marshall Sklare, "Intermarriage and the Jewish Future," in *Observing America's Jews* (Hanover, N.H.: Brandeis University Press, 1994), 234–47, 237; rpt. from *Commentary,* April 1964.

10. Jack Wertheimer, *A People Divided: Judaism in Contemporary America* (New York: BasicBooks, 1993) discusses as wings of American Judaism the following groups: Orthodox, Traditional, Conservative, Reconstructionist, and Reform, each of which has its own separate program of rabbinical ordination and its own institutional frame-

work. Some contemporary observers believe that the Orthodox world will split into right wing/hareidi versus modern Orthodox divisions, but at this date no official split has taken place.

11. Philip Roth, *Operation Shylock: A Confession* (New York: Simon & Schuster, 1993), 334.

12. Jacob Katz, *Out of the Ghetto: The Social Background of Jewish Emancipation, 1770–1870* (New York: Schocken Books, 1973); Michael Meyer, *The Origins of the Modern Jew: Jewish Identity and European Culture in Germany, 1749–1824* (Detroit: Wayne State University Press, 1976); Marion Kaplan, *The Making of the Jewish Middle Class: Women, Family, and Identity in Imperial Germany* (New York: Oxford University Press, 1991).

13. Philip Gleason, "American Identity and Americanization," *Harvard Encyclopedia of American Ethnic Groups* (Cambridge: Harvard University Press, 1980), 31.

14. Cited by Harold J. Abramson, "Assimilation and Pluralism," *Harvard Encyclopedia of American Ethnic Groups,* 152.

15. Louis Wirth, *The Ghetto* (Chicago: University of Chicago Press, 1956).

16. Horace M. Kallen, "Champion of Pluralism," in *Dialogues in Judaism: Jewish Dilemmas Defined, Debated, and Explored* (Northvale, N.J.: Jason Aranson, 1991), 155.

17. Louis D. Brandeis, "Zionism is Consistent with American Patriotism" (June 1915), in *The Jew in the Modern World: A Documentary History,* ed. Paul Mendes-Flohr and Jehuda Reinharz (New York: Oxford University Press, 1995), 496.

18. Kaufman Kohler, "The Concordance of Judaism and Americanism" (1911), in *The Jew in the Modern World: A Documentary History,* ed. Paul Mendes-Flohr and Jehuda Reinharz (New York: Oxford University Press, 1995), 471–72.

19. Jenna Wiseman Joselit, *The Wonders of America: Reinventing Jewish Culture, 1880–1950* (New York: Hill and Wang, 1994).

20. Philip Roth, *Portnoy's Complaint* (New York: Random House, 1967), 144–45.

21. Robert Bellah, Richard Madsen, William M. Sullivan, Ann Swidler, and Steve Tipton, *Habits of the Heart: Individualism and Commitment in American Life* (Berkeley: University of California Press, 1985), 153.

22. Herbert J. Gans, "Symbolic Ethnicity: The Future of Ethnic Groups and Culture in America," *Ethnic and Racial Studies* 2 (January 1979): 1–20.

23. Developed by such thinkers as Peter Berger and Thomas Luckman, *The Construction of Reality: A Treatise on the Sociology of Knowledge* (Garden City, N.J.: Anchor Books, 1967), and Malcom Spector and John Kitsuse, *Constructing Social Problems* (New York: Aldine, 1977), the constructionist theory of ethnicity has recently been reevaluated by James A. Holstein and Gale Miller, eds., *Perspectives on Social Problems: Reconsidering Social Constructionism,* 5 (New York: Aldine, 1993).

24. Joanne Nagel, "Constructing Ethnicity: Creating and Recreating Ethnic Identity and Culture," *Social Problems* 41, no. 1 (February 1994): 152–76, 153.

25. Mary C. Waters, *Ethnic Options: Choosing Identities in America* (Berkely: University of California Press, 1990), 18–19.

26. Waters, 158.

27. Peter Berger, *The Heretical Imperative* (New York: Anchor/Doubleday, 1979), 24.

28. Samuel C. Heilman and Steven M. Cohen, *Cosmopolitans and Parochials: Orthodox Jews in Modern America* (Chicago: University of Chicago Press, 1989), 98.

29. Riv-Ellen Prell, "Rage and Representation: Jewish Gender Stereotypes in American Culture," in Faye Ginsburg and Anna Lowenhaupt Tsing, eds., *Uncertain Terms: Negotiating Gender in American Culture* (Boston: Beacon Press, 1990), 248–66, 253.

30. Paula E. Hyman, *Gender and Assimilation in Modern Jewish History: The Roles and Representations of Women* (Seattle: University of Washington Press, 1995), 169.

31. Fishman, *I of the Beholder: Jews and Gender in Film.*

32. Heilman and Cohen, 17, citing Redfield, Linton, and Herkovitz (1936), 152.

33. As conceived of by nineteenth-century German neo-Orthodox thinker Samson Raphael Hirsch and championed by modern Orthodox thinkers and institutions, synthesis is often seen as an answer to the challenges posed to tradition Judaism by emancipation and by Reform Judaism. Hirsch and his followers urged Jews to cultivate Torah im derekh eretz, immersion in Judaic knowledge and law combined with familiarity with the best and finest of secular Western humanistic thinking and behavior, with the clear understanding that Judaic wisdom was superior and always had ·the final word.

34. Kaplan, *The Making of the Jewish Middle Class,* 25–63 and 117–36.

35. Marshall Sklare, *Conservative Judaism* (New York: Free Press, 1955); "The Conservative Movement: Achievements and Problems," in *Observing America's Jews,* ed. Jonathan Sarna (Hanover, N.H.: Brandeis University Press, 1993) 55–73, 68.

36. Andrew R. Heinze, *Adapting to Affluence: Jewish Immigrants, Mass Consumption, and the Search for American Identity* (New York: Columbia University Press, 1990), 84.

37. Joselit, *Wonders of America,* 225.

38. Marshall Sklare and Joseph Greenblum, *Jewish Identity on the Suburban Frontier: A Study of Group Survival in the Open Society* (New York: Basic Books, 1967).

39. Marshall Sklare, "The Image of the Good Jew in Lakeville," (1967) in *Observing America's Jews,* , 205–14, 208–213.

40. Charles S. Liebman, "American Jews: Still A Distinctive Group," *Commentary* 64, no. 2 (August 1977): 57–60, 60.

41. Indeed, the religious attitudes of traditionalist versus liberal lay and professional leadership today diverge widely. Traditionalist elites often share a worldview and behavior patterns with traditionalist folk, while many among the liberal elites display increasing similarities in attitude and behavior with the folk whom they lead. Thus, Orthodox and traditional Conservative leaders and folk both tend to aspire (to greater or lesser degrees) to behaviors such as regular observance of rabbinic dietary laws, Sabbaths and holidays, normative Jewish patterns of family formation, and ongoing adult textual study.

42. Arthur A. Cohen, *The Carpenter Years* (New York, 1967).

43. Sid Groeneman, "Beliefs and Values of American Jewish Women" (Report

by Market Facts, Inc. presented to the International Organization of B'nai B'rith Women, 1985). The data were drawn from 956 questionnaires roughly divided between Jewish and non-Jewish informants.

44. For a brilliant essay on this subject in an earlier era of American Jewish history, see Jonathan Sarna, "The Cult of Synthesis in American Jewish Culture," *Jewish Social Studies* 5, nos. 1 & 2 (Fall 1998) 52–79.

Chapter One

1. Stephen Whitfield, *American Space: Jewish Time* (Hamden, Conn.: Archon Books, 1988), 87.

2. Sklare, *Observing America's Jews,* 208–9.

3. Teresa Strasser, "Jews Take Lead in Efforts to Reform U.S. Drug Policies," Jewish Telegraphic Agency Community News Reporter, January 3, 1997, 37, no. 1.

4. *Basic Sources: Judaism and the Environment,* a publication of Shomrei Adamah, 5500 Wissahickon Avenue, Philadelphia, Pa., 1996. The publication includes a list of articles on this subject.

5. Arthur Green, "God, Prayer and Religious Language," in *Imagining the Jewish Future: Essays and Responses* (Albany: State University of New York Press, 1992), 13–28, 16, 26.

6. Wertheimer, *A People Divided,* 77.

7. A self-defined "classical Reform" congregation in Columbus, Georgia, for example, experienced conflict between older members who liked primarily English words and nonethnic melodies used in their Friday night worship, and a rabbi and younger members who preferred "soulful" traditional Hebrew words and melodies.

8. Manhattan Congregation Kehilath Jeshurun in the 1990s provided one famous example of the phenomenon of exuberant singing and aggressive communal good works revitalizing a Conservative congregation.

9. Eric Hobsbawm, "Inventing Traditions," in *The Invention of Tradition* (Cambridge: Cambridge University Press, 1983), 9.

10. Heilman and Cohen, *Cosmopolitans and Parochials,* 209.

11. Sir Immanuel Jakobovits, "Symposium on the State of Orthodoxy," *Tradition* 20, no. 1 (Spring 1982): 39–43.

12. Alexis de Tocqueville, *Democracy in America* (1835–1839), trans. George Lawrence (Garden City, N.Y.: Doubleday, 1969), 508.

13. Rabbi Berel Wein, "A Matter of Choice: Americanizing Israel," *The Jewish Parent Connection,* September/October 1995, 7. Rabbi Wein is the Dean of Yeshiva Shaare Torah in Suffern, N.Y. and is the author of a book entitled, *Triumph of Survival.*

14. Walter S. Wurzburger, Ph.D., "Confronting the Challenge of the Values of Modernity," *Torah U'Mada Journal* 1 (1989): 104–12, 106.

15. Maimonides (1135–1204), *Mishnah Torah,* Tefillah 1:1–2, 4–5. For a complete discussion of this issue, see Avraham Weiss, *Women at Prayer: A Halakhic Analysis of Women's Prayer Groups* (Hoboken, N.J.: Ktav, 1990).

16. Within traditional Jewish communities, the rabbi whom the community

takes on as its regular spiritual leader (*Morah d'asrah*) is the ultimate authority on religious questions. The organic development of the body of religious law is due to the fact that traditional Jewish individuals and communities continue to approach rabbinic authorities with large and small questions. As in any legal system, the rabbi who has been asked a question researches rabbinic legal literature for precedents and discussions, and bases his answer (*P'sak*) upon his best understanding of rabbinic law and the particular circumstances of the supplicant. Within the spiritual symbolism of the halakhic system, each rabbinic adjudicator reflects a divinely inspired authority, passed on from Moses through the great rabbinic sages of the Talmudic and medieval periods. When a rabbi delivers an halakhic decision, it is, under ideal Orthodox conditions, regarded not as a suggestion upon which the congregation votes, but as a legal ruling. Members of the community need not ask the rabbi for his judgement, but once they have asked him to adjudicate a religious question, they must abide by his answer whether or not they are happy with the answer. Traditional Jews sometimes "shop around" before they ask a rabbi to render a decision, and it is common for people to ascertain what the answer is likely to be before they ask a particular rabbi. However, once a *Posek* has been asked, especially if the adjudicator is a rabbi and a *Morah d'asrah*, his answer to the supplicants is, quite literally, Jewish law. For this reason, Jewish law often differs in its details from community to community and even from congregation to congregation.

17. Thus, women's *tefillah* group leaders have, by and large, conformed in many ways to the communal expectations of Orthodox Jewish life. However, despite the enormous care taken by Orthodox women's *tefillah* group participants to find acceptable religious authorities for their activities, their very existence has often antagonized rabbinic and lay elements within the Orthodox community. The fact that most prayer sessions of women's *tefillah* groups involve handling and reading from a Torah scroll has proved a source of great controversy in the Orthodox community. Despite the fact that women are not prescribed by Jewish law from handling or studying from a Torah scroll at any time in their reproductive cycles—the Palestinian Tosefta states that women may study the Torah even when they are menstruating or have recently given birth (Tosefta Berakhot, ch. 2, para. 12); the Babylonian Talmud disagrees, insisting that women may not study Torah (Babylonian Talmud Berakhot 22a), except in the case of exceptional women; however, it does not link the prohibition to ritual impurity, but instead to the putative intellectual poverty of females—communal customs have grown up over the centuries that viewed females touching the Torah scrolls as a highly non-normative event.

18. For a fuller discussion, see Fishman, "Praying with Women's Voices," in *A Breath of Life*, 158–70.

19. Robert Gordis, "The Ordination of Women," in *The Ordination of Women as Rabbis*, ed. Simon Greenberg (New York: The Jewish Theological Seminary of America, 1988), 60.

20. Robert Gordis, *The Jew Faces a New World*, cited in Sklare, *Observing America's Jews*, 199.

21. A 1979 letter signed by Debra S. Cantor, Nina Beth Cardin, Stephanie Dickstein, Nina Bieber Feinstein, Sharon Fliss, Carol Glass, and Beth Polebaum.

22. Gordis, "The Ordination of Women," 55. I am grateful to Meredith Woocher for bringing this passage to my attention.

23. Gordis, *ibid.*

24. Leonard D. Gordon, "Toward a Gender-Inclusive Account of Halahkah," *Gender and Judaism: The Transformation of Tradition,* ed. T. M. Rudavsky (New York: New York University Press, 1995), 3–12, 10–11.

25. T. LaFramboise, H. L. K. Coleman, and J. Gerton, "Psychological Impact of Biculturalism: Evidence and Theory," *Psychological Bulletin* 114 (1993): 395–412.

26. Haim Soloveitchik, "Rupture and Reconstruction: The Transformation of Contemporary Orthodoxy," *Tradition* 28, no. 4 (Summer 1994): 64–130.

27. Hobsbawm, "Inventing Traditions," 9.

28. Charles S. Liebman, "Orthodox Judaism Today," *Midstream* 25, no. 7 (Aug./Sept. 1979): 19–25, 25.

29. Adam Mintz, "Sushi and Other Jewish Foods," *Commentary* (October 1998): 43–47.

30. Robert Hanley, "In the Ashes of Arson at Kiryas Joel, Tensions of Bitter Factionalism," *The New York Times* Metro Section, B1–B2, July 29, 1996.

31. Some characters divide themselves into two pieces, and some go so far as to project rejected psychological pieces of themselves onto real or imaginary siblings or doubles, golems and dopplegangers in fiction such as Philip Roth's *The Counterlife* and *Operation Shylock,* Rebecca Goldstein's *The Mind-Body Problem* and *The Dark Sister,* Cynthia Ozick's "Puttermesser and Xanthippe," and Jay Neugeboren's *The Stolen Jew.*

32. Sylvia Barack Fishman, "American Jewish Fiction Turns Inward, 1960–1990," *American Jewish Year Book, 1991,* 35–69.

33. Allegra Goodman, "Variant Text," in *Writing Our Way Home* , ed. Ted Solotaroff and Nessa Rappaport (New York: Schocken Books, 1992), 86–109, 99.

34. Goodman, "Variant Text," 101.

35. Groeneman.

36. James S. Hirsch, "An Exodus From Tradition," *The Wall Street Journal,* April 5, 1996, A8.

Chapter Two

1. Milton Gordon, *Assimilation in American Life* (New York: Oxford University Press, 1964), 186.

2. Marshall Sklare, *America's Jews* (New York: Random House, 1971), 58.

3. Jacob Katz, "Educational Institutions," in *Tradition and Crisis: Jewish Society at the End of the Middle Ages* (New York: Schocken Books, 1993), 156–69.

4. "Education: In the Talmud," *Encyclopedia Judaica, Jerusalem* 6 (Jerusalem: Keter Publishing House Jerusalem, Ltd., 1972), 398–403, 399.

5. Samuel Heilman, *The People of the Book: Drama, Fellowship and Religion* (Chicago: University of Chicago Press, 1983, rt 1987), 8.

6. Jacob Katz, *Jewish Emancipation and Self-Emancipation* (Philadelphia: The Jewish Publication Society, 1986), 11.

7. Katz, *Out of the Ghetto,* 68.

8. Sander Gilman, *The Jew's Body* (New York and London: Routledge, 1991).

9. Moses Sofer (the *Hatam Sofer,* 1762–1839) founded and presided over a large, renowned *yeshiva* in Pressburg, Hungary. He battled the forces of modernization with clever polemics and sharp wit, taking particular opposition to Moses Mendelssohn and other *maskilim* (Jewish Englightenment figures). He led the Orthodox rabbis in their battle against German Reformers, and was widely considered the leader of the Orthodox community.

10. Katz, *Jewish Emancipation,* 36.

11. Ruth Jacknow Markowitz, *My Daughter the Teacher: Jewish Teachers in the New York City Schools* (New Brunswick: Rutgers University Press, 1993), 5–15.

12. Jonathan Sarna, "American Jewish Education in Historical Perspective," *Journal of Jewish Education* 64, nos. 1–2 (winter/spring 1998) 8–21.

13. Irving Howe, *World of Our Fathers: The Journey of East European Jews to America and the Life They Found and Made* (New York: Simon and Schuster, 1976), 252.

14. Markowitz, 75–93.

15. Sarna, "The Cult of Synthesis in American Jewish Culture," cites Charles Liebman, "Reconstructionism in American Jewish Life," *American Jewish Year Book 71* (1970): 68.

16. A good summary of the educational, occupational, and social obstacles which faced twentieth-century American Jews in provided in Charles E. Silberman, *A Certain People: American Jews and their Lives Today* (New York: Summit Books, 1985). See especially 30–81.

17. Herbert J. Gans, "The Origin and Growth of a Jewish Community in the Suburbs: The Jewish Community of Park Forest," in Marshal Sklare, ed., *The Jews: Social Patterns of an American Group* (New York: Free Press, 1958), 205–48.

18. Studies conducted in Manhattan, Champaign-Urbana, Illinois, and New Haven, Connecticut, cited by Marshall Sklare, "Intermarriage and the Jewish Future," 239–242.

19. Lee Siegel, reviewing *Clement Greenberg: A Life,* by Florence Rubenfeld, in *New York Times Book Review,* March 29, 1998, 8.

20. Calvin Goldscheider, *Jewish Continuity and Change: Emerging Patterns in America* (Bloomington: Indiana University Press, 1986), 117.

21. Andrew M. Greeley, "Further Commentary on the Michigan Cross-Generational Data" (National Opinion Research Center for the Study of American Pluralism, October 31, 1973).

22. Frances Kobrin Goldscheider and Calvin Goldscheider, "Generational Relationships and the Jews: Patterns of Leaving Home, 1930–1985" (Paper presented at the 1993 World Congress of Jewish Studies," Jerusalem, Israel, 1993).

23. Moshe Hartman and Harriet Hartman, *Gender Equality and American Jews* (Albany: State University of New York Press, 1996), 219–25.

24. Hartman and Hartman, 41.

25. Hartman and Hartman, 38–39.

26. For a thorough exploration of these and related phenomena, see Sidney

Goldstein and Alice Goldstein, *Jews on the Move: Implications for Jewish Identity* (Albany: State University of New York Press, 1996).

27. Hartman and Hartman, p, 121.

28. Marion A. Kaplan, "Gender and Jewish History in Imperial Germany," in *Assimilation and Community: The Jews in Nineteenth-Century Europe,* ed. Jonathan Frankel and Steven J. Zipperstein (Cambridge: Cambridge University Press, 1992), 199–224.

29. Susan Glenn, *Daughters of the Shtetl: Life and Labor in the Immigrant Generation* (Ithaca: Cornell University Press, 1990), 76–78.

30. Kaplan, *The Making of the Jewish Middle Class,* 30–36, 153–57.

31. Hyman, *Gender and Assimilation,* 8, 25–26.

32. Glenn, *Daughters of the Shtetl,* 67–79.

33. Kaplan, "Gender and Jewish History," 199–224.

34. Kaplan, "Gender and Jewish History," *ibid.* For similar patterns in respectable middle-class English and American societies, see Diane Lichtenstein, *Writing Their Nations: The Tradition of Nineteenth-Century American Jewish Women Writers* (Bloomington: Indiana University Press, 1992). Lichtenstein focuses on the ways in which Jewish women conflated the domestic angel, the "myth of true womanhood," with the figure of the "woman of valor."

35. Hartman and Hartman, 270.

36. Sklare, *America's Jews,* 115–17.

37. Fishman, "In Many Voices," 62.

38. See for example, Egon Mayer, "Why Not Judaism," *Moment,* October 1991, 28–42, which advocates creating a new, more accessible form of Judaism which seems less at odds with American culture; and Egon Mayer, "Intermarriage: Beyond the Gloom and Doom," *San Diego Jewish Press,* November 13, 1992, which urges the Jewish community to be "as open and welcoming to our own interfaith families as America has been open and welcoming to us. . . . And this requires us to be as respectful of the philosphical and life style choices of interfaith families as we would want them to be of more traditional Jewish choices."

39. Alvin Schiff, *Jewish Supplementary Schooling: An Educational System in Need of Change* (New York: The Board of Jewish Education of Greater New York: 1988).

40. In the so-called "black hat" community represented by the Agudas Yisrael and those to the right, young people are often strongly discouraged from attending college. When they do work for professional training, programs which are primarily technical in orientation and do not involve any study of the humanities are preferred.

41. Seymour Martin Lipset, "American Exceptionalism Reconfirmed: The Educational Background of American Jews" (Report prepared for the Mandel Institute in Jerusalem through a grant to the Wilstein Institute, 1990), 77.

42. Richard D. Alba, *Ethnic Identity: The Transformation of White America* (New Haven: Yale University Press, 1990), 199.

43. Goldscheider, *Jewish Continuity and Change,* used dazzling demographic comparisons of Jews and non-Jews to suggest that "Transformation and Jewish Cohesion" (Title, 1) went hand in hand.

44. Steven M. Cohen, *American Assimilation or Jewish Revival* (Bloomington: Indiana University Press, in cooperation with Brandeis University Cohen Center for Modern Jewish Studies, 1988), 125, asked whether "Assimilation or Transformation" characterized the American Jewish community, and decided pending further research that the community was basically stable: "The moderate version of transformationism—the view that Jewish expression may be changing qualitatively but not quantitatively—is the one I believe is best supported by the data at hand." Cohen has since transformed his own diagnosis subsequent to analyzing 1990 NJPS data, and his work is frequently cited in this volume.

45. Silberman, *A Certain People,* popularized Goldscheider's demographic findings and analysis. Silberman focused on the rags to riches story of the Jews in America, calling his first chapter, "The Great Transformation" (Title, 21), in a kind of homage for his debt to Goldscheider; like his source, Silberman painted an unequivocably rosy picture of the American Jewish future.

46. The demise of the "brutal bargain" is convincingly argued by Silberman, *A Certain People.*

47. Gish Jen, quoted by Sandee Brawarsky, "Lox and Egg Rolls: Gish Jen Novel about a Chinese Teen's Foray into Judaism Funny," *The Jewish Week,* August 30, 1996, 33.

48. HBO Comedy Special, Aired October 15, 1996.

49. National Public Radio Morning News, October 16, 1996.

50. Katie Couric, on NBC's morning news program, "The Today Show," interviewing pediatrician T. Berry Brazelton, September 5, 1996.

Chapter Three

1. Babylonian Talmud *Kiddushin* 29b.

2. Katz, *Tradition and Crisis,* 162.

3. Katz, *Tradition and Crisis,* 168–169.

4. Shoshana Pantel Zolty, *And All Your Children Shall Be Learned: Women and the Study of Torah in Jewish Law and History* (Northvale, N.J.: Jason Aranson Inc., 1993), 177–86.

5. Sarna, "American Jewish Education," 3.

6. Enrollments in Jewish education were hardly universal for American children early in the twentieth century. One report in 1900 asserted that only 18 percent of American Jewish children attended formal classes, reported by Charles S. Bernheimer, "A Summary of Jewish Organizations in the United States," in *American Jewish Year Book* (Philadelphia: Jewish Publication Society, 1901), 501, 506. I am grateful to Jonathan Golden for bringing this source to my attention. Another report in 1908 estimated that about 100,000 children out of a Jewish population of 1,750,000 attended any type of Jewish school (*Encyclopedia Judaica* 6, 440).

7. Sarna, "American Jewish Education," 4.

8. *Ibid.*

9. Mordecai M. Kaplan and Bernard Cronson, "Report of Committee on Jewish Education of the Kehillah Presented at its First Annual Convention," New

York, February 1910, reprinted in *Jewish Education* 20, no. 3 (Summer 1949): 113–14. I am grateful to Jonathan Golden for bringing this source to my attention.

10. Alan Mintz, *Hebrew in America* (Detroit: Wayne State University Press, 1993), 17.

11. *Encyclopedia Judaica* 6, 440.

12. Schiff, *Jewish Supplementary Schooling: An Educational System in Need of Change*, 20–21.

13. William B. Helmreich, *Against All Odds: Holocaust Survivors and the Successful Lives They Made in America* (New York: Simon & Schuster, 1992), includes rich qualitative materials on the Jewish orientation of Holocaust survivors who emigrated to the United States.

14. Samuel C. Heilman, *Portrait of American Jews: The Last Half of the 20th Century* (Seattle: University of Washington Press, 1995), provides a good sense of the cultural impact of Orthodox refugees.

15. Wertheimer, *A People Divided*, 13.

16. Mark A. Raider, *The Emergence of American Zionism* (New York: New York University Press, 1998), 69–124.

17. Marshall Sklare, "The Greening of Judaism," *Commentary* 58, no. 6 (December 1974): 51–57, reprinted in *Observing America's Jews*, 75–86, 78.

18. Sara Lee, director of the Reform Rhea Hirsch School at Hebrew Union College-Jewish Institute of Religion in Los Angeles, recalls that her Jewish education "began with Young Judea [Hadassah Summer Camp] and a trip to Israel." Her experience is especially typical for Jewish girls prior to the popularity of the Bat Mitzvah. Cited in Fishman, *A Breath of Life*, 192.

19. Sklare, "Greening of America," 79–81.

20. *Ibid.*

21. Richard Siegel, Michael Strassfeld, and Sharon Strassfeld, *The Jewish Catalogue: A Do-It-Yourself Kit* (Philadelphia: The Jewish Publication Society of America, 1974), 64.

22. Fishman, "American Jewish Fiction Turns Inward," 51–61.

23. Fishman, "I of the Beholder."

24. Sarna, "American Jewish Education," 11.

25. Some observers feel that the day school movement grew primarily because of fear: parents feared the growing drug culture in public schools, or the incursion of African American students into integrated classrooms, or the possibility that their children would lack Jewish identification and would marry out of the faith. Others stress positive motivations: as American Jewish parents themselves became more sophisticated about the factors that influence Jewish identity formation, they dedicated themselves to providing their children with a knowledge base and experiential basis for connections to Jews and Judaism.

26. Allie A. Dubb and Sergio DellaPergola, *First Census of Jewish Schools in the Diaspora, 1981/83* (Jerusalem: Institute for Contemporary Jewry, 1986), 1, 4.

27. Aspects of this section were explored in a different context in two research reports which Alice Goldstein and I published on Jewish education issues in the 1990

NJPS data. I am grateful to my colleague not only for the studies that we completed together, but also for her assistance over many years, including generous and useful insights and rigorous statistical work. Tables taken from our reports will, as appropriate, be attributed to: Sylvia Barack Fishman and Alice Goldstein, *When They Are Grown They Will Not Depart: Jewish Education and the Jewish Behavior of American Adults* (Brandeis University Cohen Center for Modern Jewish Studies and JESNA: *Research Report 8,* March 1993); and Alice Goldstein and Sylvia Barack Fishman, *Teach Your Children When They Are Young: Contemporary Jewish Education in the United States* (Brandeis University Cohen Center for Modern Jewish Studies and JESNA: *Research Report 10,* December 1993).

28. Goldstein and Goldstein, *Jews on the Move.*

29. Goldstein and Fishman, 40.

30. Fishman, "In Many Voices," 62.

31. Alvin I. Schiff and Mareleyn Schneider, *The Jewishness Quotient of Jewish Day School Graduates: Studying the Effect of Jewish Education on Adult Jewish Behavior* (New York: Yeshiva University, 1994).

32. See Menachem Brayer, *The Jewish Woman in Rabbinic Literature: A Psychological Approach* (Hoboken, N.J.: Ktav Publishing Company, 1986), 2:79–80.

33. Contradicting much classical Jewish thought, Rabbi Schneerson asserts that all women are capable of learning the Oral Law. He notes that in the past the group of women who did in fact study the Oral Law was limited because it was entirely voluntary. Today, however, he urges, women may and should be taught the complete range of Talmudic texts. Rabbi Menachem Schneerson, *Me-Sichat Shabbat Parshat Emor, Erev Lag B'Omer 5770: Al Devar Hiyyuv Neshei Yisrael Be-Hinukh Limud ha-Torah,* May 1990.

34. Paula E. Hyman and Deborah Dash Moore, eds., *Jewish Women in America: An Historical Encyclopedia* (New York: Routledge, 1997).

35. Ann R. Shapiro et. al., eds., *Jewish American Women Writers: A Bio-Biographical and Critical Sourcebook* (Wesport, Conn.: Greenwood Press, 1994).

36. Tobin Belzer, *University Courses in Jewish Women's Studies* (Waltham, Mass.: Brandeis University International Research Institute on Jewish Women Working Paper Series, No. 3), 1999.

37. Lipset, "The Educational Background of American Jews."

38. Roth, *Operation Shylock,* 311–12.

39. Fishman, "In Many Voices," 60.

Chapter Four

1. Differing patterns are found among the most right-wing sectarian (*hareidi*) communities, groups who were less represented in 1990 NJPS data, partially because of their own reticence about participating in surveys.

2. Alba, *Ethnic Identity,* 197–200.

3. Alba, 187–88.

4. Barry R. Chiswick and Carmel U. Chiswick, "The Cost of Living Jewishly

and Jewish Continuity" (Paper prepared for the Conference on the Future of the Jewish Family in America, Brandeis University, April 1998, forthcoming in *Contemporary Jewry*).

5. Fishman and Goldstein, *When They Are Grown They Will Not Depart,* Table 8, 27.

6. Fishman and Goldstein; Goldstein and Fishman, *op. cit.*

7. Schiff and Schneider, *op. cit.*

8. Mordechai Rimor and Elihu Katz, *Jewish Involvement of the Baby Boom Generation: Interrogating the 1990 National Jewish Population Survey* (Jerusalem: Louis Guttman Israel Institute of Applied Research, Publication No. MR/1185B/E, 1993).

9. Lipset, *op. cit.*

10. Fishman and Goldstein; Goldstein and Fishman, *op. cit.*

11. Steven M. Cohen, "The Impact of Varieties of Jewish Education Upon Jewish Identity: An Inter-Generational Perspective," *Contemporary Jewry* 16 (1995): 1–29.

12. Schiff and Schneider.

13. Bruce A. Phillips, *Re-examining Intermarriage: Trends, Textures, Strategies* (New York and Los Angeles: American Jewish Committee and Susan and David Wilstein Institute of Jewish Policy Studies, 1997), 16, 8.

14. Harold Himmelfarb, "Jewish Education for Naught: Educating the Culturally Deprived Jewish Child," *Analysis* (The Institute for Jewish Policy Planning and Research of the Synagogue Council of America), no. 51 (September, 1975).

15. Geoffrey E. Bock, *Does Jewish Schooling Matter* (Jewish Education and Jewish Identity Colloquium Papers for the American Jewish Committee, 1976).

16. Sol Ribner, "The Effects of Intensive Jewish Education on Adult Jewish Lifestyles," *Jewish Education* (Spring, 1987): 6–12. Since respondents were chosen from a list of subscribers to the *Jewish Exponent,* the least affiliated Jews were probably not represented in this sample.

17. Cohen, *American Assimilation or Jewish Revival.*

18. Bock, *Does Jewish Schooling Matter?;* Himmelfarb, *Jewish Education for Naught.* Bock's proposed "threshold" for effective Jewish education is far lower than Himmelfarb's—one thousand hours versus Himmelfarb's three thousand hours. In terms of the actual number of hours a student in supplementary afternoon school is likely to accumulate over a typical Jewish childhood education, Bock's threshold is attainable, while Himmelfarb's would almost certainly be limited to students in all-day Jewish schools.

19. Bock, *ibid.* See also Rela Geffen Monson, *Jewish Campus Life: A Survey of Student Attitudes Toward Marriage and Family* (New York: The American Jewish Committee, 1984), 24–28. Monson's study points out the high correlation between home ritual observance and informal Jewish education with a student's proportion of Jewish friends: Students who come from homes with more religious ritual observance and more informal Jewish educational experiences are more likely to have many Jewish friends. More than half of those students who reported homes with "very high" ritual observance and those students who had participated in both Jewish youth groups and camps said that most of their friends were Jewish; only a third of those who reported homes with "low" ritual observance and who had participated in neither Jewish youth

groups or camps had mostly Jewish friends. Formal Jewish education had a much smaller impact on the proportion of Jewish friends.

20. See Ron Kronish, "Educating for Jewish-Zionist Identity in Israel" and Elan Ezrachi, "Informal Jewish Education in Israel: A Sign of Strength or Weakness," both in *The Melton Journal*, no. 16 (Spring–Summer, 1983): 7–8, 12, 23; and Simon N. Herman, *Israelis and Jews: The Continuity of an Identity* (Philadelphia: The Jewish Publication Society, 1970), 49. Herman studied 3679 Israeli high school students in 117 schools; he found that 44 percent of nonreligious students said that being Jewish "is of little importance in their lives" and another 10 percent said it played "no part at all" in their thinking.

21. Amos Oz, "Chekhov in Hebrew," *The New Yorker*, December 25, 1995 and January 1, 1996, 50–65, 50.

22. Gabriel Berger and Lawrence Sternberg, *Jewish Child Care: A Challenge and An Opportunity* (Brandeis University: Cohen Center for Modern Jewish Studies Research Report 3, November 1988), 29–33.

23. Ruth Pinkenson Feldman, *The Impact of the Day-Care Experience on Parental Jewish Identity* (American Jewish Committee, 1987).

24. Sylvia Barack Fishman, *Educating American Jewish Teens* (Boston: Bureau of Jewish Education of Greater Boston, 1997), based on Fishman's talk to the 1995 *Al Pi Darko* Conference on North American Jewish Teens, 10.

25. Phillips, *Re-examining Intermarriage*, 17–18.

26. Steven M. Cohen, "Geographical Variations in Participation in Israel Experience Youth Programs: The CRB Foundation Geo-Coded Survey," *Journal of Jewish Communal Service* (Winter/Spring 1995) 212–20, 121.

27. Cohen, "Geographic Variations," 215, 217.

28. William B. Helmreich, *The March of the Living: A Follow-Up Study of Its Long Range Impact and Effects* (CUNY Graduate Center and City College of New York, 1993).

29. Erik H. Cohen, "Toward a Strategy of Excellence," "Summer 1994," "Existing Marketing Network: A First Review," and "A Follow-Up Survey," Publications 2, 3, 4, and 5 of The Israel Experience, Ongoing Survey and Evaluation, A Project Commissioned by the Youth & Hechalutz Department, The Joint Authority for Jewish Zionist Education, Jerusalem, 1994, 1995.

30. Samuel Heilman, "Hail the Conquering Heroes," *The Jewish Week*, July 9, 1995.

31. Steven M. Cohen, "The Impact of Varieties of Jewish Education upon Jewish Identity: An Inter-Generational Perspective" (Paper presented at the World Congress of Jewish Studies, Jerusalem 1994, research supported by a grant from the Joint Authority for Jewish-Zionist Education of the WZO).

32. Cohen, *Contemporary Jewry* 1995, 88–89.

33. Amy L. Sales and Gary A. Tobin, *Moving Toward the Future: Action Steps for Revitalizng JCC Youth Services* (Waltham, Mass.: Maurice and Marilyn Cohen Center for Modern Studies, Brandeis University, 1995), 23.

34. Nathalie Friedman, *Remarriage and Stepparenting in the Jewish Community* (New York: The American Jewish Committee, 1993), 3–18.

35. Phillips, *Re-examining Intermarriage,* 17.

36. Goldstein and Goldstein, *Jews on the Move,* 205–7.

37. Leah J. Sokoloff, "On Their Own: The Graduates of Orthodox Jewish Day Schools and their Religious Beliefs and Observances while at Brandeis University" (Unpublished Senior Honors Thesis, Brandeis University Near Eastern and Judaic Studies Department, 1994), 47–59.

38. Barry Shrage, "Jewish Studies, Jewish Community, and Jewish Literacy: Creating a Revolution in Jewish Life" (Unpublished paper presented at the Association for Jewish Studies Conference, Boston, 1995).

39. Egon Mayer, "A Misleading Jewish Learning Curve," *Forward,* August 23, 1996, 6.

40. Jack Wertheimer, Charles S. Liebman, and Steven M. Cohen, "How to Save American Jews," *Commentary* 101, no. 1 (January 1996); 47–51, 50.

Chapter Five

1. David Biale, *Eros and the Jews: From Biblical Israel to Contemporary America* (New York: Basic Books, 1992), details both the widespread emphasis on monogamous marital unions in most Jewish societies and reasons why particular societies departed from this model.

2. David Biale, "Classical Teachings and Historical Experience," in *The Jewish Family and Jewish Continuity,* ed. Steven Bayme and Gladys Rosen (Hoboken, N.J.: Ktav Publishing, 1994), 133–71, especially 148–151.

3. See, Howe; and Sidney Stahl Weinberg, *The World of Our Mothers: The Lives of Jewish Immigrant Women* (Chapel Hill: University of North Carolina Press, 1988).

4. Biale, "Classical Teachings."

5. Judith Hauptman, *Rereading the Rabbis: A Woman's Voice* (Boulder, Colo.: Westview Press, 1998), 74.

6. Rachel Adler, *Engendering Judaism: An Inclusive Theology and Ethics* (Philadelphia: The Jewish Publication Society, 1998), 148.

7. Daniel Boyarin, *Carnal Israel: Reading Sex in Talmudic Culture* (Berkely: University of California Press, 1993), especially 61–133.

8. Chaim Grade, *My Mother's Sabbath Days* (New York: Alfred A. Knopf, 1986), for example, describes how his pious widowed mother was repeatedly urged to remarry. She refrained only because she did not wish to inflict a step-father on her son, pp.78–79.

9. Zabrowsky and Herzog, *Life Is with People,* (New York: Shocken Books, by arrangement with International Universities Press, 1962), 291–360.

10. Diane Lichtenstein, *Writing Their Nations,* especially 16–35 and 60–94.

11. Howe, 169–90; Weinberg, 114–15, 125–48.

12. Glenn, 239.

13. Phyllis D. Airhart and Margaret Bendroth, eds., *Faith Traditions and the Family* (Louisville, Ky.: Westminster John Knox Press, 1996), 23–37, 53–72, 100–114.

14. Sidney Goldstein, *Profile of American Jewry: Insights from the 1990 National*

Jewish Population Survey (New York: Council of Jewish Federations and CUNY Graduate School Occasional Papers No. 6, 1993), 117.

15. Steven Martin Cohen and Paul Ritterband, "Why Contemporary American Jews Want Small Families," in *Modern Jewish Fertility,* ed. Paul Ritterband (Leiden: E.J. Brill, 1981), 209–31.

16. Data from individual city studies are drawn from the following sources: Gary A. Tobin, *Jewish Population Study of Greater Baltimore,* 1986; Sherry Israel, *Boston's Jewish Community: The 1985 CJP Demographic Study* (Boston, Combined Jewish Philanthropies of Greater Boston, May 1987); Population Research Committee, *Survey of Cleveland's Jewish Population, 1981* (Cleveland, 1981); Allied Jewish Federation of Denver, *The Denver Jewish Population Study* (Denver, 1981); Gary A. Tobin, Robert C. Levy, and Samuel H. Asher, *A Demographic Study of the Jewish Community of Greater Kansas City* (Jewish Federation of Greater Kansas City, Summer 1986); Bruce A. Phillips, *Los Angeles Jewish Community Survey Overview for Regional Planning* (Los Angeles, 1980); Ira M. Sheskin, *Population Study of the Greater Miami Jewish Community* (Miami, 1981); Bruce A. Phillips, *The Milwaukee Jewish Population Study* (Milwaukee, 1984); Lois Geer, *The Jewish Community of Greater Minneapolis 1981 Population Study* (Minneapolis, 1981); Nancy Hendrix, *A Demographic Study of the Jewish Community of Nashville and Middle Tennessee* (Nashville, 1982); Paul Ritterband and Steven M. Cohen, *The 1981 Greater New York Jewish Population Survey* (New York, 1981); Bruce Phillips and William S. Aron, *The Greater Phoenix Jewish Population Study* (Phoenix, 1983–1984); Gary A. Tobin and Sylvia Barack Fishman, *Jewish Population Study of Greater Rochester,* 1987; Gary A. Tobin, *A Demographic and Attitudinal Study of the Jewish Community of St. Louis* (St. Louis, 1982); Lois Geer, *1981 Population Study of the St. Paul Jewish Community* (St. Paul, 198 1); Gary A. Tobin and Sharon Sassler, *Bay Area Jewish Community Study* (Bay Area Jewish Federations and Cohen Center for Modern Jewish Studies, 1988); Gary A. Tobin, Joseph Waksberg, and Janet Greenblatt, *A Demographic Study of the Jewish Community of Greater Washington* (Washington, D.C., 1984); Gary A. Tobin and Sylvia Barack Fishman, *Jewish Population Study of Greater Worcester,* 1987. Percentages in this paper have been rounded from .5 to the next highest number.

17. U. O. Schmeltz and Sergio Della Pergola, "The Demographic Consequences of U.S. Population Trends," *American Jewish Year Book, 1983* (New York and Philadelphia: American Jewish Committee and Jewish Publication Society, 1983), 148–49.

18. Hartman and Hartman, 58.

19. Goldscheider, *Jewish Continuity and Change,* 92–98.

20. Sarah Silver Bunim, *Religious and Secular Factors of Role Strain in Orthodox Jewish Mothers* (Unpublished doctoral dissertation, Wurzweiler School of Social Work, 1986), 208–13, 88–89, 133–38, 172–74, 208–13.

21. Frank L. Mott and Joyce C. Abma, "Contemporary Jewish Fertility: Does Religion Make a Difference?" *Contemporary Jewry* 13, 1992, 74–94.

22. Mott and Abma, *Ibid.*

23. Goldscheider, *op. cit.,* 92–98.

24. Calvin Goldscheider and Frances K. Goldscheider, "The Transition to Jew-

ish Adulthood: Education, Marriage, and Fertility" (Paper for the Tenth World Congress of Jewish Studies, Jerusalem, 1989), 17–20.

25. Mott and Abma, *op. cit.*

26. Some of the organizations that deal the the *Agunah* issue are G.E.T.—Getting Equitable Treatment, Agunah, Inc., Kayama, and the Israel Women's Network.

27. Nathalie Friedman, "Divorced Parents and the Jewish Community," 53–102, and Eliot Gertel, "Jewish Views on Divorce," 201–30, in Steven Bayme and Gladys Rosen, eds., *The Jewish Family and Jewish Continuity* (New York: Ktav, 1994).

28. Sanford Seltzer, "When There Is No Other Alternative" (Boston: Committee on the Jewish Family, Union of American Hebrew Congregations, Undated).

29. This eventuality has prompted women in Chicago, New York, New Jersey, Ohio and Minnesota to take their husbands to secular courts to pursue a Jewish divorce. Courts in Chicago, New York, and New Jersey each ruled in favor of the woman and her *get*, "on the grounds that they [husband and wife] had entered into a contract with the signing of a ketubah" and are "bound by its stipulations"—in other words, some courts found it logically inconsistent and legally indefensible for men to wish to enter into marriage with a religious contract but dissolve the same marriage with a civil document. In contrast, judges in Minnesota and Ohio ruled against the women, saying that their interference in these disputes would constitute a violation of the separation of church and state. Reported by Todd Winder, "Despite Reconstructionist Wedding, Judge Order Orthodox Divorce," *JTA* 29, no. 10 (March 10, 1989).

30. Steve Lipman, "Orthodox Wives Are Victims of 'Get Blackmail': Lawyer," *Jewish Week*, November 22, 1985.

31. Sherry Israel, *Boston's Jewish Community.*

32. Nathalie Friedman, *Remarriage and Stepparenting in the Jewish Community* (New York: American Jewish Committee, 1993).

33. Martha Ackelsberg, "Jewish Family Ethics in a Post-halakhic Age," in *Imagining the Jewish Future: Essays and Responses,* ed. David A. Teutsch (Albany: State University of New York Press, 1992), 158–59.

34. Gary A. Tobin and Sharon Sassler, *Bay Area Jewish Community Study Special Report: Human Services Needs Assessment* (Waltham, Mass.: Brandeis University Cohen Center for Modern Jewish Studies, 1988), 81.

35. Ira Sheskin, *Jewish Demographic Study of Palm Beach, 1987* (Palm Beach, FL.: The Jewish Federation of Palm Beach County, 1987), 24.

36. Phillips (Milwaukee, 1984).

37. Tobin and Sassler, *Bay Area Jewish Community Study Special Report: Human Services Needs Assessment,* 148.

38. Christie Balka and Andy Rose, eds., *Twice Blessed: On Being Lesbian or Gay and Jewish* (Boston: Beacon Press, 1989); Evelyn Torten Beck, ed., *Nice Jewish Girls: A Lesbian Anthology* (Boston: Beacon Press, 1989, rpt. 1982); Melanie Kaye/Kantrowitz and Irena Klepfisz, eds., *The Tribe of Dina: A Jewish Woman's Anthology* (Boston: Beacon Press, 1986, 1989).

39. Jonathan Krasner, *JAGL and the 1993 Salute to Israel Parade: A Study of the Genesis of Gay Jewish Activism* (Unpublished ms., Brandeis University Near Eastern and Judaic Studies Department, 1996).

40. Rabbi Fabian Schonfeld, interview in *The Jewish Week,* April 2–8, 1993, 9.

41. Krasner, *op. cit.,* 29.

42. Douglas Sadownick, *Sacred Lips of the Bronx* (New York: St. Martin's Press, 1994), 111.

43. Lev Raphael, *Dancing on Tisha B'Av* (New York: St. Martin's Press, 1990), 120.

44. Sarah Schulman, *Empathy* (New York: A Dutton Book/Penguin Books, USA, 1992), 179.

45. Jyl Lynn Felman, *Hot Chicken Wings* (San Francisco: Aunt Lute Books, 1992).

46. Marcia Freedman, *Exile in the Promised Land: A Memoir* (Ithaca, N.Y.: Firebrand Books, 1990); Alice Bloch, *The Law of Return* (Boston: Alyson Publications, Inc., 1983).

47. Judith Plaskow, *Standing again at Sinai: Judaism from a Feminist Perspective* (San Francisco: HarperCollins, 1991), 197–210.

48. Reuven Kimelman, "Homosexuality and Family-Centered Judaism," *Tikkun* 9, no. 4, 53–57.

49. Ackelsberg, *op. cit.,* 149–64, 156–57.

50. Acklesberg, 156.

51. Many articles have been written about rising rates of Jewish problem households, even among very traditional populations. See, for example: Rabbi Dr. Abraham J. Twersky, "Denial," *The Jewish Homemaker,* December 1989, 20–21; Faith Solela, "Family Violence: Silence Isn't Golden Anymore," *Response* xiv, no. 4 (Spring 1985): 101–6; Barbara Trainin, "Facing Up to the Problem of Jewish Wife Abuse," *The Jewish Week,* January 18, 1985; Nadine Brozan, "Wife Abuse in Jewish Families," *New York Times,* December 26, 1982.

52. Debra Darvick, "To Have and to Harm: Waking Up to the Reality that Domestic Violence Happens in Nice Jewish Homes," *Forward,* November 8, 1996, 13.

53. Toby Axelrod, "A Community on Trial?" *The Jewish Week* October 11, 1996, 6.

54. Brochures produced and distributed by Ohel Children's Home and Family Services, 4514 16th Avenue, Brooklyn, NY 11219.

55. Heilman, *Portrait of American Jews,* 94.

56. Groeneman, *op. cit.* Data were drawn from 956 questionnaires roughly divided between Jewish and non-Jewish informants.

57. Mott and Abma, *op. cit.,* 74–94.

58. *Marlene Post, "President's Column: Soul Talk," Hadassah Magazine* 77, no. 10, June/July 1996, 6.

59. *Hadassah Magazine* 77, no. 10, "Table of Contents," 4.

60. Hanita Blumfield, "Letter from Washington: Synergy & Harmony," *Hadassah Magazine,* (June/July 1996) 20.

61. David Zigelman, "Babysitter or Day Care Center: That Is the Question," *The Jewish Parent Connection,* September/October 1995, 22.

62. Deena Garber, "Mom and the Machzor: Balancing Spirituality and Ma-

ternal Realities," and Sharon First, "8 Ways to Help Make the High Holy Days More Meaningful for the Whole Family," *The Jewish Parent Connection,* September/October 1995, 9, 13.

63. The "new familism" is a phrase suggested and explored in *Family Affairs* 5, nos. 1 & 2 (Summer 1992).

64. Mary Jo Bane, *Here to Stay: American Families in the Twentieth Century* (New York: Basic Books, 1976).

65. A representative collection of familist articles can be found in David Blankenhorn, Steven Bayme, and Jean Bethke Elshtain, eds., *Rebuilding the Nest: A New Commitment to the American Family* (Milwaukee, Wis.: Family Service America, 1990).

66. Sylvia Ann Hewlett, *A Lesser Life: The Myth of Women's Liberation in America* (New York: Warner Books, 1986).

67. Christopher Lash, *Haven in a Heartless World: The Family Besieged* (New York: Basic Books, 1977).

68. Mary Ann Glendon, *Abortion and Divorce and Western Law* (Cambridge: Harvard University Press, 1987).

69. David Blankenhorn, introduction, *Rebuilding the Nest,* vii–xv.

70. Bruce C. Hafen, "Individualism in Family Law," in *Rebulding the Nest,* 161–77, 171.

71. Rebecca Johnson, "The Just-Do-It Shrink," *The New York Times Magazine,* November 17, 1996, 41–45.

72. A few of the many important works on the creation of American domestic life include: Stephanie Coontz, *The Social Origins of Private Life: A History of American Families, 1600–1900* (London: Verso, 1988); Carroll Smith-Rosenberg, *Disorderly Conduct: Visions of Gender in Victorian America* (New York: Knopf, 1985); Marcia Millman, *Warm Hearts, Cold Cash: The Intimate Dynamics of Families and Money* (New York: Free Press, 1991); Elaine Tyler May, *Domestic Revolutions: A Social History of American Family Life* (New York: Free Press, 1988); Steven Mintz and Susan Kellog, *Domestic Revolutions: A Social History of American Family Life* (New York: Free Press, 1988).

73. Barbara Ehrenreich, *The Hearts of Men: American Dreams and the Flight from Commitment* (Garden City, N.Y.: Anchor Press, 1983).

74. Judith S. Wallerstein and Sandra Blakeslee, *Second Chances: Men, Women, and Children a Decade After Divorce—Who Wins, Who Loses, and Why* (New York: Ticknor & Fields, 1989), 35–53, 296.

75. Judith S. Wallerstein and Sandra Blakeslee, *The Good Marriage: How and Why Love Lasts* (Boston: Houghton Mifflin Company, 1995), 330.

76. Dana Vannoy-Hiller and William W. Philliber, *Equal Partners: Successful Women in Marriage* (Newbury Park: Sage Publications, 1989), 120–22.

77. Walter R. Grove, "Sex Differences in Mental Illness among Adult Men and Women," *Social Science and Medicine* 12B (1978); see also Mary Roth Walsh, *The Psychology of Women: Ongoing Debates* (New Haven: Yale University Press, 1987); and M. Mednick, S. Tangri, and L. Hoffman, *Women and Achievement: Social and Motivational Analysis* (New York: Halstead Press, 1975).

78. Stephanie Coontz, *The Way We Never Were: American Families and the Nostalgia Trap* (New York: Basic Books, 1992), 17.

79. Elaine Tyler May, *Homeward Bound: American Families in the Cold War Era* (New York: Basic Books, 1988), 162, 171.

80. Susan Faludi, *Backlash: The Undeclared War against American Women* (New York: Crown Publishers, 1991), 27–34, 253–54, 230, 246–91, 294–295, 313–18, 409. In contrast, see Gina Maranto, "Delayed Childbearing," *Atlantic Monthly*, June 1995.

81. Sklare, *America's Jews*, 87–88.

82. Norman Linzer, "Self and Other: The Jewish Family in Crisis," in *Crisis and Continuity: The Jewish Family in the 21st Century*, ed. Norman Linzer, Irving N. Levitz, and David J. Schnall (Hoboken, N.J.: Ktav Publishing, 1995), 1–21, 3.

Chapter Six

1. Sholem Asch, *Three Cities* (New York: Carroll & Graf, 1983, rpt. 1933), 342–59.

2. Alfred Kazin, *A Walker in the City* (1951), quoted in Steven J. Rubin, ed., *Writing Our Lives: Autobiographies of American Jews* (Philadelphia and New York: The Jewish Publication Society, 1991), 134–37.

3. Sklare, *America's Jews*, 114.

4. "Jewish Food—The Kosher Revival: Is It Health or Is It Religion?" *Forward*, February 16, 1996, 11.

5. Goldstein, *Profile*, 143. It should be noted that higher proportions of Orthodox and newly Orthodox Jews are computed from the 1990 NJPS data by Bernard Lazerwitz, J. Alan Winter, Arnold Dashefsky, and Ephraim Tabory in *Jewish Choices: American Jewish Denominationalism* (Ithaca, N.Y.: SUNY Press, 1998).

6. Kosmin et. al., *Highlights*, 8.

7. Jack Wertheimer, *Conservative Synagogues and Their Members: Highlights of the North American Survey of 1995–96* (New York: The Jewish Theological Seminary of America, 1996), p.42.

8. Sources are numerous, but see, for example: Abba Hillel Silver, *Where Judaism Differed: An Inquiry into the Distinctiveness of Judaism* (New York: The Macmillan Company, 1961), 57, 61, 63.

9. Silver, *Where Judaism Differed*, 215.

10. Abraham Joshua Heschel, *The Sabbath: Its Meaning for Modern Man* (New York: Farrar, Straus & Giroux, 1951); *God in Search of Man: A Philosophy of Judaism* (Philadelphia: The Jewish Publication Society of America, 1956), 290, 326, 351, 417–19.

11. Sklare and Greenblum, *Jewish Identity on the Suburban Frontier*, 52–53. Data in this study was gathered in 432 loosely structured interviews in a suburb of Chicago, Illinois, in 1957–1958.

12. Allen Hoffman, *Big League Dreams* (New York: Abbeville Press, 1997), 133–34, 144.

13. In coding responses to questions about kashruth, this chapter computes vegetarianism together with two sets of dishes, because vegetarianism is particularly

widespread among certain segments of Jewishly active younger adults, including but not limited to the eco-Orthodox. Given the fact that these groups see vegetarianism as a higher form of kashruth observance, that they do not consume foods prohibited by the dietary laws, and that some traditional rabbinic authorities postulate that meat consumption was only a divine concession to human frailty, this analysis makes the assumption that vegetarian observance is better matched to kosher households than to nonkosher households.

14. Variations in levels of maintaining kashruth outside the home can include: purchasing from nonkosher establishments items assumed to be non-problematic such as coffee or other beverages, brands of ice cream or frozen yogurt known not to include gelatin, or fresh salads or fruit plates. It should be noted that even in the past, letters, travel accounts, and other cultural artifacts indicate that historically the exigencies of business travel may have led punctilious Jews to compromise, when necessary, by eating the least egregious unchecked foods—fruit, vegetables, plain bread, beverages—when on the road. For many kashruth-observant Jews, the most lax norm of behavior is summed up in the phrase: "eating fish out," which includes fish or warm dairy foods prepared in nonkosher utensils and ovens.

15. Letty Cottin Pogebrin, *Deborah, Golda, and Me: Being Jewish and Female in America* (New York: Crown Publishers, 1991), 10.

16. Pogebrin, *Deborah, Golda, and Me*, 9–11.

17. Wertheimer, *Conservative Synagogues*, 35, 42.

18. Lynn Davidman, *Tradition in a Rootless World: Women Turn to Orthodox Judaism* (Berkeley and Los Angeles: University of California Press, 1991), 74–107.

19. Debra Renee Kaufman, *Rachel's Daughters: Newly Orthodox Jewish Women* (New Brunswick: Rutgers University Press, 1991), 9–10.

20. Elizabeth Powers, "A Farewell to Feminism," *Commentary* (January 1997): 23–30.

21. Anne Roiphe, *Lovingkindness* (New York: Simon & Schuster, 1987), 3, 133–34.

22. Fishman and Goldstein.

23. Wertheimer, *Conservative Synagogues*, 35.

24. Peter Y. Medding, Gary A. Tobin, Sylvia Barack Fishman, and Mordechai Rimor, "Jewish Identity in Conversionary and Mixed Marriages," *American Jewish Year Book, 1992* (New York and Philadelphia: Jewish Publication Society and American Jewish Committee, 1992), 3–76.

25. Peter Medding et. al., *Ibid.*

26. Robert Bellah, "Competing Visions of the Role of Religion in American Society," *Uncivil Religion: Interreligious Hostility in America*, ed. Robert N. Bellah and Frederick E. Greenspahn (New York: Crossroad 1987), 228.

Chapter Seven

1. Gabriel Berger, *Current Philanthropic Patterns of American Jews* (Waltham, Mass.: Brandeis University Cohen Center for Modern Jewish Studies Research Report 7, 1992), 22.

2. All members of the community, for example, were required to hear the Torah reading concerning the biblical persecutor of the Israelites, Amalek, on the Sabbath immediately preceding the holiday of Purim, and to listen to the reading of the Book of Ruth from an appropriate scroll on the holiday itself. In addition to such required attendances, many women also made a special point of attending syngagogue services on those Sabbaths preceding the new moon, during which special prayers were recited for health, financial solvency, and joy during the coming month.

3. For an excellent summary discussion of historical Jewish communal structures, see Daniel J. Elazar, "Community," *Encyclopedia Judaica*, 5: 807–853.

4. Elazar, "Community," *Encyclopedia Judaica, Ibid.*

5. In addition to Elazar's overview of Jewish communal institutions historically from biblical through modern times in the *Encyclopdia Judaica* cited above, see also Daniel J. Elazar, *Community and Polity: The Organizational Dynamics of American Jewry* (Philadelphia: The Jewish Publication Society, 1995), for detailed information on the American Jewish organizational scene.

6. Jonathan S. Woocher, *Sacred Survival: The Civil Religion of American Jews* (Bloomington and Indianapolis: Indiana University Press, 1986), 94–96.

7. Woocher, 70–71.

8. Elazar, *Community and Polity,* 275–310.

9. Sklare and Greenblum, "The Friendship Pattern of the Lakeville Jew," 269–290.

10. Herbert J. Gans, "The Origin of a Jewish Community in the Suburbs," in *American Jews: A Reader,* ed. Marshall Sklare (New York: Berman House, Inc. and Brandeis University Center for Modern Jewish Studies, 1983), 153–71, 162.

11. Gans, "Jewish Community in the Suburbs," 166.

12. Berger, *Philanthropic Patterns.*

13. Berger, *Philanthropic Patterns,* 11.

14. Berger, *Philanthropic Patterns,* 13.

15. Berger, *ibid.*

16. Berger, *o cit.*, 15.

17. Gabriel Berger, *Voluntarism Among American Jews* (Waltham, Mass.: Brandeis University Cohen Center for Modern Jewish Studies, 1991), 45.

18. Keller Freeman, "The Gender Gap in Philanthropy," *Radcliffe Quarterly* 77, no. 4 (December 1991): 3–4.

19. Gary A. Tobin and Sylvia Barack Fishman, "CJF Women's Division Leadership Survey: Executive Summary" (presented at the Council of Jewish Federations General Assembly Miami, November 1987).

20. Set into the lexicon of American Jewish terms by Woocher, *Sacred Survival.*

21. B'nai B'rith International Annual Meeting, Washington, D.C., August 31, 1996, Roundtable Discussion on "Jewish Family Values," led by Sylvia Barack Fishman and Egon Mayer.

22. For a complete report on these data, and copies of the survey and instrument and other documentation, see Fishman, "Training for a Life of Jewish Service," in Cohen, Fishman, Sarna, and Charles Liebman, *Expectations, Education and Experience,* 61–125. This Wexner Foundation Study is based on telephone interviews with

280 persons who completed their Jewish professional training after 1980. The processes of interviewing and data entry and analysis were conducted under the auspices of and with the staff support of the Cohen Center for Modern Jewish Studies at Brandeis University (CMJS). Major training institutions across the United States cooperated with the Wexner Foundation by supplying to CMJS names of students who had graduated approximately ten years (1982–1984) and approximately four years (1988–1990) before the study ensued. Some schools supplied to CMJS lists with telephone numbers; others supplied addresses only; others contacted their graduates and asked them to mail permissions forms to CMJS. The schools also varied widely in the accuracy and currency of their alumni information. The ability of the CMJS research team to contact graduates of a given institution was somewhat delimited by these factors. Graduates who agreed to participate were selected for interviewing randomly, with the exception that researchers aimed to adjust for geographical distribution. The rate of outright refusal to participate was exceedingly low; only eight persons of those contacted directly stated that they did not wish to participate in the survey. There was a more substantial rate of incomplete interviews, due to persons who initially agreed to be interviewed, but subsequently found that professional responsibilities conflicted with the interviewing process.

23. *Ibid.*

Chapter Eight

1. Ann Swidler, "Culture as Action: Symbols and Strategies," *American Sociological Review* 51 (1986), 273–86.

2. Michael Brenner, *The Renaissance of Jewish Culture in Weimar Germany* (New Haven: Yale University Press, 1996), 4–5, 197–211.

3. Paul Levesque, writing on the Jewish Studies Network on Friday, July 18, 1997, Subject: Jew as Oriental, "I have been working on two German-Jewish writers of the 1920s (Leon Feuchtwanger and Alexander Doeblin) . . ." For further information, contact "levesqup@WABASH.EDU".

4. Jonathan Sarna, *A Great Awakening: The Transformation That Shaped Twentieth Century American Judaism and Its Implications for Today* (New York: Council for Initiatives in Jewish Education, 1995), 31–32.

5. David Biale, "Objectivity and Ideology," in *Tikkun* 11, no. 3 (May/June 1996): 67–68, discussing David Myers, *Re-Inventing the Jewish Past: European Jewish Intellectuals and the Zionist Return to History* (New York: Oxford University Press, 1995).

6. Frederik Barth, *Ethnic Groups and Boundaries* (Boston: Little, Brown and Company, 1969), 38.

7. Sander Gilman, *The Jews' Body* (New York: Routledge, 1991).

8. Steven J. Zipperstein, "Ahad Ha'am and the Politics of Assimilation," in *Assimilation and Community* (Cambridge: Cambridge University Press, 1992), 344–65, 344.

9. Thomas Sowell, *Ethnic America: A History* (New York: Basic Books, 1981); Lawrence H. Fuchs, *The American Kaleidoscope: Race, Ethnicity, and the Civic Culture* (Hanover, N.H.: Wesleyan University Press, 1990), 288–289.

10. Sowell, *Ethnic America*, 9, reminds us that "Jews, who had been excluded from many top university faculties, came ultimately to be overrepresented on such faculties. Professional sports that once excluded blacks came to be dominated by black athletes. Anti-Oriental laws, which had flourished for decades in California, were repealed in popular referendums."

11. Esmerelda Santiago, "A Puerto Rican Stew," in "Hers," *The New York Times Magazine*, December 18, 1994, 34, 36.

12. Steven Drukman, "Taking Bittersweet Journeys into the Past," *New York Times*, November 10, 1996, 5, 13.

13. Roth, *Operation Shylock*, 47.

14. Stephen L. Carter, *The Culture of Disbelief* (New York: Basic Books, 1993).

15. Steven Bayme, Steven M. Cohen, and Jack Wertheimer, *Commentary,* January 1996. The same authors also drafted a "Statement on the Jewish Future" which was signed by a number of scholars and Jewish communal leaders, and ran as an ad in the *Jerusalem Report, Jerusalem Post*, and elsewhere.

16. Nagel, "Constructing Ethnicity," 168.

17. Phillip E. Hammond and Kee Warner, "Religion and Ethnicity in Late-Twentieth Century America," *Annals of the American Academy of Political and Social Science* 527 (May 1993): 55–66, 66.

18. Peter Berger, *The Sacred Canopy: Elements of a Sociological Theory of Religion* (New York: Doubleday, 1967), 114.

19. Benedict Anderson, *Imagined Communities: Reflections on the Origin and Spread of Nationalism* (London: Verso, 1991).

SUBJECT INDEX

Index of Names

Printed in the United States
1075600005B/121-147